D1274077

Edwin H. Sutherland

ON ANALYZING CRIME

THE HERITAGE OF SOCIOLOGY

A Series Edited by Morris Janowitz

Edwin H. Sutherland

ON ANALYZING CRIME

Edited and with an Introduction by
KARL SCHUESSLER

THE UNIVERSITY OF CHICAGO PRESS
CHICAGO AND LONDON

Much of this book was originally published in *The Sutherland Papers*, edited by Albert Cohen, Alfred Lindesmith, and Karl Schuessler. Copyright 1956 by Indiana University Press ©

THE UNIVERSITY OF CHICAGO PRESS, CHICAGO 60637
THE UNIVERSITY OF CHICAGO PRESS, LTD., LONDON

Printed in the United States of America
International Standard Book Number: 0-226-78055-4 (clothbound)
Library of Congress Catalog Card Number: 72-94733

CONTENTS

Acknowledgments

THE PAPERS for the original edition of *The Sutherland Papers* were selected and edited by A. K. Cohen, A. R. Lindesmith, and myself, and the contributions of Cohen and Lindesmith to this edition are therefore no less than mine. This edition contains a new introduction, a short autobiographical statement by Sutherland, an index, several changes in the bibliography, and a new title. The new title, *On Analyzing Crime*, was chosen to emphasize that Sutherland's contribution to sociological criminology lay as much in his method of analyzing crime as in his substantive conclusions about crime. The contribution of George Vold to the original edition in the form of judgments about the worth of specific papers must be mentioned again, and also the generous cooperation of Donald R. Cressey, who was instrumental in uncovering unpublished manuscripts. Sutherland's widow, Myrtle—who continues to make her home in Bloomington, Indiana—helped in many ways, and especially in the irksome task of assembling scattered materials.

With minor exceptions, the introduction to *On Analyzing Crime* is based on books and articles and various and sundry papers in my files (the latter being available to anyone doing scholarly work on Sutherland). Professor Robert E. L. Faris was kind enough to provide me with a few personal recollections about Sutherland at the University of Chicago, and Jon Snodgrass, who has recently completed a doctoral dissertation (University of Pennsylvania) on American criminologists, supplied me with items for the bibliography based on his own research. I also wish to express my appreciation to Dr. Thorsten Sellin, who kindly furnished me with a brief memoir about his Social Science Research Council project with Sutherland; also to Professor Paul J. Baker for bringing my attention to the Luther Bernard Papers, which include a short autobiographical sketch by Sutherland; and to the University Library of Pennsylvania State University for authority to print a portion of that sketch.

For permission to reprint previously published materials, I wish to acknowledge my gratitude to the University of Chicago Press, the J. B. Lippincott Company, Henry Holt and Company, the American Prison Association, the Bureau of Social Hygiene, and the publishers of *The American Journal of Sociology*, *The American Sociological Review*, the *Journal of Criminal Law and Criminology*, *The Annals of the American Academy of Political and Social Science*, and *The Cornell Law Quarterly*.

KARL SCHUESSLER

Introduction

E. H. SUTHERLAND is regarded by most American sociologists as one of the major criminologists. Sutherland himself would have resisted such attempts to establish his relative importance since he held to the view that knowledge is a collective product whose development does not depend on specific individuals. Still, he might have conceded that his efforts were instrumental in shaping the modern sociological approach to the study of crime and criminals, and he could not have noticed the attention his work drew during his lifetime. His own discomfort with personalized accounts of social behavior has had little effect on his fellow workers. They generally give him credit for major advances in criminology and continually mull over his studies for their precise meaning.

His influential position in twentieth-century criminology reflects the sustained and progressive character of his studies over a thirty-year period, culminating in his theory of differential association. Sutherland did not work in several distinct fields of sociology, but rather restricted himself with practically no deviations to the subject of crime and its causes. Furthermore, he was consistently sociological in his analysis of crime and did not broaden his theoretical model to accommodate biological and psychological factors. In fact, he was severely critical of those criminologists who stretched their framework to include every possible factor, however disparate those factors might be. Moreover, Sutherland was concerned with a scientific criminology that might, because of its capacity for prediction, have some practical value for purposes of social engineering. He showed little interest in historical trends and social movements, except insofar as they were expressive of general social forces and regularities. The explanation of his centrality in criminology thus seems to lie in his continuing and reasonably successful effort to formulate an internally consistent sociological explanation of crime with implications for both social policy and social practice.

LIFE HISTORY

Sutherland was born in Gibbon, Nebraska, August 13, 1883, and died in Bloomington, Indiana, on October 11, 1950. Although his three score and seven years were about average, his death was regarded as premature by his friends. Scarcely more than a month before, he had given a critical paper on Sheldon's *Varieties of Delinquent Youth* at a meeting of the American Sociological Society in Los Angeles, and at the time of his death he was working steadily on the fifth edition of *Principles of Criminology* (hereafter referred to as *Principles*). Sutherland was imbued with the Protestant ethic, and it was his habit to meet his commitments and obligations. His parents presided over a Protestant parsonage in a rural community, and in that setting they succeeded in giving their son a sense of the moral importance of carrying out one's duties.

Sutherland did his undergraduate work at Grand Island (Nebraska) College, getting his A.B. degree in 1903. During the next few years, he taught at both his alma mater and Sioux Falls (South Dakota) College, giving courses in, among others, shorthand, geometry and Greek. But his heart was apparently not in his work, as he presently (1906) enrolled as a graduate student at the University of Chicago. His training there was largely in the hands of Charles Henderson, Albion Small, and

W. I. Thomas, whose collective influence is quite evident in Sutherland's earlier writing, with its emphasis on social process.[1] It is also evident in his theory of criminal behavior, which may be regarded as an adaptation of interactional sociology as expounded by W. I. Thomas; it is further evident in his empirical research, which is based on those techniques of careful investigation that came to be known as the hallmark of the Chicago school of sociology. He received a doctorate in sociology in 1913, having in the meantime completed his dissertation, entitled "Unemployment and Public Employment Agencies."

Upon receiving the doctorate, Sutherland accepted a post at William Jewell College in Liberty, Missouri, where he taught until 1919. In that year he moved to the University of Illinois to join a sociology faculty that included such notables of the day as E. C. Hayes and E. T. Hiller. In 1925 Sutherland left Illinois for the University of Minnesota, staying until 1929, when he was given leave of absence to work at the Bureau of Social Hygiene in New York. During the course of that year, which included research in England, he resigned from Minnesota to accept a research professorship at the University of Chicago. In announcing his appointment, President Robert M. Hutchins stated that the step was taken to strengthen the university's crime-study program.

Sutherland stayed at Chicago until 1935 when he moved to Indiana University as head of the sociology department. Although the reasons for his move from the University of Chicago to Indiana University are obscure, we can imagine that he was more or less dissatisfied with his dispensation in the department at Chicago, which did not include permanent tenure. There was probably more push than pull.

Sutherland was somewhat restless and peripatetic. He was affiliated with five different schools (excluding his predoctoral positions), with an average stay of around seven years. However, he covered no great distances and remained within a

[1] See "Crime and the Conflict Process" and "Social Process in Behavior Problems," pp. 99 and 112 of this volume.

rather restricted geographical area throughout his academic career. This pattern is of no special significance, except that it kept him within easy distance of his friends in Chicago (McKay, Ogburn, and Hughes) and relatively distant from sociologists outside the Midwest. Thus the biases of his graduate training were reenforced by his somewhat provincial pattern of contacts.

MAJOR CONTRIBUTIONS

Sutherland's reputation as a leading contributor to sociological criminology rests largely on his *Principles*, his theory of differential association, and his concept of white-collar crime. However, he made numerous but less visible contributions through his persistent activity behind the scenes. At the peak of his career, in fact, no major discussion appears to be free of his influence, as we shall later endeavor to show.

Principles of Criminology. The publication in 1924 of *Criminology*, as the first edition of *Principles* was titled, marks Sutherland's official entry into the field. In a 1928 vita it appears as the earliest publication on the topic of crime. According to Sutherland's own testimony, the idea for the book came from Hayes, who believed that the younger faculty, for their own good, should be engaged in some major project.[2] Since Hayes was both chairman of the department and editor of the Lippincott Sociological Series, Sutherland had to give some weight to his opinion. In any event, Sutherland did the book for Lippincott.

Although this somewhat cynical version appealed to Sutherland's puckish humor, and he enjoyed repeating it, it is probably something of an oversimplification. It is unlikely that Hayes, who was not considered a reckless man, would have offered much encouragement if he had had scant confidence in Sutherland's competence and dependability. Whatever its

[2] See p. 13, this volume.

auspices, *Criminology* had the effect of binding Sutherland to the field of criminology, which he cultivated until his death.

It is instructive to speculate on the success of *Principles*, which has dominated the field for the last forty-five years. (The fifth and subsequent editions have been done by Donald R. Cressey, the last student to complete a doctoral dissertation under Sutherland.) Its reputation as a scholarly work rests mainly on two characteristics: (1) its striving toward a unified sociological interpretation, free of internal inconsistencies, and (2) its judicial tone and unpretentious style.

The development of *Principles* reflects Sutherland's struggle with the problem of causation and his continual efforts to reach a more adequate solution to that problem. Once a revision was out, Sutherland would immediately turn to its logical flaws and to the ways in which they might be eliminated. In the second edition (1934), he sought to introduce a measure of theoretical order by means of the principles of social process and cultural conflict. It was in that edition, too, that the elements of differential association, scattered here and there, made their first appearance. Differential association was set forth in propositional form in the third edition (1939) and refined in the fourth edition (1947), according to Sutherland's latest judgments and insights. There was thus an evolution from an ordinary textbook in 1924 to a rather remarkable analysis of crime and social process in 1947. Sutherland used to say that his interest in crime was as an approach to sociology rather than the other way around. That view is borne out by *Principles*.

Principles is a scholarly work in that no hypothesis is facilely dismissed and all issues are weighed and evaluated according to their merits. The reader gets an impression of careful analysis and logical inference rather than mindless dogma and clever sophistry. The writing is plain rather than fancy, concise rather than prolix, and generally free of elements that detract from the points to be made. Sutherland had a preference for unadorned expression, based on the assumption that ideas would be lost in ornate writing. Similarly, the writing is never for purposes of presenting self or for purposes of literary effect;

rather it is consistently for the sake of communicating ideas to the reader.

During Sutherland's lifetime, *Principles* was translated from English into several languages. However flattered he may have been by these translations, he did not overlook their significance for comparative sociology. In his preface to the Japanese edition, he stated that his book gives a general theory which presumably holds in Japan as well as in the United States. But the generality of that theory, he went on to say, can be judged only by scrutinizing it under cultural situations different from the one in which it was developed. In these simple words, he gives the main idea of what has come to be known as comparative sociology. Although he carried out no comparative studies himself, he did appreciate the fact that claims for the universality of his theory would have to be checked against comparative data.

Differential Association. The theory of differential association was launched as a set of seven propositions in the third edition of *Principles* (1939), and expanded into nine in the fourth edition (1947).[3] It did not appear out of nowhere but was, as has been said, an extension of ideas contained in the second edition (1934). In particular, it was an elaboration of the idea that "the conflict of cultures is the fundamental principle in the explanation of crime."[4] Sutherland's point was that social groups differ in the importance they attach to respect for the law, and that the individual will tend toward or away from crime according to the cultural standards of his associates, especially his intimate ones. This is a rough version of the theory of differential association.

Sutherland had some misgivings about assembling his scattered ideas and calling them a theory, although there was ample warrant for that step. He was concerned that not enough was known to justify a general theory and that the mere presence

[3] See "A Statement of the Theory," p. 7 of this volume.

[4] E. H. Sutherland, *Principles of Criminology*, 2d ed. (Philadelphia: Lippincott, 1934), p. 50.

of a theory might foster an unhealthy perseveration of thought, possibly in the wrong direction. He understood that a theory might gain adherents not because of its truth but because of its mere existence as a rallying point in a jumbled field. Accordingly, he preferred to think of his propositions as an approach rather than a theory, as working hypotheses rather than universal laws. In its original form, the theory asserted that crime is attributable to differential association in a situation of culture conflict produced by social disorganization. This summary statement was divided into the following seven propositions:[5]

First, the processes which result in systematic criminal behavior are fundamentally the same in form as the processes which result in systematic lawful behavior.

Second, systematic criminal behavior is determined in a process of association with those who commit crime, just as systematic lawful behavior is determined in a process of association with those who are law-abiding.

Third, differential association is the specific causal process in the development of systematic criminal behavior.

Fourth, the chance that a person will participate in systematic criminal behavior is determined roughly by the frequency and consistency of his contacts with the patterns of criminal behavior.

Fifth, individual differences among people in respect to personal characteristics or social situations cause crime only as they affect differential association, or frequency and consistency of contacts with criminal patterns.

Sixth, cultural conflict is the underlying cause of differential association and therefore of systematic criminal behavior.

Seventh, social disorganization is the basic cause of systematic criminal behavior.

The elucidation of the theory was largely at the urging of Henry McKay, Hans Riemer, and Harvey Locke, all members of Sutherland's intellectual circle. With modesty, Sutherland would say that he was hardly aware of his theory until it had been brought to attention by his perceptive friends. But he

[5] E. H. Sutherland, *Principles of Criminology*, 3d ed. (Philadelphia: Lippincott, 1939), pp. 4–8.

was aware that a general theory would be premature in the absence of more factual information about crime and criminals. His ideal was a general theory of crime consistent with the widest possible range of data, and he realized that the factual materials on crime were fragmentary and unreliable and generally insufficient to bear the weight of broad generalizations. As late as 1937, he wrote Sellin: "I am opposed to an effort at this time to make criminology highly scientific (in the sense of universal propositions) because I think we will be trying to define things about which we do not have enough information."[6] And in 1940, speaking before a graduate seminar at the University of Illinois, he commented that his theory should have been called a point of view, or at least no more than a hypothesis. With a touch of wryness, he went on to say that it was brazen and dangerous to tag his explanation of criminal behavior a theory, considering the fate of other theories in sociology.

Thus far Sutherland's theory has not suffered "the fate of other theories," and today it is the subject of much study and discussion. Since no plausible alternative of comparable scope has been advanced, it has no close rival at the moment.[7] It has been the object of much critical scrutiny, but that scrutiny has not led to its rejection and abandonment. Sutherland anticipated the substance of much of the criticism that would eventually materialize, since he reflected a great deal on the weaknesses of, and prospects for, his theory.[8]

One criticism is that the theory is not a sociological theory, since it explains individual differences in criminality rather than differences between groups. Possibly to forestall this objection, Sutherland reiterated in his writing that a theory of criminal behavior could take either the person or the group as its unit of analysis. In focusing on the person, as he did, Sutherland tended to slight the way in which society is organized to con-

[6] For details of this correspondence, see p. xxv, this volume.

[7] For an elaboration of this point, see Don C. Gibbons, "The Study of Crime Causation," *American Journal of Sociology*, LXXVII (September 1971), 262–78.

[8] See "Critique of the Theory," p. 30 of this volume.

trol crime, although he was aware of the importance of that factor. In analyzing the effect of war on domestic crimes, for example, he noted that the crime rate is generally a function of community organization for and against crime, and he used that principle to explain the changes in specific crime rates during the Second World War.[9] He recognized that attitudes and techniques were needed, but that these were not enough to produce criminal behavior, and that a complete explanation would have to incorporate the variation in social organization.

Another criticism leveled against the theory is that its psychology is faulty in at least two respects: (1) in its implication that learning depends simplistically on a pattern of external contacts, and (2) in its neglect of personality as a factor in crime. On the first point, Sutherland defined his concern as being the special social circumstances under which criminal attitudes and techniques are acquired, not the mechanisms of learning on the level of the individual. Working today, he might, for example, have availed himself of B. F. Skinner's reenforcement theory, not because of an interest in operant conditioning, but rather because of its possible utility in differentiating between persons with identical contacts but varying attitudes toward crime.

His case against personality rested on the general finding that mental traits were uncorrelated with criminal behavior. He did, however, have a bias against psychiatry—possibly acquired from W. I. Thomas, who was anti-Freudian—with its tendency to explain social behavior by emotional complexes.[10] He took cognizance of that bias and regularly reexamined his position, although he never changed it. In his seminars he regularly pursued the possibility that the facts in the case of Stanley "The Jack Roller"[11] were more in harmony with the theory that criminality is an expression of personality needs than with his own theory of social learning.

9 See "Wartime Crime," p. 120 of this volume.

10 See p. 199, this volume.

11 C. R. Shaw, *The Jack-Roller: A Delinquent Boy's Own Story* (Chicago: University of Chicago Press, 1930; Phoenix ed. 1966).

The criticism has been made that the theory merely explains the manner in which criminal attitudes and techniques are acquired, but not how such attitudes and techniques arise in the first place. This is reminiscent of the slightly banal point that Tarde's theory of social imitation fails to account for the form and substance of what is imitated. Sutherland must have been aware of the charge that his theory was tautological (crime causes crime), since it was voiced by several of his contemporaries,[12] but he seems to have prepared no full-fledged rebuttal. He did discuss it with his students, and Albert Cohen's attempt[13] to get beyond the problem of how delinquency is transmitted to the problem of how delinquency is invented may have been influenced by such discussions.

The scope of the theory has also come in for some critical appraisal, but more by way of clarification than by way of refutation. That it does not apply to all offenders is generally conceded, although the evidence for this assertion is usually circumstantial. For example, there is indirect evidence that some shoplifters have relatively few criminal contacts prior to their apprehension, with the implication that such contacts are not essential to some forms of stealing.[14] Such empirical findings, which have gradually mounted during the last twenty years, do not refute the theory, but rather serve to fix its outer limits.

Since Sutherland was a man of some pride, he would probably be pleased with the critical attention his theory has received posthumously, and its implication that he was on the right track. He would doubtless have been disappointed with little or no attention, with its implication that he was on the wrong track. The inability of sociologists to come up with a more adequate formulation, in spite of their critical reservations, attests to the difficulty of the task facing differential association in particular and theoretical criminology in general.

12 Hans Von Hentig, *Crime: Causes and Conditions* (New York: McGraw-Hill, 1947), p. 8.

13 A. K. Cohen, *Delinquent Boys* (Glencoe, Ill.: Free Press, 1955).

14 M. B. Cameron, *The Booster and the Snitch* (Glencoe, Ill.: Free Press, 1964).

White Collar Crime. Sometime in the 1920s, Sutherland became interested in the occupational crimes of persons of respectability and high social status. Later, mainly as a convenience, he called them "white-collar crimes." The expression has become standard terminology in sociology, although the theoretical analysis remains at the level where Sutherland left it in 1949 with the publication of *White Collar Crime.*[15] (The efforts of Ralph Nader and his associates in the late 1960s and early 1970s to protect the consumer from false advertising and various types of commercial fraud represent a popular concern with white-collar crime and its causes.)

The merits of *White Collar Crime* aside, it interestingly reflects the discontinuity between Sutherland's theory of differential association and his own research on business crimes. In that research, his unit of study was the corporation rather than the person, and his conclusions apply to the behavior of corporations rather than to the behavior of persons. There is a rather obvious explanation for this incongruity: the design of his research was set, and much data were collected, before he had formulated his general theory. True, in his analysis he made an effort to show that white-collar criminals undergo the same process of learning as blue-collar criminals, but that effort is so incidental as to slur the importance of differential association.

The seeming neglect of white-collar crime since 1950 is of interest, and a few clues are present in Sutherland's writing. First, the affluence of American society in recent times may have diverted attention from business crimes and generally brought about a flagging interest in the subject. Sutherland started his investigation during the depression when the standing of business was low and public skepticism about its social worth was high. The times favored an analysis of business crime. Second, the study of white-collar crime, by reason of its legal complexities, requires a competence in law that few sociologists possess, although the number may be increasing. Sutherland himself spent many, many hours in the law library, not only to track down cases, but also to obtain that technical

[15] W. H. Sutherland, *White Collar Crime* (New York: Dryden, 1949).

knowledge essential to the analysis of complex and ambiguous administrative decisions. Possibly reacting to the deficiencies of his own training, he encouraged his doctoral students to minor in law. Third, the study of white-collar crime is regarded by some as a veiled attack on business with the aim of reforming it, rather than a serious sociological enterprise. Sutherland disclaimed any interest in reforming business and held that the violations of corporations were relevant data for criminology, even though they were not so regarded by the general public. Nevertheless, the view that white-collar crime is not crime has persisted and possibly has retarded its analysis.[16]

Sutherland's efforts at defending his work on white-collar crime, particularly the concept itself, are contained in his paper entitled "Is 'White-Collar Crime' Crime?"[17] They are displayed more informally in the following exchange with the late Paul Tappan, professor of law and sociology at New York University and in his day the leading critic of white-collar crime.

At a meeting of the American Sociological Society in December 1946, Tappan expressed some general reservations about white-collar crime as follows:

> Grave weakness in the concept [of white-collar crime] results from the apparent inability of writers in this area to determine whether the term should be predicated upon social class differentials, upon the inherent wrongfullness of the behavior involved, or only upon violation of formal statutory specifications of social injury, upon the purposes for which the acts are committed, upon civil as well as criminal law violations, upon "punishability" in the abstract or "penal sanctions" specifically, upon wilfullness or merely upon the consequences of the particular behavior. The term has been weakened by the apparent indecision of writers who define the term differently each time they use it. The consequent con-

[16] While Sutherland claimed to have no interest in exposing business crimes, he was, nevertheless, quite indignant over the publisher's (The Dryden Press) demand that corporations not be identified by name in the published version of *White Collar Crime*. After much futile correspondence, he not only conceded, but even supplied a rationalization to the effect that the anonymity of subjects must be preserved in scientific research.

[17] Reprinted in this volume, p. 62.

fusion would not be too serious were the effects confined to the limited area of research in white collar criminality. The real evil lies in the fact that convenient stereotypes, speculation, and emotive tirades against "economic injustice" come to contaminate the objectivity of theory in criminology and sociology more generally.

Although Sutherland attended that session, he apparently had no opportunity to confront Tappan face-to-face, and shortly after returning to Bloomington, he wrote to Tappan as follows:[18]

> . . . I agree with you as to the desirability of clear definition of criminal behavior and agree also that the concept of white collar crime is especially apt to be appropriated for propagandistic purposes. My own belief is that crime is a legal concept and that its definition must, therefore, be found in the law, and that a "white collar crime" which does not fall within a proper general definition of crime is not a "white collar crime."
>
> . . . It is certainly not necessary that the word "crime" be used in the legislative definition, otherwise some of the acts in some penal codes would be excluded from "crimes." Also, it is certainly unnecessary that a particular act be dealt with under criminal procedures in order to justify its classification as a criminal act. The Sherman anti-trust law is particularly significant in this connection. In that law restraint of trade is defined as a misdemeanor, punishable by fine or imprisonment or both. However, the law provides that procedures under this law may be either criminal, civil, or injunctive, and courts have held in both equity and civil cases under this law that the behavior is criminal even though the procedure used is not criminal procedure. . . .
>
> I believe that the concept of white-collar crime is questionable in certain respects and I hope to elaborate these in a later publication. I may mention here one or two of these. First, so far as the "white collar" element is concerned, no clear-cut line can be drawn to distinguish it from "blue collar" or "no collar" crimes. This, I think, makes no significant difference. Second, the concept of "punishment" is indefinite. Penal sanctions are variable. At the present time various agencies are searching for new penal sanctions which will be more efficacious than fine or imprisonment.

[18] Letter of December 31, 1946, in editor's file.

Behavior which is defined legally as crime will not cease to be crime if new penal sanctions are devised and used or even if non-penal methods are authorized as alternative methods of control.

I must say that I am uncertain regarding the definition of damages in relation to punishment. "Restitution" is sometimes authorized and used by criminal courts regarding the old line crimes, and larceny does not cease to be larceny, or assault and battery cease to be assault and battery when a criminal court orders restitution or reparation. Punitive damages ordered by a civil court seem to me to fall definitely within the area of punishment. This leaves a considerable area of damages regarding which the definition is uncertain and I have found no general criteria which can be used in limiting this area.

Other questions regarding the concept of white collar crime seem to me are potentially much more damaging to the concept than these questions of definition and anyone interested in fighting this concept would be much more effective if he raised these other questions. As I said previously, I plan to state these questions in another connection.

I do not know whether you had me in mind when referring to emotional criticisms of business and reformist attitudes. As a matter of fact, I am not at all certain that the antitrust law, on which I have concentrated, is not a bad law and should not be repealed. Consequently I am not at all certain that violations of the antitrust law may not be contributions to social welfare. That, however, is beside the point for a theory of criminal behavior, since it is necessary to take the legal definition of crime rather than one's own conception of social welfare.

I realize that these remarks are not likely to change your evaluation of the concept of white collar crime. If we had had time for an hour's discussion during the conference, both of us might have changed our evaluations to some extent. At any rate, I thought you might be interested in my reaction to your discussion.

Tappan responded with a rigorous rebuttal of some 500 words, in a letter dated January 9, 1947. He did concede in the very last sentence that, "since my thinking in this area has been far shorter than your own, I readily admit to the possibility that where differences continue I may come to be persuaded to your point of view." But Sutherland remained convinced that Tappan wanted to confine criminology to the study of convicted criminals.

CRITICAL PERSPECTIVES

As previously noted, Sutherland's contribution to criminology consisted as much in his informal papers and letters as in his published writing. Either on his own initiative or by invitation, Sutherland managed to say something on practically every topic engaging the attention of criminologists during the period 1925–50. It is not practicable to give extensive documentation for this claim, and the following fragments will have to suffice: his comment (circa 1929) on E. W. Burgess's method for predicting success on parole; his part in a 1931 Social Science Research Council conference on treatment of offenders; his contribution to Thorsten Sellin's study of culture conflict and crime; and his reaction to legal realism, as expounded by Jerome Hall in his *Principles of Criminal Law*.

Parole Prediction. Although Sutherland was skeptical about the actuarial method of predicting criminality, he was intimately familiar with its details, and he gave his views on its utility and promise when the opportunity arose. A meeting of the Society for Social Research at University of Chicago in the late 1920s afforded one such opportunity. At that meeting, E. W. Burgess presented a paper on the feasibility of predicting success on parole from an experience table, using his study of 3,000 parolees in Illinois to illustrate his main points.

Speaking as a discussant, Sutherland noted that such studies do not indicate whether prisoners should be paroled or released unconditionally without parole, since they consider only prisoners who have been paroled.[19] He also noted that some violations of parole go undetected, while others are disregarded or misrepresented, and that consequently the prediction of success from an experience table is ambiguous. Continuing, he

[19] Unpublished manuscript in editor's file.

wondered whether it was possible to establish the predictive utility of personal and social traits, since no standard method of known validity for measuring those traits is presently available. Finally, he observed that the population of parolees, and in consequence their violation rate, is affected by the policies of the parole board. If the board is very strict, the violation rate will tend to zero, and likewise the predictive efficiency of the actuarial table. However trite these points may seem today, they illustrate Sutherland's impact on criminological thought through his steady activity behind the scenes.

View of Treatment. Sutherland is considered more criminologist than penologist, and his writings on crime are more highly developed than his writings on punishment. He was not oblivious to the close link between crime and punishment, and he devoted considerable thought to that topic, particularly during his years at the University of Minnesota, where he was affiliated with social workers as well as sociologists.

That concern is reflected in his participation in a conference on the individualization of treatment of offenders, held under the auspices of the Social Science Research Council in 1931. He helped to arrange that conference and presided over its meetings as chairman. Papers by such well-known figures as Sheldon Glueck, Harvard Law School; A. W. Stearns, Commissioner of Corrections for Massachusetts; and Mark A. May, Yale University, were addressed to questions of how individualized treatment might be made more effective.

In his opening remarks, Sutherland touched on a point he was later to elaborate; namely, that to evaluate methods of treatment, it is necessary to take into account their relationship to society as a whole.[20] The effectiveness of a specific method of treatment depends not only on its intrinsic features, he maintained, but also on the public's concern in controlling crime, and on the way in which society is organized for purposes of enforcing its laws. It is thus essential to investigate "treatment"

20 Unpublished manuscript in editor's file.

in order to assess the effectiveness of a given program of treatment. In this view, with its stress on interaction among social components, Sutherland was very much in harmony with sociologists today calling for a "sociology of punishment." His part in the conference also bears out the claim that he was usually at the site of the action.

Culture Conflict and Crime. In 1935 the Social Science Research Council set up a two-man committee on crime and delinquency, with Thorsten Sellin as chairman and Sutherland as the other member. As a first step, in order to provide a basis for planning for future research, the committee gathered several hundred generalizations about the causes of crime. However, before proceeding with these plans, Sellin (with Sutherland's assent) prepared early in 1936 a statement on the sociological approach to criminology. This statement underwent several revisions during the year and was presented to the Sociological Research Association at Chicago in December. During 1937, additional chapters were drafted which, together with the original statement, culminated in the 1938 SSRC bulletin on crime and culture conflict.[21]

The exchange of communications between Sellin and Sutherland in the development of this bulletin reveals Sutherland's basic perspectives toward crime and criminal behavior. In his initial statement on crime as a field of sociological study, Sellin held that conduct norms and violations of those norms are more universal than criminal law and crime and therefore are more adequate for scientific purposes. In a letter dated May 6, 1936, Sutherland raised a number of questions about Sellin's formulation:

1. Can the sociologist define the conduct norms or must he take them as he finds them just as he does the criminal laws?

2. In what sense are conduct norms more universal than criminal laws—in the variety of groups in which they are found or in con-

[21] Thorsten Sellin, *Culture Conflict and Crime* (New York: Social Science Research Council, 1938).

tent? Is it not universality in content that is needed in scientific categories?

3. Should study be concentrated on the violations of the norms of the groups with which the person most completely identifies himself?[22]

During the summer of 1936, Sellin undertook a substantial revision, which he sent to Sutherland in late August. In that revision he attached considerable importance to the resistance potential of conduct norms. Sutherland's reaction to the revision is contained in a letter written on August 29, parts of which follow:

I am not clear as to your meaning of group norms and resistance potentials. I had assumed that they were something which were conceived as external to any particular person and as capable of study as group entities. At one point, however, you describe these resistance potentials as attributes of persons, varying from person to person. . . . In any case it seems to me that it is going to be very difficult to get any measurement, or method of measurement, or resistance potentials.

Let me summarize my views this way: your statement points to the desirability of making some studies of the non-legal violation of conduct norms. The value of such studies is likely to consist not in the attainment of a science of criminology but in the development of some more hypotheses that may at some much later date point the way. I am opposed to an effort at this time to make criminology highly scientific . . . because I think we will be trying to define things about which we do not have enough information. Your paper is a statement of Mortimer Adler's position, though without his extreme demands. . . . My own position is much more eclectic and empirical; keep on getting information, searching for ideas and hypotheses by intimate contacts with criminals and with violators of non-legal norms, but do not subordinate this at present to a highly organized rational scheme.[23]

In acknowledging Sutherland's letter, Sellin indicated that he would undertake no major revision before the Chicago SRA

22 Correspondence between Sellin and Sutherland quoted here is in editor's file.

23 See "The Michael-Adler Report," p. 229 of this volume.

meeting, where he expected to encounter constructive criticism and advice. Holding to this schedule, he forged a much longer document during the spring and summer of 1937 and sent a draft of that monograph to Sutherland in November.

Sutherland's first thoughts on the monograph are contained in a letter dated December 14; his second thoughts are given in a letter dated December 16. He begins his initial letter by suggesting that the elaborate analysis of criminal statistics in the latter part of the book might be dropped, since that analysis is only remotely related to the thesis that criminology is essentially the study of conduct norms and resistance potentials. As a way out of the difficulty, he suggests that current methods in criminology be examined for their possible use in the study of conduct norms and their violations. In particular, he suggests that studies of sociologically unified groups, such as the professional thieves, and logically unified acts, such as white-collar crimes, be undertaken for the light they shed on deviant social conduct generally.

His second letter, of December 16, in which he confesses to some afterthoughts, carries the suggestion that the analysis of crime and delinquency might be retained if it were restated in terms of conduct norms. Expanding on this suggestion, he wrote:

> If this were done, there might first be a review of the general theory and of some of the general studies, but this should be followed by an attempt to isolate a certain part of the conduct norms which have uniform or identical resistance potentials (perhaps as measured in terms of legal penalties) and a comparison of immigrants and native be made on that basis. It should be possible, then, to go beyond these legal norms and study some of the other conduct norms, which have no legal connotation, or a minor connotation, such as Sabbath violation, use of alcohol, wearing whiskers, etc., to see how immigrants compare with native born on such types of behavior, and how or to what extent the violations are related to culture conflicts.

In closing, he reiterates that the report in its present form is long on theory and short on suggestions for research.

Sellin's answer to these letters does not appear in the correspondence files, but we may assume that the two men discussed the whole business at the 1937 meeting of the American Sociological Society at Atlantic City in December. In any case, in a letter in February of 1938 Sutherland gave his reaction to Sellin's suggestions for research, suggestions which were to be a vital part of the final report for SSRC. He again expresses some uncertainty about the meaning of culture conflict, wonders about limiting the analysis to the problems of immigration, and hypothesizes that inconsistencies in informal codes may undermine the general criminal code. Here are excerpts from that letter:

There has been some analysis and doubt as to the concept "cultural conflict." When are cultures in conflict? There was a conflict between the church and the artists on nudity in art, but nudity became "conventionalized" and was regarded as no longer in conflict. May not any two things which seem to be in conflict thus become integrated or accommodated in some manner? . . . I am recording the question, so that we may say the point has been recognized. I think there is an answer to the question, but in general I have shifted to "social disorganization" as preferable to "cultural conflict."

I have wondered somewhat about limiting the problems definitely to immigration, as constituting a more unified group of problems. Your statement now goes beyond that to rural-urban migrations. Should there be a more general consideration of mobility in relation to crime rates?

. . . [I]t seems to me that the relatively low rate of the large [immigrant] colonies is due to "isolation" from conflicting patterns. They live their own life in the midst of an American city almost as in their home community. Consequently they have few conflicts. Conflicts must grow out of cultural contacts. Moreover, the family and the neighborhood in such situations work together consistently in the direction of control of the individual member, while in the smaller [immigrant] groups, there may be no such harmony between the patterns of these two primary groups, and consequently there may be a high delinquency rate. . . . The probable conflict of cultures does not consist merely in the fact that the law of one group says thus-and-thus, while the law of the other group says so-and-so. Rather more important I believe is the fact that the informal codes differ on hundreds of other things, thus undermining the legal codes of both groups.

To this rather critical letter, Sellin replied on February 14 as follows:

> I am enclosing some substitute pages. . . . If you think this stuff is all right I shall send it on. . . . Of course, it will not be too late to make any changes, for I do not want to give you the impression that I close my mind against any suggestions. But if you want to make changes I hope that you will embody them in specific research questions which can be fitted into the general scheme.

In his reply of February 18, Sutherland raised additional questions:

> Your point regarding indigenous origin of conflicts is interesting and important. I believe conflicts may arise in this manner. But I am not sure that your interpretation of Shaw represents correctly his view. I know that he has indicated in conversation, although perhaps not in the literature, that a new immigrant group in a delinquency area has a period of several years of very low rates and then gradually or suddenly the rate approaches the usual rate for other national groups in that and similar areas. His interpretation as I have understood it is that it takes a period of years for the children of the incoming group to form contacts and assimilate the culture of the area. It might, of course, be interpreted also as a period required for the development of attitudes toward the situation in which they are located. . . .
>
> The general tone of the analysis seems atomistic [rather than molecular]. Your statement that a lower rate for a concentrated group than for a scattered group is paradoxical illustrates what I have in mind. I can conceive of an immigrant group with conduct norms exactly the same as those of the general native born population, a part of the immigrant group being located in a closely knit community, and a part scattered among other national groups. I should expect the second to have a higher rate of juvenile delinquency in part because the divergent norms of the national groups (some of them deviating from the native born norms) would produce a personal disorganization in the children, but partly because

of the [pattern of] reënforcement of the family standards by the similar standards of neighbors. . . . It seems to me the question involves not merely what the norms are, but how they are presented to the individual, as consistently by family and neighborhood as contrasted with presentation by the family in one way and by the neighborhood in a conflicting way.

. . . I should be content to have the report go in substantially as at present. Moreover, I should be proud to have my name attached, although I feel very strongly that the names should be attached in such a way that it is clear you are primarily responsible for the work, "Thorsten with the collaboration of Edwin" or something like that.

This letter marks the end of Sutherland's express contribution to the Social Science Research Committee report, which was published during the summer of 1938 under the title "Culture Conflict and Crime."[24]

On Legal Realism. Although Sutherland has been criticized recently for his preoccupation with the etiology of criminal behavior and his neglect of the legal process, he was by no means ignorant of the latter. His attitude was that both matters

[24] In a recent (May 13, 1972) letter from Professor Sellin, he comments on his work with Sutherland as follows: "The SSRC mandate was a headache for both of us. We were supposed to make criminology more 'scientific'; how to do it was left up to us. In hunting for a focus we finally settled on 'culture conflict,' a not uncommon concept forty years ago. Ed felt that since I was chairman of the committee I should start the ball rolling even though neither of us had a clear idea of what the goal was. As it turned out, the onus of writing the monograph fell on me. The result was that instead of a dissertation on criminological theory with a new twist, it ended in an exercise in logic and scientific method. . . .

"Ed was not happy about this. He tried to set me thinking in other directions and was no doubt annoyed because I did not take his advice. I was unable to do so without completely re-orienting my own thinking and rewriting the monograph. I may have been incapable of doing that. Anyway, I was unwilling because I had already spent an inordinate amount of time on the project. . . .

"One good thing may have come out of Ed's dissatisfaction with my production. I strongly suspect that this formulation of the differential association concept in the 1939 edition of his *Principles* crystallized out of his earnest efforts to set me straight."

were important and that one would suffer if the other were disregarded. His concentration on criminal behavior is quite consistent with, and perhaps explained by, the concern of his generation with countering the biological explanation of social behavior, which was in vogue at the time. From this standpoint, Sutherland's work was part and parcel of a wider effort to advance the sociological explanation of man's behavior.

Sutherland's effort to grasp the essentials of legal realism and not to slight it is evident in a letter to Jerome Hall, a professor of law at Indiana University with whom Sutherland had formed one of his most important relationships. In many ways, it was a critical relationship in that Hall stood for a somewhat different approach to criminology. He was an exponent of classical criminology and took the position that criminology should focus on criminal law rather than on criminal behavior. In fact, it was Hall's view that criminology is synonymous with the sociology of criminal law. The exchanges between these two "giants," who were good friends, forced Sutherland to examine his positivistic views and to evaluate their logical adequacy. This process of evaluation and refinement is reflected in the above-mentioned letter, in which he gives his reactions to Hall's *Principles of Criminal Law*, which had recently been published.[25] Pertinent parts of that letter, dated February 6, 1947, are as follows:

> Dear Jerome:
>
> I have read your "Principles" with much pleasure and enlightenment. I find that I understand your point of view and system of thought much better than I did from the reading of scattered articles.
>
> I believe it is important that we understand each other, regardless of whether we agree. On that account I am going to state, somewhat briefly and without much systematization, some of my reactions to your book.
>
> I agree that the fundamental problem, if we are to secure an integration of knowledge in the various disciplines (specifically

[25] Jerome Hall, *Principles of Criminal Law* (Indianapolis: Bobbs-Merrill, 1946).

criminal law and criminology), is the question of determinism, voluntarism, free will, positivism, or what not. Your fundamental thesis seems to rest on "voluntary" behavior, and I believe you make a good case for it, so far as concerns the criminal law. On the other hand, a criminologist who is attempting to explain or understand criminal behavior must, I believe, take a deterministic hypothesis: choice or the will undoubtedly exist but, from the point of view of explanation, they are interim processes and they, in turn, must be explained. . . .

Many of your statements seem to be dogmatic, as is doubtless true of any system of thought with which a person has some disagreement. You seem to see the lack of consensus among psychiatrists and social scientists and you utilize this lack of consensus in rebuttal of their theories. Your opponent could use precisely this tactic in rebuttal of the principles of criminal law, namely, point out the great disagreement among scholars in the field of criminal law. . . .

I agree with you in the criticism of the loose identification of crime and injury to social welfare. I believe that crime is defined in the criminal law and should not be extended beyond that definition. Perhaps our principal point of difference here is that I believe "white collar crime" is real crime. If I understand your argument, you believe that the violation of some laws is criminal behavior but ought not to be. If that is your meaning, your position does not conflict with my ideas of white collar crime.

But I am inclined to differ so far as policy is concerned. In general, it seems to me that you are thinking principally about society of two centuries ago, when social relations were confined almost entirely to direct relations between two persons. We have passed into a society in which social relations are much more impersonal. . . . Our society has made some attempt to protect its members through new regulations, and the violations of these regulations constitute the greatest damage to persons; the damage, however, is not direct, immediate, personal, but is diffused over the marketplace and frequently over a long time. Consequently, no particular act or violation of such regulations arouses wide-spread emotion, but there is a great deal of diffused antagonism against such behavior. Also, I am pesuaded that most of the behavior which is actually brought before courts or commissions under these regulations would meet your criterion of voluntary, culpable, and immoral behavior. These violations during the last three or four generations have made fundamental alterations in our social structure . . . ; perhaps they are forcing us into a better system but they have done so by violating the criminal law.

While agreeing with your criticism of the loose usage of the term crime, I believe it is highly desirable for criminologists to study behavior in two related fields: (a) the violation of other codes, on the assumption that from the point of view of causation the same processes will be discovered; (b) behavior which is sometimes criminal and sometimes not criminal, which can be identified as behavior and explained as such; drug addiction is an illustration of the latter and Lindesmith has undertaken to explain it regardless of whether the law prohibits it.

I find your views on punishment somewhat confusing. My own belief is that punishment is one way in which a society expresses its antagonism to specified behaviors and that behavior of a person is determined primarily by the several definitions of behavior which confront him; consequently, punishment does have values for purposes of control. . . .

However, a great mass of factual evidence makes it clear that punishment is not *very* effective in the regulation of behavior, and it tends to perpetuate criminal behavior in various ways. If we can devise other social reactions to crime which protect society against crime more effectively than punishment does, let us by all means do so. The theoretical problem, therefore, is not whether punishment has some value but whether, in specific circumstances, it has as much value as some other social reaction does. . . .

I could go on and on, but this is enough of a reaction at this time.[26]

METHODS OF WORK

Sutherland As Teacher. While Sutherland was writing his books and articles, notes and memos, he was carrying on as a teacher. In thinking back on Sutherland as teacher, one is naturally inclined to remember his good points and to forget his limitations. The ensuing account, in my opinion, is colored more by the omission of facts rather than the slanting of them.

[26] This letter from Sutherland to Jerome Hall is in the editor's file.

As with all persons regularly sought out for opinions and advice, Sutherland's teaching took a variety of forms and occurred outside as well as inside the classroom. In fact, because of his sincere manner, free of affectation, his impact was probably greater in small, informal gatherings than in large impersonal classes. But even in small seminars and the like, he did not relax his logical standards in the interest of smooth social relations and a high group rating. He always spoke his mind according to the way he saw things.

Sutherland had no silver tongue and was considered a drab lecturer by many students, probably because he made no effort to entertain them. Undeniably, his metier was the Socratic dialogue rather than the oratorical lecture. At Indiana, much of that dialogue took place in his office, which was quite accessible and which featured an old wicker rocking chair. At ease in the rocker, Sutherland's protégés (such as Albert Cohen, Donald Cressey, and Lloyd Ohlin) would hold forth with bold confidence on what they regarded as the logical flaws in Sutherland's criminology. Indiana's reputation for the tutorial method in sociology may have had its origin in Sutherland's rocking chair. In his friendly encounters with students, Sutherland was perfectly democratic, and he continually sought to learn from them. In preparing his papers, he regularly solicited their advice and sometimes revised his thinking on the basis of that advice. In much the same spirit, he helped his students and his younger colleagues in their own efforts and tended to excuse, but not overlook, their initial blunders and mistakes. In contrast, he did not excuse the blunders of an established man of reputation, particularly one given to pretense, scientism, and sophistry. In this sense, he was anti-Establishment and in tune with the Age of Aquarius.

Sutherland as Methodologist. Sutherland's methodology, like his teaching, was simple but effective, plain but productive. He was no statistician, although he regularly used statistics in his research. His conclusions on white-collar crime, for example, rest on a statistical analysis of almost 1,000 decisions against

70 large corporations. Moreover, he was uncanny in his ability to spot errors in statistical logic and patient in locating the trouble—witness his unravelling of the Gluecks. Shortly after his death, William Ogburn wrote to Mrs. Sutherland, saying (among other things) that although Edwin had not been a trained statistician, he could not be fooled by figures, the implication being that trained statisticians might be fooled.

Sutherland's competence in method consisted of more than a skepticism about calculations remote from the data. Most social scientists share that skepticism. Rather, it consisted in two habits of work: (1) his method of collecting, recording, and maintaining data, and (2) his requirement of a good fit between conclusions and data. Sutherland had no special method for collecting data, except his working rule that all elements in the data be open to inspection and that the process of data collection be reproducible. Thus, from Sutherland's files on white-collar crime, it is possible to examine the raw data in every detail and to reconstruct the operations by which those data were produced. In line with this principle, he regarded a graduate term paper as incomplete unless accompanied by a package of field notes, face sheets, interview schedules, tallies and counts, and the like. These matters are deserving of notice since at the moment sociologists appear to be less concerned with meticulous methods of data collection—a hallmark of Chicago in the 1920s—and more concerned with data manipulation by glamorous techniques. In reacting to this, Sutherland might have observed that you cannot turn bad data into good data by elaborate statistics, but you may ruin them by that means.

Few if any sociologists would dissent from Sutherland's working principle of a good fit between conclusions and data, and most would regard it as axiomatic and its expression in words as needless. But for Sutherland it was a reminder of these human failings: (1) maintaining one's theory in the face of negative evidence of proven reliability, and (2) improperly handling one's data so as not to reject one's hypothesis. Sutherland struggled against these tendencies and was concerned that others struggle against them as well. That concern is reflected in his criticism of the Gluecks, Hooton, and Sheldon—all guilty, in his opinion, of these undesirable habits.

His requirement of a good fit between data and theory may seem at odds with his attempt to construct a general theory of crime. For, in that attempt, he evidently substituted the principle of best fit for the principle of good fit; he was content to construct a best-fitting, but not necessarily good-fitting, theory. As previously noted, however, he did have misgivings about this grandiose undertaking with its connotation of excessive abstraction from reality. It perhaps would comfort him to know that his work was consistent with the current emphasis on a synthesis of generalizations arrived at inductively, and theoretical implications reached deductively. But then much of his work has a contemporary ring.

The papers in this volume, as noted in the introduction to the original edition, were chosen primarily for the light they shed on Sutherland's work and thought. However, some special consideration was given to unpublished manuscripts and to articles appearing in relatively inaccessible journals, with the thought of making such papers conveniently available to students and scholars. This bias, though slight, will explain the omission of some of Sutherland's better known pieces.

Although there was a temptation to tinker with Sutherland's prose here and there, presumably in the interest of greater clarity, in the end practically no textual changes were made, in order not to take the chance of disturbing the sense of his ideas. Sutherland's footnotes are referred to by superior numbers and letters; those added by the editors are referred to by asterisks. An index has been added to this edition, and the entries interestingly reflect Sutherland's close connection with the Chicago school of sociology.

KARL SCHUESSLER

Edwin H. Sutherland

ON ANALYZING CRIME

Edwin H. Sutherland

PART ONE

Differential Association

In the first chapter of the 1939 edition of his *Principles of Criminology* Sutherland set forth his "theory of differential association," a bold and compact set of propositions purporting to account for all "systematic criminal behavior." This theory conceives of criminality as participation in a cultural tradition and as the result of association with representatives of that culture. It is in contrast to all those schools that conceive of criminality as a consequence of some abnormality, physical or psychological, of the person. In the 1947 edition of the *Principles* Sutherland presented a revised formulation of the theory incorporating, among other significant changes, the generalization of the theory to include all criminal behavior rather than "systematic" criminal behavior alone.

Although this theory has generated a good deal of discussion, the two statements in the *Principles* are Sutherland's only published formulations of his position. This unfortunately gave rise in some quarters to the impression that Sutherland conceived of the theory in its published form as complete and definitive and to a conception of Sutherland himself as inflexible and resistant to change.

Papers here published for the first time should rectify these misconceptions. They are of great value in several respects.

First, they include a remarkably candid autobiographical revelation of the continuous intellectual growth of an outstanding criminological theorist. Second, they reveal the complexity of Sutherland's own thinking, his ability to recognize effective criticism, and his efforts to take that criticism into account. Third, they provide a more systematic and exhaustive assessment of the theory of differential association than any yet published. Fourth, they present, in the context of a searching self-evaluation, a trenchant formulation of many of the leading issues of criminological theory.

From these papers it will be evident that Sutherland conceived of the published versions of the theory of differential association as tentative formulations, subject to revision in the light of criticism and research. At the same time, they help to explain his reluctance to abandon the theory in the face of criticism. Sutherland was committed to the principle that the goal of science is general theory applicable to all events of a given class. He did not think of a potpourri of unrelated theoretical notions as a genuine alternative, and he did not believe that any of his critics could offer a truly general theory which met the tests of parsimony, logical coherence, and consistency with data better than the theory of differential association. Although prepared to recognize the force of criticism, he preferred to operate with a unitary theory and to strive to deal with criticism by modifying the original theory rather than to take the easy way of a "multiple-factor" approach. This method highlights the limitations of the theory, but Sutherland considered this a virtue rather than a defect. It forces the theoretical issues; it counters the tendency for criminological theory to deteriorate into a catalogue of disparate and unco-ordinated "causes"; and it stimulates the quest for a more adequate, inclusive, and internally consistent system of thought.

A Statement of the Theory

THE SCIENTIFIC explanation of a phenomenon may be stated either in terms of the factors which are operating at the moment of the occurrence of a phenomenon or in terms of the processes operating in the earlier history of that phenomenon. In the first case the explanation is mechanistic, in the second historical or genetic; both are usable. The physical and biological scientists favor the first of these methods, and it would probably be superior as an explanation of criminal behavior. Efforts at explanations of the mechanistic type have been notably unsuccessful, perhaps largely because they have been concentrated on the attempt to isolate personal and social pathologies. Work from this point of view has, at least, resulted in the conclusion that the immediate factors in criminal behavior lie in the person-situation complex. Person and situation are not factors exclusive of each other, for the situation which is important is the situation as defined by the person who is involved.

Reprinted by permission from Edwin H. Sutherland's *Principles of Criminology* (4th ed.; Philadelphia: J. B. Lippincott Company, 1947), pp. 5-9. This excerpt from the *Principles* is the last published version of the theory of differential association and is provided as a context for the papers which follow.

Subsequent footnotes supplied by the editors will be referred to, as here, by asterisks. Professor Sutherland's footnotes are indicated by superior numbers or letters.

The tendencies and inhibitions at the moment of the criminal behavior are, to be sure, largely a product of the earlier history of the person, but the expression of these tendencies and inhibitions is a reaction to the immediate situation as defined by the person. The situation operates in many ways, of which perhaps the least important is the provision of an opportunity for a criminal act. A thief may steal from a fruit stand when the owner is not in sight but refrain when the owner is in sight; a bank burglar may attack a bank which is poorly protected but refrain from attacking a bank protected by watchmen and burglar alarms. A corporation which manufactures automobiles seldom or never violates the Pure Food and Drug Law, but a meat-packing corporation violates this law with great frequency.

The second type of explanation of criminal behavior is made in terms of the life experience of a person and is a historical or genetic explanation of criminal behavior. This, to be sure, assumes a situation to be defined by the person in terms of the inclinations and abilities which the person has acquired up to that date. The following paragraphs state such a genetic theory [i.e., the theory of differential association] of criminal behavior on the assumption that a criminal act occurs when a situation appropriate for it, as defined by a person, is present.

(1) *Criminal behavior is learned.* Negatively, this means that criminal behavior is not inherited, as such; also, the person who is not already trained in crime does not invent criminal behavior, just as a person does not make mechanical inventions unless he has had training in mechanics.

(2) *Criminal behavior is learned in interaction with other persons in a process of communication.* This communication is verbal in many respects but includes also "the communication of gestures."

(3) *The principal part of the learning of criminal behavior occurs within intimate personal groups.* Negatively, this means that the impersonal agencies of communication, such as picture shows and newspapers, play a relatively unimportant part in the genesis of criminal behavior.

(4) *When criminal behavior is learned, the learning includes* (a) *techniques of committing the crime, which are sometimes very complicated, sometimes very simple;* (b) *the specific direction of motives, drives, rationalizations, and attitudes.*

(5) *The specific direction of motives and drives is learned from definitions of legal codes as favorable and unfavorable.* In some societies an individual is surrounded by persons who invariably define the legal codes as rules to be observed, whereas in others he is surrounded by persons whose definitions are favorable to the violation of the legal codes. In our American society these definitions are almost always mixed, and consequently we have culture conflict in relation to the legal codes.

(6) *A person becomes delinquent because of an excess of definitions favorable to violation of law over definitions unfavorable to violation of law.* This is the principle of differential association. It refers to both criminal and anti-criminal associations and has to do with counteracting forces. When persons become criminals, they do so because of contacts with criminal patterns and also because of isolation from anti-criminal patterns. Any person inevitably assimilates the surrounding culture unless other patterns are in conflict; a Southerner does not pronounce "r" because other Southerners do not pronounce "r." Negatively, this proposition of differential association means that associations which are neutral so far as crime is concerned have little or no effect on the genesis of criminal behavior. Much of the experience of a person is neutral in this sense, e.g., learning to brush one's teeth. This behavior has no negative or positive effect on criminal behavior except as it may be related to associations which are concerned with the legal codes. This neutral behavior is important especially as an occupier of the time of a child so that he is not in contact with criminal behavior during the time he is engaged in neutral behavior.

(7) *Differential associations may vary in frequency, duration, priority, and intensity.* This means that associations with criminal behavior and also associations with anti-criminal be-

havior vary in those respects. "Frequency" and "duration" as modalities of associations are obvious and need no explanation. "Priority" is assumed to be important in the sense that lawful behavior developed in early childhood may persist throughout life, and also that delinquent behavior developed in early childhood may persist throughout life. This tendency, however, has not been adequately demonstrated, and priority seems to be important principally through its selective influence. "Intensity" is not precisely defined, but it has to do with such things as the prestige of the source of a criminal or anti-criminal pattern and with emotional reactions related to the associations. In a precise description of the criminal behavior of a person these modalities would be stated in quantitative form and a mathematical ratio be reached. A formula in this sense has not been developed, and the development of such a formula would be extremely difficult.

(8) *The process of learning criminal behavior by association with criminal and anti-criminal patterns involves all of the mechanisms that are involved in any other learning.* Negatively, this means that the learning of criminal behavior is not restricted to the process of imitation. A person who is seduced, for instance, learns criminal behavior by association, but this process would not ordinarily be described as imitation.

(9) *Though criminal behavior is an expression of general needs and values, it is not explained by those general needs and values since non-criminal behavior is an expression of the same needs and values.* Thieves generally steal in order to secure money, but likewise honest laborers work in order to secure money. The attempts by many scholars to explain criminal behavior by general drives and values, such as the happiness principle, striving for social status, the money motive, or frustration, have been and must continue to be futile since they explain lawful behavior as completely as they explain criminal behavior. They are similar to respiration, which is necessary for any behavior but which does not differentiate criminal from non-criminal behavior.

It is not necessary, on this level of discussion, to explain why a person has the associations which he has; this certainly involves a complex of many things. In an area where the delinquency rate is high a boy who is sociable, gregarious, active, and athletic is very likely to come in contact with the other boys in the neighborhood, learn delinquent behavior from them, and become a gangster; in the same neighborhood the psychopathic boy who is isolated, introvert, and inert may remain at home, not become acquainted with the other boys in the neighborhood, and not become delinquent. In another situation, the sociable, athletic, aggressive boy may become a member of a scout troop and not become involved in delinquent behavior. The person's associations are determined in a general context of social organization. A child is ordinarily reared in a family; the place of residence of the family is determined largely by family income; and the delinquency rate is in many respects related to the rental value of the houses. Many other factors enter into this social organization, including many personal group relationships.

The preceding explanation of criminal behavior was stated from the point of view of the person who engages in criminal behavior. It is also possible to state theories of criminal behavior from the point of view of the community, nation, or other group. The problem, when thus stated, is generally concerned with crime rates and involves a comparison of the crime rates of various groups or the crime rates of a particular group at different times. One of the best explanations of crime rates from this point of view is that a high crime rate is due to social disorganization. The term "social disorganization" is not entirely satisfactory, and it seems preferable to substitute for it the term "differential social organization." The postulate on which this theory is based, regardless of the name, is that crime is rooted in the social organization and is an expression of that social organization. A group may be organized for criminal behavior or organized against criminal behavior. Most communities are organized both for criminal and anti-criminal behavior, and in that sense the crime rate is an expression of the differential group organization. Differential group organization as an explanation of a crime rate must be consistent with the explanation of the criminal behavior of the person, since the crime rate is a summary statement of the number of persons in the group who commit crimes and the frequency with which they commit crimes.

Development of the Theory

I SHALL present a personal account of the hypothesis that criminal behavior is caused by differential association. This is to be a biography of the hypothesis and a report on its present status or its rise and decline. It is a story of confusion, inconsistencies, delayed recognition of implicit meanings, and of much borrowing from and stimulation by colleagues and students. The hypothesis has changed rapidly and frequently, for which I am doubly thankful, first because the hypothesis at any rate is not dead, and second because I have been able to retract many ideas about it before they were published.

My organized work in criminology began in 1921, when E. C. Hayes, head of the Department of Sociology in the University of Illinois, asked me to write a text on criminology for the Lippincott series. My principal interest up to that time had been in labor problems. Hayes's request turned my career in the direction of criminology. I had taken a course in criminology in 1906 under Charles Richmond Henderson, in which we used as a text his *Dependents, Defectives, and Delinquents*, first edition, 1893, second, 1901. I had taught a course in criminology each year from 1913 to 1921. Fortunately the only texts, Parmelee and Wines, were inadequate, and I was compelled to

Address given by Professor Sutherland as retiring president of the Ohio Valley Sociological Society at the annual dinner of the Society, April, 1942.

make some investigations of the literature rather than depend entirely on the texts.

My principal theoretical interest in criminology at that time was the controversy between heredity and environment. The inherited factor had shifted somewhat from morphology, which Lombroso had emphasized, to feeble-mindedness, which Goddard was emphasizing, and inherited psychopathies were beginning to claim more attention.

Preliminary to writing a manuscript, I attempted to review all of the literature on criminology and especially the research studies. I organized the results topically—economic factors, political factors, physiological factors, etc.—rather than abstractly or logically. I made no effort to generalize, and consequently I had a congeries of discrete and co-ordinate factors, unrelated to each other, which may be called the multiple-factor theory. I was not aware that the relations among these factors constituted a problem, except as to the relative importance of the several factors. I took pride in my broadmindedness in including all kinds of factors and in not being an extremist like the geographic determinists, the economic determinists, the biological determinists, or the mental-tester determinists.

My other principal interest at that time was opposition to the view of Hayes and others that sociology is a synthetic science, organizing and interpreting the findings of other sciences. In contrast I insisted that sociology is a specialized science with special problems. I did not realize that this conception of general sociology was inconsistent with my synthetic view of criminal behavior; I was not even vaguely aware that the two positions were inconsistent.

I made some effort from the first to apply sociological concepts to criminal behavior, especially Thomas's attitude-value and four wishes, but also imitation, isolation, culture-conflict (implicitly rather than explicitly), and a little later Park's and Burgess' four processes. I was especially interested in the four wishes as a substitute for instincts, which were biological and inherited. And I made explicit use of the concept of isolation, partly because of the dramatic quality of the literature regarding feral men and partly because I worked somewhat intensively on that concept when Burgess asked me to write a paper on "The Isolated Family" for the Illinois conference of social work. For the most part these sociological concepts were used in restricted areas and became additional factors rather than generalizations from other factors. I made no effort to extend these sociological concepts to explain all criminal behavior.

More significant for the development of a theory were certain questions which I raised in class discussions. One of these questions was, Negroes, young-adult males, and city dwellers all have relatively high crime rates: What do these three groups have in common that places them in this position? Another question was, Even if feeble-minded persons have a high crime rate, why do they commit crimes? It is not feeble-mindedness as such, for some feeble-minded persons do not commit crimes. Later I raised another question which became even more important in my search for generalizations. Crime rates have a high correlation with poverty if considered by areas of a city but a low correlation if considered chronologically in relation to the business cycle; this obviously means that poverty as such is not an important cause of crime. How are the varying associations between crime and poverty explained? Largely in connection with the relation between crime and poverty, I began about 1928 to make investigations of white-collar crimes.

Almost all the ideas in the 1939 edition of my criminology are present in the 1924 edition, but they are implicit rather than explicit, appear in connection with criticisms of other theories rather than as organized constructive statements.

The second edition of my criminology in 1934 shows some progress toward a point of view and a general hypothesis. I was surprised in 1935 when Henry McKay referred to my theory of criminal behavior, and I asked him what my theory was. He referred me to pages 51–52 of my book. I looked this up and read

The hypotheses of this book are as follows: First, any person can be trained to adopt and follow any pattern of behavior which he is able to execute. Second, failure to follow a prescribed pattern of behavior is due to the inconsistencies and lack of harmony in the influences which direct the individual. Third, the conflict of cultures is therefore the fundamental principle in the explanation of crime.

I assure you that I was surprised to learn that I had stated a general hypothesis regarding criminal behavior. I undoubtedly owed much to Wirth's 1931 paper. My thinking was compartmentalized rather than integrated. I wrote one section of the book and forgot it when working on another section. I feel that I am not unique in this respect and that culture is generally compartmentalized rather than integrated in the person and the society. In spite of the statement about hypotheses, if anyone had caught me in my usual frame of mind and asked me what my theory of criminal behavior was, I would have answered, "The multiple-factor theory," and in that theory I would have left the multiple factors co-ordinate and unrelated to each other. I was not aware that I was approaching generalizations of an abstract nature.

I had been affected, however, by several incidents which turned my attention toward abstract generalizations, and these occurred about the time I was preparing the manuscript for the 1934 edition, or perhaps a little later. Michael and Adler had published their critical appraisal of criminological research. My first reaction, lasting for a couple of years, was emotional antagonism. But I wish now to admit that it had a very important influence on me and turned my attention toward abstract generalizations. Second, Dean Ruml of the University of Chicago called together several persons interested in criminology and asked us, "What do you know about criminal behavior?" The best I could say was that we had certain facts about the incidence of high crime rates and that we had proved that certain propositions were false. I could state no verified positive generalizations. This turned me somewhat more toward a search for such propositions. Third, in a doctoral examination of a candidate, whose name I do not remember,

Louis Wirth asked, "What is the closest approach you know to a general theory of criminal behavior?" After the stumbling often characteristic of such occasions, the candidate answered "cultural conflict," which was the right answer, since Wirth had published an article to that effect. Fourth, I supervised the work of Ching-Yueh Yen on a dissertation on crime in China which had the thesis that crime is due to cultural conflict. That work and, perhaps even more, Burgess's sharp criticisms during the examination, helped to clarify my position. Fifth, Sellin and I were appointed members of a committee of the Social Science Research Council to organize a report on a nuclear problem in criminology. We selected culture conflict as the problem and spent considerable time organizing the data and problems of criminal behavior around that concept. Although Sellin is almost entirely responsible for the report, it had an additional influence on me.

In the third edition of my criminology in 1939 I stated the hypothesis of differential association and placed it in the first chapter. I did this under the insistent prodding of Henry McKay, Hans Riemer, and Harvey Locke. I was reluctant to make the hypothesis explicit and prominent even after I realized that I had stated it, for I knew that every criminological theory which had lifted its head had been cracked down by everyone except its author. In spite of the danger I accepted the advice, probably because of the following influences.

First, I had worked for several years with a professional thief and had been greatly impressed by his statement that a person cannot become a professional thief merely by wanting to be one; he must be trained in personal association with those who are already professional thieves. There I seemed to see in magnified form the process that occurs in all crime. Second, Lindesmith had come to Indiana University, and I became acquainted with his conception of methodology as developed in his study of drug addiction. According to this conception, an hypothesis should fit every case in the defined universe, and the procedure to use is: State the hypothesis and try it out on one case; if it does not fit the facts, modify the hypothesis or else redefine the universe to which it applies, and try it on another case, and so on for case after case. This methodology consists in searching for negative cases, one negative case disproving the hypothesis. Although this involves several cases, it is not concerned with averages, standard deviations, or coefficients of correlation. This conception of methodology assisted me greatly in formulating problems and in testing hypotheses. I had long felt dissatisfied with work which consisted in finding a high correlation, say .72, and then regarding that problem as solved and passing to another problem. A third event was that some of us organized a non-credit seminar which met monthly in Indianapolis for two years and was attended by members of the professional staff of the penal institutions and by Lindesmith, Sweetser, and me. We were concerned principally with neighborhood influences on delinquency. One evening as we drove home from Indianapolis Sweetser asked, "Why doesn't the explanation of juvenile delinquency in a slum area apply in principle to murders in the South?" That question was the specific occasion for the formulation of the statement of differential association. The statement was mimeographed, distributed to the Indianapolis seminar and to some of my classes, criticized, re-formulated, and then included in the first chapter of the 1939 edition of my criminology. I made little effort in the text to organize the factual data regarding causes of crime around this hypothesis. This would have delayed publication for another year, and I was unwilling to disturb the somewhat standardized organization of the book in order to make the materials consistent with an hypothesis which might quickly be murdered or commit suicide.

It was my conception that a general theory should take account of all the factual information regarding crime causation. It does this either by organizing the multiple factors in relation to each other or by abstracting from them certain common elements. It does not, or should not, neglect or eliminate any factors that are included in the multiple factor theory.

The statement of that hypothesis of differential association as the explanation of the criminal behavior of a person marked the turning point in my thinking; previously I had used abstract processes as co-ordinate with concrete conditions, or had used them in certain compartments of my thinking but not in others. I had sufficient acquaintance with reports of research in criminology to know that hundreds of concrete conditions have something to do with criminal behavior, are associated with it in some way or other. But every one of them had a relatively small degree of association. Some Negroes commit crimes, some do not; some people who reside in delinquency areas commit crimes, some do not. Any concrete condition is sometimes associated with criminal behavior and sometimes not. Perhaps there is nothing that is so frequently associated with criminal behavior as being a male. But it is obvious that maleness does not explain criminal behavior. I reached the general conclusion that a concrete condition cannot be a cause of crime, and that the only way to get a causal explanation of criminal behavior is by abstracting from the varying concrete conditions things that are universally associated with crime.

With the general point of view which I had acquired as a sociologist and used particularly in relation to criminal behavior, it seemed to me that learning, interaction, and communication were the processes around which a theory of criminal behavior should be developed. The theory of differential association was an attempt to explain criminal behavior in that manner.

The hypothesis of differential association seemed to me to be consistent with the principal gross findings in criminology. It explained why the Moloccan children became progressively delinquent with the length of residence in the deteriorated area of Los Angeles, why the city crime rate is higher than the rural crime rate, why males are more delinquent than females, why the crime rate remains consistently high in deteriorated areas of cities, why the juvenile delinquency rate in a foreign nativity is high while the group lives in a deteriorated area and drops when that group moves out of that area, why second-generation Italians do not have the high murder rate that their fathers had, why Japanese children in a deteriorated area of

Seattle had a low delinquency rate even though in poverty, why crimes do not increase greatly in a period of depression. All of the general statistical facts seem to fit this hypothesis.

I wish now to pass to the second part of this history and describe some of the problems which have arisen in regard to the hypothesis, some of the research work that has been done, and the present state of my belief in the hypothesis.

One of the first questions concerned the relations among the concepts of differential association, social disorganization, and culture conflict. The published statement is very far from clear. The view that emerged from discussions is: First, culture relating to criminal law is not uniform or homogeneous in any modern society. This lack of homogeneity is illustrated in extreme form in the criminal tribes of India. Two cultures are in sharp conflict there. One is the tribal culture which prescribes certain types of assault on persons outside the tribe, in some cases with religious compulsions. The other is the legal culture as stated by the Indian and provincial governments and made applicable to the criminal tribes. Two conflicting codes of behavior impinge upon these tribes. When members of the tribe commit crimes, they act in accordance with one code and in opposition to the other. According to my theory, the same principle or process exists in all criminal behavior, although the conflict may not be widely organized or sharply defined as in the Indian tribes. Culture conflict in this sense is the basic principle in the explanation of crime. This culture conflict was interpreted as relating specifically to law and crime; and as not including conflicts in relation to religion, politics, standard of living, or other things. At an earlier date I had used the concept of culture conflict in this broader sense on the assumption that any kind of culture conflict caused crime. Principally because of criticisms by Mary Bess (Owen) Cameron I restricted the concept to the area of law and crime. This may be called the principle of specificity in culture conflict. The second concept, differential association, is a statement of culture conflict from the point of view of the person who commits the crime. The two kinds of culture impinge on him or he has associations with the two kinds of cultures, and this is differential association. The third concept, social disorganization, was borrowed from Shaw and McKay. I had used it but had not been satisfied with it because the organization of the delinquent group, which is often very complex, is social disorganization only from an ethical or some other particularistic point of view. At the suggestion of Albert K. Cohen, this concept has been changed to differential group organization, with organization for criminal activities on one side and organization against criminal activities on the other. This concept was designed to answer the question, Why does not criminal behavior, once initiated, increase indefinitely until everyone participates in it? The answer was: Several criminals perfect an organization and with organization their crimes increase in frequency and seriousness; in the course of time this arouses a narrower or a broader group which organizes itself against crime, and this tends to reduce crimes. The crime rate at a particular time is a resultant of these opposed organizations. Differential group organization, therefore, should explain the crime rate, while differential association should explain the criminal behavior of a person. The two explanations must be consistent with each other.

A second question was related to the distinction between systematic and adventitious crimes. This distinction had been made for practical rather than logical reasons, in order to postpone consideration of the very trivial criminal acts. I soon learned that different persons made very different definitions of the distinction. A psychiatrist in the Indiana State Prison accepted the theory as it related to systematic criminal behavior but asserted that not more than two of the two thousand prisoners there were systematic criminals. My idea had been that practically all of the prisoners were systematic criminals. However, when some of our graduate students were attempting to test the validity of the hypothesis by case studies of prisoners, they found that the most difficult part of the work was to determine objectively whether a prisoner was a criminal systematically or adventitiously. Since the distinction had been made for practical purposes and did not seem to have practical utility,

I abandoned it and stated the hypothesis as applying to every crime, regardless of its systematic quality. Some of my friends, especially Lindesmith, have insisted that I shall need to re-adopt this distinction or something much like it.

A third question had to do with the significance of "differential." I was asked, Why not say criminal behavior is due to association? The answer was that some persons who have many intimate contacts with criminals refrain from crime and that this is probably due to the counteracting influence of associations with anti-criminal behavior. Actual participation in criminal behavior is a resultant of two kinds of associations, criminal and anti-criminal, or the associations directed toward crime and the associations directed against crime. This eliminates a large portion of our experiences which are neutral so far as crime is concerned. The elimination of non-criminal culture was required by the principle of the specificity of culture conflict. I concluded that these non-criminal experiences were significant in restricted ways: (*a*) They may occupy time and thereby prevent frequent and intimate associations with criminal or anti-criminal patterns. (*b*) They may develop lawful techniques which may be utilized later in criminal or anti-criminal behavior in a different context. (*c*) They may determine the prestige of certain kinds of persons, e.g., the athletic person, and this may in a different context make the criminality of a person of that type more attractive. (*d*) They may provide training for legal behavior, which is later made illegal by a change in laws. The general conclusion was that training is transferred from the non-criminal area to the criminal or anti-criminal area so far as there are common elements.

A fourth question was, Is differential association merely a restatement of Tarde's theory that crime is due to imitation? My answer was that differential association takes into account not only imitation but all other processes of learning. For instance, seduction into illegal sexual behavior or other illegal behavior is not imitation.

A fifth question was, What specific things are learned in this association? Techniques of criminal behavior may be learned, but since many techniques of criminal behavior are also techniques of non-criminal behavior, other things must be acquired. The most important of the other elements is the evaluation of the behavior. Evaluation, which may be called rationalization, is concerned with motivation in a restricted sense. Another element is the definition of the situation in which criminal behavior is appropriate. The professional thief learns to define the situation in which criminal behavior is appropriate, but for him the situations are extensive and objects of theft somewhat substitutable. For many other offenders the situations and objects are not substitutable. Thus, a man kills his wife's lover in accordance with a code acquired from his associations; he would not be satisfied by killing some other person.

A sixth question was, Do non-criminals sometimes invent simple crimes? In other words, is criminal behavior possible without criminal associations? We have learned in social psychology that at least a slight element of invention is present in practically all behavior. The situation is a little different here, for both the legal code and the criminal pattern must be learned or acquired. But the question cannot be answered except by research studies. Some of our graduate students have made case studies of 125 adult prisoners and have found only one case in which associations with other criminals had not preceded their own crimes; although no measurement of the modalities of association were made, their associations with criminal patterns appeared to be much more frequent and intimate than those customary for people such as university students and faculty members. In the one exception, a student had been shortchanged by a storekeeper, almost certainly by mistake. The student called attention to it, but later used the same method as a student prank and then as the basis of a criminal career, with little association with other criminals. Another research project on this question of the invention of criminal behavior was to inquire of students regarding the circumstances of the first theft they could remember. Approximately three fourths of the students reported that their first thefts were subsequent to and presumably the result of association with others who had stolen previously. The other fourth described their first thefts as: "I saw something, I wanted it, I took it, although I knew it was wrong." My own first recollected theft is of that nature. But I am sure that in my own case I had stolen many things before the first one that I now recollect and that memories are not a reliable source of information as to the first theft. They will need to be studied at the time they occur. Two families have agreed to make reports to me regarding the first thefts of their children when the children reach the age when thefts may occur. I hope some of you will collect similar cases. The invention of criminal behavior may occur also in certain extreme cases of kleptomania or other compulsive crimes or of psychotic crimes. I shall deal with this at a later point.

A seventh question was, How did crime begin in the first place? How did it get into the culture? It can't be diffused until it originates, and differential association does not explain its origin. My explanation was that behavior of a certain kind goes on before the law prohibits it, and that pre-legal behavior constitutes the pattern for subsequent violation of the law. The new crimes defined by our defense and war legislation are of this nature, and I think that all other crimes are.

An eighth question was, What are the variables, modalities, or exponents of association with criminal patterns or with anti-criminal patterns? The 1939 edition refers to two such variables, frequency and consistency. Consistency is the same as "differential" association and therefore is not a variable, which leaves nothing except frequency. At least two other variables should be included, namely, intimacy and the prestige of the source of the pattern; to some extent the latter duplicates the first, and such duplication is the principal difficulty in adding to the number of variables. I have been asked, How do you explain the relatively low crime rate of prison guards and policemen who come into contact with criminals with great frequency? In the first place, I am not sure that they have a low crime rate, and second, they may not have frequent contacts with criminal patterns even though they have contact with criminals, for a prisoner seldom displays his criminal behavior to a prison guard. But waiving those points, we may say that policemen and prison guards seldom have intimate contact with criminals, and that criminals have little prestige with these agents of justice. A policeman or a prison guard has his most frequent, intimate, and prestigious associations with others in the same occupation and with members of the police machine; and when he participates in criminal behavior, it is most frequently in graft, which he learns from these associates. No attempt has been made to measure these exponents of association, and this certainly must be done if the hypothesis is to be used extensively, or progressively.

The ninth, last, and most difficult question was, What is the relation of personal traits to these culture patterns in the genesis of criminal behavior? This, to some extent, is the question of the invention of criminal behavior. I believe it is the most important and crucial question in criminological theory. When I prepared the first edition of the statement of differential association and submitted it for criticisms, I believed that the person's susceptibility to the criminal pattern was a factor. Under criticism this was dropped, on the ground that his susceptibility was largely, if not wholly, a product of his previous associations with criminal and anti-criminal patterns, and another proposition was substituted: Personal traits have a causal relation to criminal behavior only as they affect the person's associations. This proposition has been questioned more frequently and more vigorously than any other part of the theory. In view of the extent of the disagreement I must be wrong. In fact I am fairly convinced that the hypothesis must be radically changed at this point. My difficulty is that I do not know what to change it to. I am convinced that the basic principle is sound and that modification is preferable to abandonment.

The modification most frequently suggested is "Emphasize personal traits." Professor Reckless suggests that criminal behavior is due to contacts with criminal patterns plus reactive tendencies of persons. This can't be done, because the two are not in the same frame of reference. One is a genetic process, the other a static factor. The result is that the two overlap, the reactive tendencies being to a considerable extent the result of previous contacts.

I have worked with the idea that certain personal traits might be segregated to avoid this overlapping, particularly the so-called psychogenic traits which are regarded as developing independently of associations with criminal and anti-criminal patterns. The difficulty I have found with this is that there is no satisfactory definition of the psychogenic traits and no way of differentiating them from the sociogenic traits. One criterion often suggested is origin in early childhood, but language originates in early childhood and is not regarded as a psychogenic trait. Another criterion suggested is pervasiveness in other behavior; e.g., bashfulness is acquired in early childhood and appears in very much of the behavior of the person. This is equally true of the English language. Probably the method of learning is the most important differentiating characteristic of psychogenic and sociogenic traits, but that is the thing we wish to explain, and we can't use it at the same time as a criterion and an explanation. Even if the distinction were clear-cut, the question of how a psychogenic trait enters into criminal behavior would remain. It is possible that the bashful person might commit crimes bashfully, but the bashfulness would have nothing to do with the selection of the criminal behavior. The important question is whether a psychogenic trait is significant in the selection of criminal versus non-criminal patterns presented to him with equal frequency, intimacy, and prestige. If two patterns, one criminal and one non-criminal, are presented to a bashful person with equal frequency, etc., and if one pattern involves responsibility for manipulating other people and intimate contacts and the other does not, the bashful person would doubtless select the latter. In this manner bashfulness would have something to do with the genesis of the criminal behavior of a person.

The same may be said regarding sociogenic traits. This question of sociogenic traits is the same question raised previously regarding the specificity of culture conflict: Does one culture element cut across another? Are culture elements segregated from each other, or are they completely integrated with each other? There is no question that the non-criminal neutral culture elements may enter into criminal behavior in particular cases through influences on prestige. I recently read a case history of a boy in an institution for juvenile delinquents. The boy was practically a model boy until he reached the age of eight. Shortly before that the father had been converted to a Holy Roller church, had moved from a rural area to Terre Haute, and was operating a restaurant there and taking the family to church two or three times a week for many hours a day. The family lived in a district in which few other families were members of the Holy Roller church. This boy was ridiculed by the other boys in school; they called him preacher and reverend because he went to church so much. By the boy's own account he developed because of this an antagonism against the parents, and as a part of that antagonism began to steal. There seems to be no doubt, at any rate, that the prestige of the source of a pattern may be affected by cultural elements outside the field of the criminal code, and in that respect at least the principle of specificity of culture conflict breaks down. This applies equally to the sociogenic traits of a person.

I wish to suggest that this relation between personal traits and culture patterns is the most important problem in regard to criminal behavior. In order to answer the question, we might re-work some of the old research studies and undertake some new studies.

Healy and Bronner report a much greater frequency of emotional disturbances in delinquents than in their non-delinquent siblings and imply that emotional disturbance is the cause of delinquency. I have several criticisms of their methodology, which I shall not mention, and wish to point out only that they do not present organized evidence that emotional disturbance is a cause rather than an effect of the delinquent behavior. Waiving those questions, I cannot see that emotional disturbance is the cause of delinquency since some non-delinquents were emotionally disturbed and some delinquents were not emotionally disturbed. I believe it would be possible, if the original data were available and were found to be reliable, to show that delinquency in these cases originated in this manner: Emotional disturbances, originating from frustration at home, drive boys away from home for companionship and recreation. Such cases are in the lower economic group, and the juvenile delinquency rate is high in such neighborhoods. Consequently there is a probability that they will come into contact with boys who are delinquent with greater frequency and intimacy than they would if they were not frustrated at home and that they will on that account become delinquent. The boys who became delinquent were more active, gregarious, and athletic than the boys who did not become delinquent; the others were content with their homes, their schools, and their libraries and had less contact with delinquency. It is possible that emotional disturbance was significant in the genesis of delinquent behavior only as it resulted in increasing the frequency and intimacy of associations with delinquent patterns or the prestige of those patterns, or in isolating the individual from the patterns of anti-criminal behavior. Whether this would provide a clear-cut distinction between the delinquents and the non-delinquents I do not know, but I suspect that it would make a more complete distinction than is made by emotional disturbance as such.

Terman and Miles have suggested that femininity is the cause of passive male homosexuality. They found by tests that passive male homosexuals have higher scores for femininity than did a random sample of the male population. The scores were based on present activities and interests and also on childhood recreations and other earlier interests. The authors concluded that passive male homosexuality was a part of a general feminine pattern that characterized most of the behavior of these persons and that therefore the personal trait was the explanation. These tests, however, were given to passive male homosexuals who had been practically commercial prostitutes for an average period of ten years. Consequently their answers to the test questions may have been greatly affected by their experiences after homosexual behavior began and very little by their prior experiences. Even if we assume that the scores reflected their earlier personal traits accurately, it is probable that the feminine traits attracted active male homosexuals and that they were subjected to the pattern of homosexuality with greater frequency and intimacy, and more persuasive salesmanship than are males with ordinary masculine traits. It is probable that their passive male homosexuality originated from their associations and that the personal trait was significant only in determining their associations. Finally, even if femininity explains passive male homosexuality, masculinity obviously does not explain active male homosexuality.

Thus some questions about the relations between personal traits and cultural patterns in the genesis of criminal behavior may be answered tentatively by repeating former research studies. I have suggested that extreme cases should be selected for new research by sociologists. These extreme cases have been studied heretofore almost exclusively by psychiatrists who were interested only incidentally in the person's associations, and who also were interested only incidentally in the criminality of the behavior. I have suggested that sociologists study kleptomania, pyromania, the criminal behavior which is interpreted by psychoanalysts as symbolic incest, the psychotic criminal, the black sheep, and crimes committed under the influence of alcohol by persons who do not behave in similar manner under other conditions.

If these studies are made, they may result in a conclusion that criminal behavior is homogeneous in its genesis, or that there are types of criminal behavior, each with a distinct genetic process. I am confident, however, that the explanations either of the homogeneous process or the heterogeneous processes, whichever may be supported by the evidence, will be concerned primarily with the relations between personal traits and differential association.

And so, this is my account of how my theory of differential association has been produced by my own differential associations.

Critique of the Theory

THE THEORY of differential association as the explanation of criminal behavior postulated criminal behavior as a closed system. Differential association was regarded as both the necessary and the sufficient cause of a person's entrance into the closed system of criminal behavior. Association with criminal patterns was defined as the necessary cause because it was felt that no person could enter the system of criminal behavior unless he had associated with criminal patterns. This was regarded as analogous to learning the English language: a person acquires the English language only by associating with it; he does not invent it, and he does not acquire it by associating with Republican politics or Presbyterian theology except as those cultural systems involve the English language. Also, differential association was regarded as the sufficient cause, in the sense that all persons who associate with criminal patterns participate in

This previously unpublished paper, written in 1944, was intended only for circulation among Sutherland's associates. The manuscript was entitled "The Swan Song of Differential Association," but the title is not to be taken as a reflection of disillusionment on Sutherland's part. The paper is Sutherland's own effort to make the strongest case for the critics of the theory. That he continued to be in the main—but not altogether—unconvinced is evidenced by the statement in the *Principles* (1947), which set forth the theory with the same vigor as the 1939 edition, although the exposition was substantially modified in some respects.

criminal behavior unless inhibited by associations with anti-criminal patterns. According to this hypothesis, whether a person enters or does not enter the closed system of criminal behavior is determined entirely by the ratio between associations with criminal patterns and associations with anti-criminal patterns, with their varying modalities of frequency, intensity, prestige of the source of the pattern, and other modalities. Variations in other social conditions and in personal characteristics were regarded as factors in the causation of criminal behavior only as they affected differential association with criminal and anti-criminal patterns.

While some questions have been raised regarding the necessity of association with criminal patterns, these questions are largely verbal and can be answered with approximate finality. The crucial questions and criticisms have been directed at the sufficiency of differential association as a cause of criminal behavior. Certain of the factors in the causation of crime which are extraneous to differential association will be considered in this analysis, which results in the conclusion that differential association is not a sufficient cause of criminal behavior. In the methodology which is used, with the explanation postulated as universal, the only thing needed to disprove an hypothesis is a single exception.

OPPORTUNITY

One factor in criminal behavior which is at least partially extraneous to differential association is opportunity. Criminal behavior is partially a function of opportunities to commit specific classes of crimes, such as embezzlement, bank burglary, or illicit heterosexual intercourse. Opportunities to commit crimes of these classes are partially a function of physical factors and of cultures which are neutral as to crime. Consequently criminal behavior is not caused entirely by association with criminal and anti-criminal patterns, and differential association is not a sufficient cause of criminal behavior.

This argument will be elaborated and illustrated. First, criminal behavior is partially a function of opportunity. Persons in prisons seldom commit illicit heterosexual intercourse because they are physically segregated from persons of the opposite sex and thus have little opportunity to commit this crime. Convictions of public intoxication in Germany during World War I decreased almost to zero because intoxicating beverages were not manufactured and were not available for consumption, and the Germans consequently had no opportunity to become intoxicated. Negroes are seldom convicted of embezzlement because they are seldom in positions of financial trust, in which alone embezzlement is possible. It is true, of course, that certain crimes, such as petty theft, may be committed by practically anyone in modern society and that opportunity is practically always present. The only thing necessary for the present purpose, however, is to indicate that criminal behavior is sometimes limited by lack of opportunity. It is axiomatic that persons who commit a specific crime must have the opportunity to commit that crime. On the other hand, opportunity is not a sufficient cause of crime, since some persons who have opportunities to embezzle, become intoxicated, engage in illicit heterosexual intercourse or to commit other crimes do not do so. Consequently opportunity does not differentiate all persons who commit a particular crime from all persons who do not commit that crime.[1]

Second, the opportunity to commit a specific crime is partially a function of physical factors and of the non-criminal culture. The illustrations presented previously show that physical barriers, including physical space, interfere with crimes of certain types and also that occupational and general social positions are generally determined by cultural elements which are

[1] The complexity of the problem is increased, but the conclusion is not altered by introducing the concepts of attempts or conspiracies to commit a particular crime. It is difficult to conceive of a situation in which a person may not attempt or conspire with others to commit a specific crime. While the opportunities to attempt or conspire to commit a particular crime are much less limited than the opportunities to perform the primary tasks of a successfully consummated crime, the fact remains that variations in opportunities are associated with variations in crimes committed.

neutral so far as crime is concerned. For instance, the opportunity for a Negro to obtain a position of financial trust is limited by race prejudice, and consequently the low rate of embezzlement among Negroes is explained by race prejudice. While opportunity may be partially a function of association with criminal patterns and of the specialized techniques thus acquired, it is not determined entirely in that manner, and consequently differential association is not the sufficient cause of criminal behavior.

INTENSITY OF NEED

Another criticism of differential association as a sufficient cause of crime is that criminal behavior varies with the intensity of a particular need independently of variations in differential association with criminal and anti-criminal patterns. This criticism is illustrated by the following types of evidence. Thefts are most frequent in the lower socioeconomic class, which is in greater poverty than the upper socioeconomic class. The members of the Donner party, caught in the snow in the mountains during their trip to the Pacific Coast in the forties, with their food supply exhausted, generally resorted to cannibalism. Fathers who engage in incest with their daughters are concentrated in the age group between forty and sixty and in families in which the mothers have died, are sick, or are for other reasons not available for legitimate sex relations. Prisoners who are segregated from the other sex and unable to engage in legitimate heterosexual relations frequently resort to homosexual relations.

This evidence is not derived from careful studies of situations in which differential association is held constant, and it can to some extent be harmonized with the theory of differential association. While thefts, as conventionally treated, are concentrated in the lower socioeconomic class, which is in the greatest poverty, more subtle forms of illegal appropriation of property flourish, perhaps with equal frequency, in the upper socioeconomic or white-collar class. Also, thefts do not increase appreciably in periods of depression, when poverty increases, presumably because a depression does not appreciably modify the associations of persons; this indicates that when associations are held constant, increased poverty does not result in increased thefts. Fathers whose wives are dead or sick often spend an increased portion of their time in low resorts where they may have more contact with various forms of illicit sex behavior, and this may include contact with the pattern of incest.

Furthermore, it is unnecessary to postulate an increase in the number of associations with criminal behavior in order to account for an increase in the crime rate. A person may learn, through association with a criminal pattern, a definition of the situation in which it is appropriate to commit a particular crime. He commits this crime, however, only when the situation defined as appropriate arises or can be located. Having learned through association with others that he should murder his wife if he catches her in an unfaithful relationship, he does so, in accordance with the learned definition, only when the situation arises. Even the general culture of the modern community includes a definition of theft as appropriate in conditions of great emergency. The statement has been frequently made by respectable persons: "If I could find no alternatives except starvation or theft, I would steal." Practically everyone in the modern community has come in contact with that definition of theft and may, without additional contact with thieves, engage in theft when he reaches that situation.

This rebuttal of the evidence that crimes vary with the intensity of needs, independently of differential association, is presumably to some extent justified. Neither the evidence for this criticism nor the evidence against it is conclusive. The conclusion may be reached, however, that the sufficiency of differential association as an explanation of crime is questionable.

CRIME AND ALTERNATE BEHAVIORS

In many situations, at least, criminal behavior is not absolutely determined but only in relation to other behaviors, against which it may be balanced in the process of making choices. The relativity of criminal behavior in this sense may be illustrated in the following cases.

An isolated and unattractive girl was taken into an intimate friendship by another girl and was being gradually inducted into a homosexual relationship. In time the first girl became vaguely aware that the relationship was progressing beyond the conventional limits and became disturbed. She secured books on homosexuality and discovered with horror that the relationship was defined in the literature as the early stages of sex perversion. She went to the other girl with a firm determination to sever the relationship. But as she talked with the other girl and thought about it in more detail, she was confronted with two alternatives: isolation and loneliness without homosexuality, or a much desired intimate friendship that involved homosexuality. She chose the latter and became a confirmed homosexual not only because of her initial contacts with that pattern but also because she could find no other way of satisfying the need for intimacy and friendship. If she had been an attractive and gregarious girl, she would presumably, given the same contacts with the pattern of homosexuality, have severed this initial relationship without hesitation.

McCracken, the owner of a new newspaper in a California community, began a campaign of vilification of French, the owner of an established newspaper in the same community. For months McCracken used great ingenuity in ridiculing French. French went to McCracken and remonstrated, but this did no good. He consulted an attorney as to the possibility of a suit against McCracken, and also consulted the postal authorities as to the possibility of prosecuting under the postal regulations; but these efforts were futile. He considered fisticuffs, but McCracken weighed over two hundred pounds and was over six feet tall, whereas French weighed one hundred and thirty pounds and was five feet seven. The irritations continued, and French's anger accumulated. Finally he secured a gun, killed McCracken, and then surrendered himself to the police.

French had tried several alternatives and had found them futile. Presumably, if one of the legal methods had been successful, French would not have committed the murder. The case history gives no information as to French's contact with patterns of murder, and it is possible that some of his friends may have said repeatedly, "If he treated me that way, I would kill him." Even if this is true, the murder was caused not only by association with patterns of murder but by the failure of alternate ways of behavior.

The theory of differential association postulated the ratio between criminal patterns and anti-criminal patterns as the cause of criminal behavior. No organized effort has been made to develop that formula in a quantitative form, but the possibility of quantifying it is implicit in the abstract proposition. If a scoring method were developed, it might show, for instance, that association with a particular criminal pattern, such as murder or homosexuality, had a score of five, that association with the anti-criminal pattern also had a score of five, and that the differential association quotient was unity, which would be the ideal borderline between committing a particular crime and not committing that crime. Since associations with various patterns of crimes vary, the quotient would vary from one crime to another. A quotient in excess of unity would mean that the person would engage in crime, whereas a quotient of less than unity would mean that the person would not engage in crime.

The abstracts of case histories which have been presented demonstrate that a person does not engage in or refrain from a particular crime because of his criminal associations alone but because of those associations plus tendencies toward alternate ways of satisfying whatever needs happen to be involved in a particular situation. Consequently it is improper to view criminal behavior as a closed system, and participation in criminal behavior is not to be regarded as something that is determined exclusively by association with criminal patterns.

In the general area of juvenile delinquency it is probable that the most significant difference between juveniles who engage in delinquency and those who do not is that the latter are provided abundant opportunities of a conventional type for satisfying their recreational interests, while the former lack those opportunities or facilities. The ordinary child in the middle-class family presumably may have no more contacts with anti-delinquent patterns than the child in the slum areas, but his time is occupied more completely with activities which are neutral so far as the criminal code is concerned.

METHODOLOGIES

For the reasons that have been outlined and doubtless for additional reasons differential association as a sufficient explanation of criminal behavior is invalid. Consequently, questions arise as to the procedures that may be used in the future. Several possibilities may be considered.

First, the effort to state universal causes of criminal behavior might be abandoned and a retreat made to the "multiple-factor" approach (which should not be called a theory) to explanation. This method consists of the listing of all of the variables associated with criminal behavior, with a minimum of attention to the interrelations among these variables. For instance, needs and opportunities have been found to be associated with criminal behavior in ways which are not included in differential association. The multiple factor approach would merely add these two variables to differential association, regardless of the lack of discreteness in the factors and regardless of the fact that they overlap differential association in many respects. In many stages this approach may be the best that can be made, but it is regarded by some students as an interim condition, as a make-shift to be tolerated only until a more adequate approach can be developed. Knowledge which results from this approach has a limited utility either from the point of view of understanding or of control.

A second suggestion is that two approaches to the explanation of behavior supplement each other, one in terms of needs, wishes, values, goals, etc., which generally are oriented to the future, the other in terms of the genesis of those needs, wishes, etc., which are oriented to the past. According to this position, the first step in explanation is to analyze the overt behavior in terms of these needs, values, and goals, and the next step to trace the genesis of these factors, perhaps in terms of association with various patterns of behavior. This position has a certain plausibility, but analysis shows that it is fundamentally unsound.

In a study of a case history, such as those presented above for illustrative purposes, it is possible to analyze the alternate behaviors under consideration in terms of values and goals, and it is also possible to trace the genesis of each of these values. The difficulty arises when one attempts to go beyond an individual case and reach generalizations regarding a class of overt behaviors, such as all murders, or all thefts, or, outside the field of criminal behavior, all divorces or all church-goings. One person may go to church for the satisfaction of needs which another person satisfies by murder. Persons steal to satisfy hunger, to provide medical care for a sick child, to go to the movies, to secure flashy clothes, to make contributions to the USO, to acquire status in a certain group, to injure certain other persons. Also, they engage in lawful employment for all of the above reasons. These evaluations consequently do not differentiate one class of behaviors from another class of behaviors. The evaluations—needs, goals, etc.—are necessary in behavior of any kind, but they do not differentiate behavior of one kind from behavior of another kind if the behaviors are defined in terms such as crime, church-going, political action. The place of these needs and values in behavior is in this respect analogous to the place of muscular processes. Behavior would not occur without muscular processes, but the muscular processes do not differentiate stealing from lawful work. The study of muscular processes, of course, is desirable for certain purposes, but since the muscular processes in criminal behavior are not unique, their study contributes nothing to the understanding of criminal behavior. Similarly the needs, values, goals, etc., in criminal behavior are not unique, and explanations cannot be made in terms of them.

If the needs or goals are taken as specific, e.g., the need to dance, rather than the need to secure exercise, the procedure is tautological. The dancing behavior of a person many be "explained" by his "need to dance," but such an "explanation" contributes nothing to the understanding of the behavior. On the other hand, the dancing behavior cannot be explained by the need to secure exercise, since the need for exercise might be expressed in swimming, walking, playing golf, or sawing wood, as well as in dancing. If the psychological dynamism is stated as a specific drive, it explains nothing; and if it is stated as a general drive, it does not differentiate between one class of behaviors and another class of behaviors. The problem of criminal behavior is precisely the problem of differentiating one class of behaviors from another class.

The frustration-aggression hypothesis is a particular case of the attempt to explain behavior by a general psychological dynamism. Frustration is essentially another name for "need," and certain theorists postulate aggression as the universal reaction to frustration. In order to make this postulation they are compelled to define aggression in a manner which makes it include submission, ordinarily regarded as the opposite of aggression. Even if the concept, as defined, be accepted, the fact of frustration does not explain why lawful methods of aggression are used on some occasions and unlawful methods of aggression on others. That is, frustration does not differentiate between lawful and unlawful behavior and is therefore not an explanation of unlawful behavior. Many psychiatrists have been prone to conclude, when they find a maladjusted person to be frustrated, that the frustration is the explanation of the maladjustment. This procedure has no more logical justification than the explanation that someone sings well "because he is a Negro" or is guilty of sharp practices "because he is a Jew."

The conclusion is that a class of behaviors, such as all crimes, or all murders, cannot be explained by needs, goals, values, etc. If the analysis of behaviors in terms of needs and values is to be valid, the problems must be formulated in terms of needs and values rather than in terms of crimes, murders, or divorces.

It is possible that if the problems are stated as value-units, generalizations may be made in terms of values, but if they are stated in other terms (e.g., crimes, murders, or divorces) generalizations cannot be made in terms of values.

Another procedure is to regard differential association as one of the very important processes in the genesis of criminal behavior. In situations like those of the criminal tribes of India, where the differential association quotient may be presumed to be far above unity, differential association is essentially the total explanation; but the hypothesis becomes increasingly uncertain in its operation as the quotient approaches unity. This might then be regarded as a statement of a law which is valid only in ideal conditions, as the law of falling bodies is valid only in a vacuum, and efforts might be made to determine and perhaps measure the various extraneous factors which enter into the genesis of criminal behavior when the ideal conditions do not prevail. Perhaps this is not different from the present stage in the explanation of tuberculosis, in which the tubercle bacilli are demonstrated to be necessary factors but not sufficient factors, and in which the other factors, which may be vaguely generalized as "susceptibility," have not been definitely formulated. Just as continued work on these factors of "susceptibility" may be expected to result in a generalization at some future time, so continued work on the factors which interfere with the operation of the hypothesis of differential association may result in a valid generalization regarding these other things. The two variables which have been discussed previously are opportunities and needs. It may be possible to describe in general the factor of opportunities as Stouffer has, regarding mobility as a law of intervening opportunities for crimes. Similarly, it may be possible to include with differential association those factors of need which have to be included to provide a valid generalization regarding crime.

If these efforts do not succeed, and it is very probable that they will not, the methodology must either remain at the multiple-factor stage of development, or else the attempt to explain criminal behavior must be abandoned and problems formulated in terms of value units. It is perhaps suggestive that Lindesmith, who has been one of the foremost proponents of this methodology, adopts substantially the latter procedure in his study of drug addiction. In his explanations of the person who ceases the use of narcotic drugs, perhaps for many years, Lindesmith insists that this person is still an "addict" and is so regarded by himself and by other addicts. This shows that his unit, which he has attempted to explain, is a psychological or value unit rather than a unit of overt behavior.

Susceptibility and Differential Association

It is possible to concentrate on the end-product, overt crime, or on a preliminary stage of behavior, which may be called susceptibility. Susceptibility is merely incomplete criminality, assimilation of a part of a culture complex into which other details may then fit readily. Susceptibility is due to the same processes as overt crime and is merely a preliminary and incomplete form of criminality.

There may be an advantage in analyzing susceptibility, for it gives a basis for prediction. It may be possible to determine susceptibility by a test of some sort, in which case one would merely be describing the person's history of differential associations in that form. Susceptibility and the frequency necessary to produce overt crime bear an inverse ratio to each other. If a person has a high degree of susceptibility, it will take relatively little more association with criminal patterns to make

This undated and previously unpublished fragment, like the preceding paper in this collection, was not originally intended for publication. It is included here for two reasons. First, it is a forceful summary statement of one of the major problems of criminological theory, the relationship between personality characteristics and association with criminal patterns as factors in the genesis of criminality. Second, it illustrates Sutherland's method of dealing with a factor which the theory does not seem to take into account by trying to reformulate that factor within the same frame of reference rather than by tacking it on as an appendage.

him engage in overt crime; if he has relatively low susceptibility, it will take a great deal of association with criminal patterns to make him deal overtly in crime. At a particular time, criminal behavior can be predicted as likely to result from a combination of a particular amount of susceptibility and a particular increment of association with criminal patterns.

This explanation makes persons substitutable. If a person is self-determinative, science is impossible and criminal behavior cannot be explained. But if a person with a given amount of susceptibility can be assumed, any other person with the same susceptibility can be substituted, and the same behavior will result. It is necessary to state the personal factor in that manner. The person in this sense is passive. He is not self-integrating. This assumes that the integration is in the culture. There is a culture complex, manifested partially in the behavior of a person; if he goes further, he will have the entire complex, which is already integrated outside of the person. The only thing necessary is that the person have association with the pattern or complex.

A person may have a number of different cultures or culture complexes, one as a professor, another as a golf player. They are not integrated. Personality in general is not integrated as personality. His crime may be committed as a golf player or as a professor, and in either case he will be filling out the pattern of the culture when he has the sufficient amount of association.

PART TWO

White-Collar Crime

SUTHERLAND was regarded by contemporary American criminologists as the foremost exponent of the idea of white-collar crime. Although his first paper on this subject was published rather late in his career, when he was fifty-seven, he had actually been concerned with this problem for many years. In the preface to his book, *White Collar Crime* (published in 1949), he stated that his study had been twenty-five years in progress, which would place its beginning around 1925.

The first selection, entitled "White-Collar Criminality," sets out in somewhat informal fashion the major characteristics of white-collar crime and also what Sutherland believed to be its significance. This paper, following its publication in 1940, stimulated a great deal of critical discussion in both nonacademic and academic circles. His reply to this initial wave of criticism is contained in "Is 'White-Collar Crime' Crime?" included as the second paper of this group. The third selection, previously unpublished, was given before a group of sociology students and faculty members at DePauw University in the spring of 1948. This article, less abstract and less technical than the first two, is an informal report on the results of his investigation of criminality in seventy corporations. It reveals his ideas through a wealth of concrete detail rather than by means of formal propositions.

Although hazardous to conjecture, the motivation behind Sutherland's interest in white-collar crime appears to have had two principal components. First, he was impressed, as all who study crime must surely be, by the manner in which the legal processes operate to the distinct advantage of the privileged and influential social classes. It is reasonable to assume that his interest in business crime was aroused in part by his recognition and appreciation of this patent social fact. The second, and perhaps the major, incentive was his dissatisfaction, often expressed, with conventional theories of crime. Conventional theories, Sutherland felt, placed an undue emphasis on poverty and other conditions concentrated in the lower socioeconomic classes. In his opinion this emphasis obstructed the development of a theory sufficiently general to cover the whole range of crime. Thus his concern with occupational crimes of the upper social classes, as with differential association, exemplifies his persistent drive toward a comprehensive sociological theory, free of contradictions and consistent with empirical knowledge.

Criticism of Sutherland's concept of "white-collar crime" has taken two principal forms. Sociologists have objected that the concept tends to blur the distinction between violators of the criminal law who are publicly stigmatized as criminals and those who are not, while legal criticism makes the point that this concept has been misapplied to actions that are essentially civil wrongs and that the terms tort and crime are confused. The legal argument is that offenses handled by the civil courts or administrative agencies should not be called "crimes." Sutherland, on the other hand, maintained that, at least for the present, criminology should study all violations of criminal law no matter how processed or named.

White-Collar Criminality

This paper is concerned with crime in relation to business. The economists are well acquainted with business methods but are not accustomed to consider them from the point of view of crime; many sociologists are well acquainted with crime but are not accustomed to consider it as expressed in business. This paper is an attempt to integrate these two bodies of knowledge. More accurately stated, it is a comparison of crime in the upper or white-collar class, composed of respectable or at least respected business and professional men, and crime in the lower class, composed of persons of low socioeconomic status. The comparison is made for the purpose of developing the theories of criminal behavior, not for the purpose of muckraking or of reforming anything except criminology.

The criminal statistics show unequivocally that crime, *as popularly conceived and officially measured*, has a high incidence in the lower class and a low incidence in the upper class; less than two per cent of the persons committed to prisons in a year belong to the upper class. These statistics refer to criminals handled by the police, the criminal and juvenile courts, and the prisons, and to such crimes as murder, assault,

Reprinted by permission from the *American Sociological Review*, V (1940), 1-12.

burglary, robbery, larceny, sex offenses, and drunkenness, but exclude traffic violations.

The criminologists have used the case histories and criminal statistics derived from these agencies of criminal justice as their principal data. From them, they have derived general theories of criminal behavior. These theories are that, since crime is concentrated in the lower class, it is caused by poverty or by personal and social characteristics believed to be associated statistically with poverty, including feeble-mindedness, psychopathic deviations, slum neighborhoods, and "deteriorated" families. This statement, of course, does not do justice to the qualifications and variations in the conventional theories of criminal behavior, but it presents correctly their central tendency.

The thesis of this paper is that the conception and explanations of crime which have just been described are misleading and incorrect, that crime is in fact not closely correlated with poverty or with the psychopathic and sociopathic conditions associated with poverty, and that an adequate explanation of criminal behavior must proceed along quite different lines. The conventional explanations are invalid principally because they are derived from biased samples. The samples are biased in that they have not included vast areas of criminal behavior of persons not in the lower class. One of these neglected areas is the criminal behavior of business and professional men, which will be analyzed in this paper.

The "robber barons" of the latter half of the nineteenth century were white-collar criminals, as almost everyone now agrees. Their attitudes are readily illustrated. Commodore Vanderbilt asked, "You don't suppose you can run a railroad in accordance with the statutes, do you?" A. B. Stickney, a railroad president, said to sixteen other railroad presidents in the home of J. P. Morgan in 1890, "I have the utmost respect for you gentlemen, individually, but as railroad presidents I wouldn't trust you with my watch out of my sight." Charles Francis Adams said, "The difficulty in railroad management . . . lies in the covetousness, want of good faith, and low moral tone of railway managers, in the complete absence of any high standard of commercial honesty."

The present-day white-collar criminals, who are more suave and deceptive than the "robber barons," are represented by Kreuger, Stavisky, Whitney, Mitchell, Foshay, Insull, the Van Sweringens, Musica-Coster, Fall, Sinclair, and many other merchant princes and captains of finance and industry and by a host of lesser followers. Their criminality has been demonstrated again and again in the investigations of land offices, railways, insurance, munitions, banking, public utilities, stock exchanges, the oil industry, real estate, reorganization committees, receiverships, bankruptcies, and politics. Individual cases of such criminality are reported frequently, and in many periods more important crime news may be found on the financial pages of newspapers than on the front pages. White-collar criminality is found in every occupation, as can be discovered readily in casual conversation with a representative of an occupation by asking him what crooked practices are found in his occupation.

White-collar criminality in business is expressed most frequently in the form of misrepresentation in financial statements of corporations, manipulation in the stock exchange, commercial bribery, bribery of public officials directly or indirectly in order to secure favorable contracts and legislation, misrepresentation in advertising and salesmanship, embezzlement and misapplication of funds, short weights and measures and dishonest grading of commodities, tax frauds, misapplication of funds in receiverships and bankruptcies. These and many others are found in abundance in the business world. They are what Al Capone called "the legitimate rackets."

In the medical profession, which is here used as an example because it probably displays less criminality than some other professions, are found illegal sale of alcohol and narcotics, abortion, illegal services to underworld criminals, fraudulent reports and testimony in accident cases, extreme cases of unnecessary treatment, fake specialists, restriction of competition, and fee-splitting. Fee-splitting is a violation of specific laws in many states and a violation of the conditions of admission to the practice of medicine in all. The physician who participates in fee-splitting tends to send his patients to the surgeon who will give him the largest fee rather than to the surgeon who will do the best work. It has been reported that two thirds of the surgeons in New York City split fees, and that more than half of the physicians in a central western city who answered a questionnaire on this point favored fee-splitting.

These varied types of white-collar crimes in business and the professions consist principally of violation of delegated or implied trust, and many of them can be reduced to two categories: misrepresentation of asset values and duplicity in the manipulation of power. The first is approximately the same as fraud or swindling; the second is similar to the double-cross. The latter is illustrated by the corporation director who, acting on inside information, purchases land which the corporation will need and sells it at a fantastic profit to the corporation. The principle of this duplicity is that the offender holds two antagonistic positions; one of them is a position of trust which is violated, generally by misapplication of funds, in the interest of the other position. A football coach permitted to referee a game in which his own team was playing would illustrate this antagonism of positions. Such situations cannot be completely avoided in a complicated business structure, but many concerns make a practice of assuming such antagonistic functions and of regularly violating a trust thus delegated to them. When compelled by law to make a separation of their functions, they make a nominal separation and continue by subterfuge to maintain the two positions.

An accurate statistical comparison of the crimes of the two classes is not available. The most extensive evidence regarding the nature and prevalence of white-collar criminality is found in the reports of the larger investigations to which reference was made. Because of its scattered character, that evidence is assumed rather than summarized here. A few statements will be presented, as illustrations rather than as proof of the prevalence of this criminality.

The Federal Trade Commission in 1920 reported that commercial bribery was a prevalent and common practice in many industries. In certain chain stores, the net shortage in weights was sufficient to pay 3.4 per cent on the investment in those commodities. Of the cans of ether sold to the Army in 1923–1925, 70 per cent were rejected because of impurities. In Indiana, during the summer of 1934, 40 per cent of the ice-cream samples tested in a routine manner by the Division of Public Health were in violation of law. The Comptroller of the Currency in 1908 reported that violations of law were found in 75 per cent of the banks examined in a three-months' period. Lie-detector tests of all employees in several Chicago banks showed that 20 per cent of them had stolen bank property, and these tests were supported in almost all cases by confessions. A public accountant estimated, in the period prior to the Securities and Exchange Commission, that 80 per cent of the financial statements of corporations were misleading. James M. Beck said, "Diogenes would have been hard put to it to find an honest man in the Wall Street which I knew [in 1916] as a corporation lawyer."

White-collar criminality is generally recognized as fairly prevalent in politics and has been used by some as a rough gauge by which to measure white-collar criminality in business. James A. Farley pointed out that "the standards of conduct are as high among officeholders and politicians as they are in commercial life," and Cermak, while mayor of Chicago, said, "There is less graft in politics than in business." According to John Flynn, "The average politician is the merest amateur in the gentle art of graft, compared with his brother in the field of business." And Walter Lippmann wrote, "Poor as they are, the standards of public life are so much more social than those of business that financiers who enter politics regard themselves as philanthropists."

These statements obviously do not give a precise measurement of the relative criminality of the white-collar class. They do not mean that all businessmen and professional men are criminals, just as the usual theories do not mean that every man in the lower class is a criminal. The statements are adequate evidence, however, that crime is not so highly concentrated in the lower class as the usual statistics indicate, and they refer in many cases to leading corporations in America and are not restricted to quacks, ambulance chasers, bucket-shop operators, dead beats, fly-by-night swindlers, and the like.[1]

The financial cost of white-collar crime is probably several times as great as the financial cost of all the crimes which are customarily included in the "crime problem." An officer of a chain grocery store in one year embezzled $600,000, which was six times as much as the annual losses from five hundred burglaries and robberies of the stores in that chain. Public enemies numbered one to six secured $130,000 by burglary and robbery in 1938, while the sum stolen by Kreuger is estimated at $250,000,000, or nearly two thousand times as much. The *New York Times* in 1931 reported four cases of embezzlement in the United States with a loss of more than a million dollars each and a combined loss of nine million dollars. Although a million-dollar burglary or robbery is practically unheard of, million-dollar embezzlers are small fry among white-collar criminals. The estimated loss of investors in one investment trust from 1929 to 1935 was $580,000,000. This loss was due primarily to the fact that 75 per cent of the values in the portfolio were in securities of affiliated companies, although the firm in question had advertised the importance of diversification in investments and had provided an investment-counseling service. In Chicago, the claim was made six years ago that householders had lost $54,000,000 in two years during the administration of a city sealer who granted immunity from in-

[1] Perhaps it should be repeated that "white-collar" (upper) and "lower" classes merely designate persons of high and low socioeconomic status. Income and amount of money involved in the crime are not the sole criteria. Many persons of "low" socioeconomic status are "white-collar" criminals in the sense that they are well-dressed, well-educated, and have high incomes, but "white-collar" as used in this paper means "respected," "socially accepted and approved," "looked up to." Some people in this class may not be well-dressed or well-educated, nor have high incomes, although the "upper" usually exceed the "lower" classes in these respects as well as in social status.

spection to stores which provided Christmas baskets for his constituents.

The financial loss from white-collar crime, great as it is, is less important than the damage to social relations. White-collar crimes violate trust and therefore create distrust, which lowers social morale and produces social disorganization on a large scale. Other crimes have relatively little effect on social institutions or social organization.

White-collar crime is real crime. It is not ordinarily called crime, and calling it by this name does not make it worse, just as not calling it crime does not make it better. It is called crime here because it is in violation of the criminal law and belongs within the scope of criminology. The crucial question in this analysis is the criterion of violation of the criminal law. Conviction in the criminal court, which is sometimes suggested as the criterion, is not adequate because a large proportion of those who commit crimes are not convicted in criminal courts. This criterion, therefore, needs to be supplemented. When it is supplemented, the criterion of the crimes of one class must be kept consistent in general terms with the criterion of the crimes of the other class. The definition should not be the spirit of the law for white-collar crimes and the letter of the law for other crimes, or in other respects be more liberal for one class than for the other. Since this discussion is concerned with the conventional theories of the criminologists, the criterion of white-collar crime must be justified in terms of the procedures of those criminologists in dealing with other crimes. The criterion of white-collar crimes, as here proposed, supplements convictions in the criminal courts in four respects, in each of which the extension is justified because the criminologists who present the conventional theories of criminal behavior make the same extension in principle.

First, other agencies than the criminal court must be included, for the criminal court is not the only agency which makes official decisions regarding violations of the criminal law. The juvenile court, dealing largely with offenses of the children of the poor, is not in many states under criminal jurisdiction. The criminologists have made much use of case histories and statistics of juvenile delinquents in constructing their theories of criminal behavior. This justifies the inclusion of agencies other than the criminal court which deal with white-collar offenses. The most important of these agencies are the administrative boards, bureaus, or commissions; and much of their work, although certainly not all, consists of cases which are in violation of the criminal law. The Federal Trade Commission ordered several automobile companies to stop advertising their interest rate on installment purchases as 6 per cent, since it was actually 11½ per cent. Also, it filed complaint against *Good Housekeeping*, one of the Hearst publications, charging that its seals led the public to believe that all products bearing those seals had been tested in their laboratories, which was contrary to fact. Each of these involves a charge of dishonesty which might have been tried in a criminal court as fraud. A large proportion of the cases before these boards should be included in the data of the criminologists. Failure to do so is a principal reason for the bias in their samples and for the errors in their generalizations.

Second, for both classes, behavior which would have a reasonable expectancy of conviction if tried in a criminal court or in a substitute agency should be defined as criminal. In this respect, convictability rather than actual conviction should be the criterion of criminality. The criminologists would not hesitate to accept as data the verified case history of a person who was a criminal but had never been convicted. Similarly, it is justifiable to include white-collar criminals who have not been convicted, provided reliable evidence is available. Evidence regarding such cases appears in many civil suits, such as stockholders' suits and patent-infringement suits. These cases, which might have been referred to the criminal court, were referred to the civil court because the injured party was more interested in securing damages than in seeing punishment inflicted. This also happens in embezzlement cases, regarding which surety companies have much evidence. In a short consecutive series of embezzlements known to a surety company, 90 per cent were not prosecuted because prosecution would have interfered with restitution or salvage. The evidence in cases of embezzlement is generally conclusive, and would probably have been sufficient to justify conviction in all the cases in this series.

Third, behavior should be defined as criminal if conviction is avoided merely because of pressure which is brought to bear on the court or substitute agency. Gangsters and racketeers have been relatively immune in many cities because of their pressure on prospective witnesses and public officials; and professional thieves, such as pickpockets and confidence men who do not use strong-arm methods, are even more frequently immune because of their ability to influence police action. The conventional criminologists do not hesitate to include the life histories of such criminals as data, because they understand the generic relation of the pressures to the failure to convict. Similarly, white-collar criminals are relatively immune because of the class bias of the courts and the power of their class to influence the implementation and administration of the law. This class bias not only affects present-day courts but to a much greater degree affected the earlier courts which established the precedents and rules of procedure of the present-day courts. Consequently, it is justifiable to interpret the actual or potential failures of conviction in the light of known facts regarding the pressures brought to bear on the agencies which deal with offenders.

Fourth, persons who are accessory to a crime should be included among white-collar criminals as they are among other criminals. When the Federal Bureau of Investigation deals with a case of kidnapping, it is not content with catching the offenders who carried away the victim; it may arrest and the court may convict twenty-five other persons who assisted by secreting the victim, negotiating the ransom, or putting the ransom money into circulation. On the other hand, the prosecution of white-collar criminals frequently stops with one offender. Political graft almost always involves collusion between politicians and businessmen, but prosecutions are generally limited to the politicians. Judge Manton was found guilty of accepting $664,000 in bribes, but the six or eight important commercial concerns that paid the bribes have not been prosecuted. Pendergast, the late boss of Kansas City, was convicted for failure to report as a part of his income $315,000 received in bribes from insurance companies, but the insurance companies which paid the bribes have not been prosecuted. In an investigation of embezzlement by the president of a bank, at least a dozen other violations of law which were related to this embezzlement and involved most of the other officers of the bank and the officers of the clearinghouse were discovered, but none of the others was prosecuted.

This analysis of the criterion of white-collar criminality results in the conclusion that a description of white-collar criminality in general terms will also be a description of the criminality of the lower class. The crimes of the two classes differ in incidentals rather than essentials. They differ principally in the implementation of the criminal laws which apply to them. The crimes of the lower class are handled by policemen, prosecutors, and judges with penal sanctions in the form of fines, imprisonment, and death. The crimes of the upper class either result in no official action at all or result in suits for damages in civil courts or are handled by inspectors and by administrative boards or commissions with penal sanctions in the form of warnings, orders to cease and desist, occasional rescinding of a license, and in extreme cases with fines or prison sentences. Thus, the white-collar criminals are segregated administratively from other criminals, and largely as a consequence of this are not regarded as real criminals by themselves, by the general public, or by the criminologists.

This difference in the implementation of the criminal law is due chiefly to the disparity in social position of the two kinds of offenders. Judge Woodward, when imposing sentence upon the officials of H. O. Stone and Company (a bankrupt real estate firm in Chicago), who had been convicted in 1933 of the use of the mails to defraud, said to them, "You are men of affairs, of experience, of refinement and culture, of excellent reputation and standing in the business and social world." That statement might be used as a general characterization of white-collar criminals, for they are oriented basically to legitimate and respectable careers. Because of their social status they have a loud voice in determining what goes into the statutes and how the criminal law as it affects themselves is implemented and administered. This may be illustrated from the Pure Food and Drug Law. Between 1879 and 1906, 140 pure food and drug bills were presented in Congress, and all failed because of the importance of the persons who would be affected. It took a highly dramatic performance by Dr. Wiley in 1906 to induce Congress to enact the law. The law, however, did not create a new crime, just as the Federal kidnapping law which grew out of the Lindbergh case did not create a new crime; the Pure Food and Drug Law merely provided a more efficient implementation of a principle which had been formulated previously in state laws. When an amendment to this law, which would have brought within the scope of its agents fraudulent statements made over the radio or in the press, was presented to Congress, the publishers and advertisers organized support and sent a lobby to Washington which successfully fought the amendment principally under the slogans of "freedom of the press" and "dangers of bureaucracy." This proposed amendment, also, would not have created a new crime, for the state laws already prohibited fraudulent statements over the radio or in the press; it would have implemented the law so that it could have been enforced. Finally, the administration has not been able to enforce the law as it has desired because of the pressures by the offenders against the law, sometimes brought to bear through the head of the Department of Agriculture, sometimes through congressmen who threaten cuts in the appropriation, and sometimes by others. A statement made by Daniel Drew describes the criminal law with some accuracy: "Law is like a cobweb; it's made for flies and the smaller kinds of insects, so to speak, but lets the big bumblebees break through. When technicalities of the law stood in my way, I have always been able to brush them aside as easy as anything."

The preceding analysis should be regarded neither as an assertion that all efforts to influence legislation and its administration are reprehensible nor as a particularistic interpretation of the criminal law. It means only that the upper class has greater influence in molding the criminal law and its administration to its own interests than does the lower class. The privileged position of white-collar criminals before the law results to a slight extent from bribery and political pressures, but largely from the respect in which such men are held and without special effort on their part. The most powerful group in medieval society secured relative immunity by "benefit of clergy," and now our most powerful groups secure relative immunity by "benefit of business or profession."

In contrast with the power of the white-collar criminals is the weakness of their victims. Consumers, investors, and stockholders are unorganized, lack technical knowledge, and cannot protect themselves. Daniel Drew, after taking a large sum of money by sharp practice from Vanderbilt in the Erie deal, concluded that it was a mistake to take money from a powerful man on the same level as himself and declared that in the future he would confine his efforts to outsiders, scattered all over the country, who wouldn't be able to organize and fight back. White-collar criminality flourishes at points where powerful businessmen and professional men come in contact with persons who are weak. In this respect, it is similar to stealing candy from a baby. Many of the crimes of the lower class, on the other hand, are committed, in the form of burglary and robbery, against persons of wealth and power. Because of this difference in the comparative power of the victims, the white-collar criminals enjoy relative immunity.

Embezzlement is an interesting exception to white-collar criminality in this respect. Embezzlement is usually theft from an employer by an employee, and the employee is less capable of manipulating social and legal forces in his own interest than is the employer. As might have been expected, the laws regarding embezzlement were formulated long before laws for the protection of investors and consumers.

The theory that criminal behavior in general is due either to poverty or to the psychopathic and sociopathic conditions associated with poverty can now be shown to be invalid for three reasons. First, the generalization is based on a biased sample which omits almost entirely the behavior of white-collar criminals. For reasons of convenience and ignorance rather than of principle, criminologists have restricted their data largely to cases dealt with in criminal courts and juvenile courts, and these agencies are used principally for criminals from the lower economic strata. Consequently, the criminologists' data are grossly biased in respect to the economic status of criminals, and the generalization that criminality is closely associated with poverty is not justified.

Second, the generalization is inapplicable to white-collar criminals. With a small number of exceptions, they are not poor, were not reared in slums or badly deteriorated families, and are not feeble-minded or psychopathic. The proposition, derived from the data used by the conventional criminologists, that "the criminal of today was the problem child of yesterday," is seldom true of white-collar criminals. The idea that the causes of criminality are to be found almost exclusively in childhood is also fallacious. Even if poverty is extended to include the economic stresses which afflict business in a period of depression, it is not closely correlated with white-collar criminality. Probably at no time within the last fifty years have white-collar crimes in the field of investments and corporate management been so extensive as during the boom period of the twenties.

Third, the generalization does not explain lower-class criminality. The sociopathic and psychopathic factors which have been emphasized doubtless have something to do with crime causation, but these factors have not been related to a general process which is found both in white-collar criminality and lower-class criminality; therefore, they do not explain the criminality of either class, though they may explain the manner or method of crime—why lower-class criminals commit burglary or robbery rather than crimes involving misrepresentation.

In view of these defects in the conventional theories, a hypothesis that will explain both white-collar criminality and lower-class criminality is needed. For reasons of economy, simplicity, and logic, the hypothesis should apply to both classes, for this will make possible the analysis of causal factors freed from the encumbrances of the administrative devices which have led criminologists astray. Shaw and McKay and others, working exclusively in the field of lower-class crime, have found the conventional theories inadequate to account for variations within the data of lower-class crime and with that difficulty in mind have been working toward an explanation of crime in terms of a more general social process. Such efforts will be greatly aided by the procedure which has been described.

The hypothesis suggested here as a substitute for the conventional theories is that white-collar criminality, just as other systematic criminality, is learned; that it is learned in direct or indirect association with those who already practice criminal behavior; and that those who learn this criminal behavior are segregated from frequent and intimate contacts with law-abiding behavior. Whether a person becomes a criminal or not is determined largely by the comparative frequency and intimacy of his contacts with the two types of behavior. This may be called the process of differential association. It is a genetic explanation both of white-collar criminality and lower-class criminality. Those who become white-collar criminals generally start their careers in good neighborhoods and good homes, graduate from colleges with some idealism, and, with little selection on their part, get into particular business situations in which criminality is practically a folkway, and are inducted into that system of behavior just as into any other folkway. The lower-class criminals generally start their careers in deteriorated neighborhoods and families, find delinquents at hand from whom they acquire the attitudes toward, and techniques of, crime. The essentials of this process are the same for the two classes of criminals. This is not entirely a process of assimilation, for inventions are frequently made, perhaps more frequently in white-collar crime than in lower-class crime. The inventive geniuses for the lower-class criminals are generally professional criminals, while the inventive geniuses for many kinds of white-collar crime are generally lawyers.

A second general process is social disorganization in the community. Differential association culminates in crime because the community is not organized solidly against that form of behavior. The law is pressing in one direction, and other forces are pressing in the opposite direction. In business, the "rules of the game" conflict with the legal rules. A businessman who wants to obey the law is driven by his competitors to adopt their methods. This is well illustrated by the persistence of commercial bribery in spite of the strenuous efforts of business organizations to eliminate it. Groups and individuals, however, are more concerned with their specialized group or individual interests than with the larger welfare. Consequently it is not possible for the community to present a solid front in opposition to crime. The better business bureaus and crime commissions, composed of professional men and businessmen, attack burglary, robbery, and cheap swindles but overlook the crimes of their own members. The forces which impinge on the lower class are similarly in conflict. Social disorganization affects the two classes in similar ways.

I have presented a brief and general description of white-collar criminality on a framework of argument regarding theories of criminal behavior. That argument, stripped of the description, may be stated in the following propositions:

(1) White-collar criminality is real criminality, being in all cases in violation of the criminal law.

(2) White-collar criminality differs from lower-class criminality principally in an implementation of the criminal law which segregates white-collar criminals administratively from other criminals.

(3) The theories of the criminologists that crime is due to poverty or to psychopathic and sociopathic conditions statistically associated with poverty are invalid for three reasons: first, they are derived from samples which are grossly biased with respect to socioeconomic status; second, they do not apply to white-collar criminals; and third, they do not even explain the criminality of the lower class, since the factors are not related to a general process characteristic of all criminality.

(4) A theory of criminal behavior which will explain both white-collar criminality and lower-class criminality is needed.

(5) An hypothesis of this nature is suggested in terms of differential association and social disorganization.

Is "White-Collar Crime" Crime?

THE ARGUMENT has been made that business and professional men commit crimes which should be brought within the scope of the theories of criminal behavior.[1] In order to secure evidence as to the prevalence of such white-collar crimes an analysis was made of the decisions by courts and commissions against the seventy largest industrial and mercantile corporations in the United States under four types of laws, namely, antitrust, false advertising, National Labor Relations, and infringement of patents, copyrights, and trademarks. This resulted in the finding that 547 such adverse decisions had been made, with an average of 7.8 decisions per corporation and with each corporation having at least 1. Although all of these were decisions that the behavior was unlawful, only 49 or 9 per cent of the total were made by criminal courts and were *ipso facto* deci-

Reprinted by permission from the *American Sociological Review*, X (1945), 132-39. This paper had been prepared for the Thirty-Ninth Annual Meeting of the American Sociological Society, which was scheduled to be held in Chicago, Illinois, December, 1944, but was canceled at the request of the Office of Defense Transportation.

1 Edwin H. Sutherland, "White Collar Criminality," *American Sociological Review*, V (1940), 1-12; Edwin H. Sutherland, "Crime and Business," *Annals of the American Academy of Political and Social Science*, CCXVII (1941), 112-18.

sions that the behavior was criminal. Since not all unlawful behavior is criminal behavior, these decisions can be used as a measure of criminal behavior only if the other 498 decisions can be shown to be decisions that the behavior of the corporations was criminal.

This is a problem in the legal definition of crime and involves two types of questions: May the word "crime" be applied to the behavior regarding which these decisions were made? If so, why is it not generally applied and why have not the criminologists regarded white-collar crime as cognate with other crime? The first question involves semantics; the second, interpretation or explanation.

A combination of two abstract criteria is generally regarded by legal scholars as necessary to define crime, namely, legal description of an act as socially injurious and legal provision of a penalty for the act.[2]

When the criterion of legally defined social injury is applied to these 547 decisions, the conclusion is reached that all the classes of behaviors regarding which the decisions were made are legally defined as socially injurious. This can be readily determined by the words in the statutes—"crime" or "misdemeanor" in some and "unfair," "discrimination," or "infringement" in all the others. The persons injured may be divided into two groups: first, a relatively small number of persons engaged in the same occupation as the offenders or in related occupations and, second, the general public either as consumers or as constituents of the general social institutions which are affected by the violations of the laws. The antitrust laws are designed to protect competitors and also to protect the institution of free competition as the regulator of the economic system and thereby to protect consumers against arbitrary prices

[2] The most satisfactory analysis of the criteria of crime from the legal point of view may be found in the following papers by Jerome Hall: "Prolegomena to a Science of Criminal Law," *University of Pennsylvania Law Review*, LXXXIX (1941), 549-80; "Interrelations of Criminal Law and Torts," *Columbia Law Review*, XLIII (1943), 735-79, 967-1001; "Criminal Attempts—A Study of the Foundations of Criminal Liability," *Yale Law Review*, XLIX (1940), 789-840.

and to protect the institution of democracy against the dangers of great concentration of wealth in the hands of monopolies. Laws against false advertising are designed to protect competitors against unfair competition and also to protect consumers against fraud. The National Labor Relations Law is designed to protect employees against coercion by employers and also to protect the general public against interferences with commerce caused by strikes and lockouts. The laws against infringements are designed to protect the owners of patents, copyrights, and trademarks against deprivation of their property and against unfair competition, and also to protect the institution of patents and copyrights, which was established in order to "promote the progress of science and the useful arts." Violations of these laws are legally defined as injuries to the parties specified.

Each of these laws has a logical basis in the common law and is an adaptation of the common law to modern social organization. False advertising is related to common law fraud, and infringement to larceny. The National Labor Relations Law, as an attempt to prevent coercion, is related to the common-law prohibition of restrictions on freedom in the form of assault, false imprisonment, and extortion. For at least two centuries prior to the enactment of the modern antitrust laws the common law was moving against restraint of trade, monopoly, and unfair competition.

Each of the four laws provides a penal sanction and thus meets the second criterion in the definition of crime, and each of the adverse decisions under these four laws, except certain decisions under the infringement laws to be discussed later, is a decision that a crime was committed. This conclusion will be made more specific by analysis of the penal sanctions provided in the four laws.

The Sherman Antitrust Law states explicitly that a violation of the law is a misdemeanor. Three methods of enforcement of this law are provided, each of them involving procedures regarding misdemeanors. First, it may be enforced by the usual criminal prosecution, resulting in the imposition of fine or imprisonment. Second, the attorney general of the United States and the several district attorneys are given the "duty" of "repressing and preventing" violations of the law by petitions for injunctions, and violations of the injunctions are punishable as contempt of court. This method of enforcing a criminal law was an invention and, as will be described later, is the key to the interpretation of the differential implementation of the criminal law as applied to white-collar criminals. Third, parties who are injured by violations of the law are authorized to sue for damages, with a mandatory provision that the damages awarded be three times the damages suffered. These damages in excess of reparation are penalties for violation of the law. They are payable to the injured party in order to induce him to take the initiative in the enforcement of the criminal law and in this respect are similar to the earlier methods of private prosecutions under the criminal law. All three of these methods of enforcement are based on decisions that a criminal law was violated and therefore that a crime was committed; the decisions of a civil court or a court of equity as to these violations are as good evidence of criminal behavior as is the decision of a criminal court.

The Sherman Antitrust Law has been amended by the Federal Trade Commission Law, the Clayton Law, and several other laws. Some of these amendments define violations as crimes and provide the conventional penalties, but most of the amendments do not make the criminality explicit. A large proportion of the cases which are dealt with under these amendments could be dealt with, instead, under the original Sherman Law, which is explicitly a criminal law. In practice, the amendments are under the jurisdiction of the Federal Trade Commission, which has authority to make official decisions as to violations. The Commission has two principal sanctions under its control, namely, the stipulation and the cease-and-desist order. The Commission may, after the violation of the law has been proved, accept a stipulation from the corporation that it will not violate the law in the future. Such stipulations are customarily restricted to the minor or technical violations. If a stipulation is violated or if no stipulation is accepted, the Commission may issue a cease-and-desist order; this is equivalent to a court's injunction except that violation is not punishable as contempt. If the Commission's desist order is violated, the Commission may apply to the court for an injunction, the violation of which is punishable as contempt. By an amendment to the Federal Trade Commission Law in the Wheeler-Lea Act of 1938 an order of the Commission becomes "final" if not officially questioned within a specified time and thereafter its violation is punishable by a civil fine. Thus, although certain interim procedures may be used in the enforcement of the amendments to the antitrust law, fines or imprisonment for contempt are available if the interim procedures fail. In this respect the interim procedures are similar to probation in ordinary criminal cases. An unlawful act is not defined as criminal by the fact that it is punished, but by the fact that it is punishable. Larceny is as truly a crime when the thief is placed on probation as when he is committed to prison. The argument may be made that punishment for contempt of court is not punishment for violation of the original law and that, therefore, the original law does not contain a penal sanction. This reasoning is specious since the original law provides the injunction with its penalty as a part of the procedure for enforcement. Consequently all the decisions made under the amendments to the antitrust law are decisions that the corporations committed crimes.[3]

The laws regarding false advertising, as included in the decisions under consideration, are of two types. First, false advertising in the form of false labels is defined in the Pure Food and Drug Law as a misdemeanor and is punishable by a fine. Second, false advertising generally is defined in the Federal Trade Commission Act as unfair competition. Cases of the second type are under the jurisdiction of the Federal Trade Commission, which uses the same procedures as in antitrust cases.

[3] Some of the antitrust decisions were made against meat packers under the Packers and Stockyards Act. The penal sanctions in this act are essentially the same as in the Federal Trade Commission Act.

Penal sanctions are available in antitrust cases, as previously described, and are similarly available in these cases of false advertising. Thus, all of the decisions in false advertising cases are decisions that the corporations committed crimes.

The National Labor Relations Law of 1935 defines a violation as "unfair labor practice." The National Labor Relations Board is authorized to make official decisions as to violations of the law and, in case of violation, to issue desist orders and also to make certain remedial orders, such as reimbursement of employees who had been dismissed or demoted because of activities in collective bargaining. If an order is violated, the Board may apply to the court for enforcement and a violation of the order of the court is punishable as contempt. Thus, all of the decisions under this law, which is enforceable by penal sanctions, are decisions that crimes were committed.

The methods for the repression of infringements vary. Infringements of a copyright or a patented design are defined as misdemeanors, punishable by fines. No case of this type has been discovered against the seventy corporations. Other infringements are not explicitly defined in the statutes on patents, copyrights, and trademarks as crimes, and agents of the state are not authorized by these statutes to initiate actions against violators of the law. Nevertheless, infringements may be punished in either of two ways: First, agents of the State may initiate action against infringements under the Federal Trade Commission Law as unfair competition, and they do so, especially against infringements of copyrights and trademarks; these infringements are then punishable in the same sense as violations of the amendments to the antitrust laws. Second, the patent, copyright, and trademark statutes provide that the damages awarded to injured owners of those rights may be greater than (in one statute as much as threefold) the damages actually suffered. These additional damages are not mandatory, as in the Sherman Antitrust Law, but on the other hand they are not explicitly limited to wanton and malicious infringements. Three decisions against the seventy corporations under the patent law and one under the copyright law included awards of such additional damages and on that account were classified in the tabulation of decisions as evidence of criminal behavior of the corporations. The other decisions, 74 in number, in regard to infringements were classified as not conclusive evidence of criminal behavior and were discarded. However, in 20 of these 74 cases the decisions of the court contain evidence which would be sufficient to make a *prima facie* case in a criminal prosecution; evidence outside these decisions which may be found in the general descriptions of practices regarding patents, copyrights, and trademarks, justifies a belief that a very large proportion of the 74 cases did, in fact, involve willful infringement of property rights and might well have resulted in the imposition of a penalty if the injured party and the court had approached the behavior from the point of view of crime.

In the preceding discussion the penalties which are definitive of crime have been limited to fine, imprisonment, and punitive damages. In addition, the stipulation, the desist order, and the injunction, without reference to punishment for contempt, have the attributes of punishment. This is evident both in that they result in some suffering on the part of the corporation against which they are issued and also in that they are designed by legislators and administrators to produce suffering. The suffering is in the form of public shame, as illustrated in more extreme form in the colonial penalty of sewing the letter "T" on the clothing of the thief. The design is shown in the sequence of sanctions used by the Federal Trade Commission. The stipulation involves the least publicity and the least discomfort, and it is used for minor and technical violations. The desist order is used if the stipulation is violated and also if the violation of the law is appraised by the Commission as willful and major. This involves more public shame; this shame is somewhat mitigated by the statements made by corporations, in exculpation, that such orders are merely the acts of bureaucrats. Still more shameful to the corporation is an injunction issued by a court. The shame resulting from this order is sometimes mitigated and the corporation's face saved by taking a consent decree.[4] The corporation may insist that the consent decree is not an admission that it violated the law. For instance, the meat packers took a consent decree in an antitrust case in 1921, with the explanation that they had not knowingly violated any law and were consenting to the decree without attempting to defend themselves because they wished to co-operate with the government in every possible way. This patriotic motivation appeared questionable, however, after the packers fought during almost all of the next ten years for a modification of the decree. Although the sequence of stipulation, desist order, and injunction indicates that the variations in public shame are designed, these orders have other functions, as well, especially a remedial function and the clarification of the law in a particular complex situation.

The conclusion in this semantic portion of the discussion is that 473 of the 547 decisions are decisions that crimes were committed.

This conclusion may be questioned on the ground that the rules of proof and evidence used in reaching these decisions are not the same as those used in decisions regarding other crimes, especially that some of the agencies which rendered the decisions did not require proof of criminal intent and did not presume the accused to be innocent. These rules of criminal intent and presumption of innocence, however, are not required in all prosecutions under the regular penal code and the number of exceptions is increasing. In many states a person may be committed to prison without protection of one or both of these rules on charges of statutory rape, bigamy, adultery, passing bad checks, selling mortgaged property, defrauding a hotelkeeper, and other offenses.[5] Consequently the criteria which have been used in defining white-collar crimes are not categorically different from the criteria used in defining other

[4] The consent decree may be taken for other reasons, especially because it cannot be used as evidence in other suits.

[5] Livingston Hall, "Statutory Law of Crimes, 1887-1936," *Harvard Law Review*, L (1937), 616-53.

crimes, for these rules are abrogated both in regard to white-collar crimes and other crimes, including some felonies. The proportion of decisions rendered against corporations without the protection of these rules is probably greater than the proportion rendered against other criminals, but a difference in proportion does not make the violations of law by corporations categorically different from the violations of laws by other criminals. Moreover, the difference in proportion, as the procedures actually operate, is not great. On the one side, many of the defendants in usual criminal cases, being in relative poverty, do not get good defense and consequently secure little benefit from these rules; on the other hand, the commissions come close to observing these rules of proof and evidence although they are not required to do so. This is illustrated by the procedure of the Federal Trade Commission in regard to advertisements. Each year it examines several hundred thousand advertisements and appraises about 50,000 of them as probably false. From the 50,000 it selects about 1,500 as patently false. For instance, an advertisement of gum-wood furniture as "mahogany" would seldom be an accidental error and would generally result from a state of mind which deviated from honesty by more than the natural tendency of human beings to feel proud of their handiwork.

The preceding discussion has shown that these seventy corporations committed crimes according to 473 adverse decisions, and also has shown that the criminality of their behavior was not made obvious by the conventional procedures of the criminal law but was blurred and concealed by special procedures. This differential implementation of the law as applied to the crimes of corporations eliminates or at least minimizes the stigma of crime. Such differential implementation began with the Sherman Antitrust Law of 1890. As previously described, this law is explicitly a criminal law, and a violation of the law is a misdemeanor no matter what procedure is used. The customary policy would have been to rely entirely on criminal prosecution as the method of enforcement. But a clever invention was made in the provision of an injunction to enforce a criminal law; this was not only an invention but a direct reversal of previous case law. Also, private parties were encouraged by treble damages to enforce a criminal law by suits in civil courts. In either case, the defendant did not appear in the criminal court, and the fact that he had committed a crime did not appear in the face of the proceedings.

The Sherman Antitrust Law, in this respect, became the model in practically all the subsequent procedures authorized to deal with the crimes of corporations. When the Federal Trade Commission bill and the Clayton bill were introduced in Congress, they contained the conventional criminal procedures; these were eliminated in committee discussions, and other procedures which did not carry the external symbols of criminal process were substituted. The violations of these laws are crimes, as has been shown above, but they are treated as though they were not crimes, with the effect and probably the intention of eliminating the stigma of crime.

This policy of eliminating the stigma of crime is illustrated in the following statement by Wendell Berge, at the time assistant to the head of the antitrust division of the Department of Justice, in a plea of abandonment of the criminal prosecution under the Sherman Antitrust Law and the authorization of civil procedures with civil fines as a substitute.

> While civil penalties may be as severe in their financial effects as criminal penalties, yet they do not involve the stigma that attends indictment and conviction. Most of the defendants in antitrust cases are not criminals in the usual sense. There is no inherent reason why antitrust enforcement requires branding them as such.[6]

If a civil fine were substituted for a criminal fine, a violation of the antitrust law would be as truly a crime as it is now. The thing which would be eliminated would be the stigma of crime. Consequently, the stigma of crime has become a penalty in itself, which may be imposed in connection with other penalties or withheld, just as it is possible to combine imprisonment

[6] Wendell Berge, "Remedies Available to the Government under the Sherman Act," *Law and Contemporary Problems*, VII (1940), 111.

with a fine or have a fine without imprisonment. A civil fine is a financial penalty without the additional penalty of stigma, while a criminal fine is a financial penalty with the additional penalty of stigma.

When the stigma of crime is imposed as a penalty, it places the defendant in the category of criminals, and he becomes a criminal according to the popular stereotype of "the criminal." In primitive society "the criminal" was substantially the same as "the stranger,"[7] while in modern society "the criminal" is a person of less esteemed cultural attainments. Seventy-five per cent of the persons committed to state prisons are probably not, aside from their unesteemed cultural attainments, "criminals in the usual sense of the word." It may be excellent policy to eliminate the stigma of crime in a large proportion of cases, but the question at hand is why the law has a different implementation for white-collar criminals than for others.

Three factors assist in explaining this differential implementation of the law, namely, the status of the businessman, the trend away from punishment, and the relatively unorganized resentment of the public against white-collar criminals. Each of these will be described.

First, the methods used in the enforcement of any law are an adaption to the characteristics of the prospective violators of the law, as appraised by the legislators and the judicial and administrative personnel. The appraisals regarding businessmen, who are the prospective violators of the four laws under consideration, include a combination of fear and admiration. Those who are responsible for the system of criminal justice are afraid to antagonize businessmen; among other consequences, such antagonism may result in a reduction in contributions to the campaign funds needed to win the next election. Probably much more important is the cultural homogeneity of legislators, judges, and administrators with business-

[7] On the role of the stranger in punitive justice, see Ellsworth Faris, "The Origin of Punishment," *International Journal of Ethics*, XXV (1914), 54-67; George H. Mead, "The Psychology of Punitive Justice," *American Journal of Sociology*, XXIII (1918), 577-602.

men. Legislators admire and respect businessmen and cannot conceive of them as criminals; that is, businessmen do not conform to the popular stereotype of "the criminal." The Legislators are confident that these businessmen will conform as a result of very mild pressures.

This interpretation meets with considerable opposition from persons who insist that this is an egalitarian society in which all men are equal in the eyes of the law. It is not possible to give a complete demonstration of the validity of this interpretation, but four types of evidence are presented in the following paragraphs as partial demonstration.

The Department of Justice is authorized to use both criminal prosecutions and petitions in equity to enforce the Sherman Antitrust Law. The Department has selected the method of criminal prosecution in a larger proportion of cases against trade unions than of cases against corporations, although the law was enacted primarily because of fear of the corporations. From 1890 to 1929 the Department of Justice initiated 438 actions under this law with decisions favorable to the United States. Of the actions against business firms and associations of business firms, 27 per cent were criminal prosecutions, while of the actions against trade unions 71 per cent were criminal prosecutions.[8] This shows that the Department of Justice has been comparatively reluctant to use a method against business firms which carries with it the stigma of crime.

The method of criminal prosecution in enforcement of the Sherman Antitrust Law has varied from one presidential administration to another. It has seldom been used in the administrations of the presidents who are popularly appraised as friendly toward business, namely, McKinley, Harding, Coolidge, and Hoover.

Businessmen suffered their greatest loss of prestige in the depression which began in 1929. It was precisely in this period of low status of businessmen that the most strenuous efforts were made to enforce the old laws and enact new laws for the

8 Percentages compiled from cases listed in the report of the Department of Justice "Federal Antitrust Laws, 1938."

regulation of businessmen. The appropriations for this purpose were multiplied several times, and persons were selected for their vigor in administration of the laws. Of the 547 decisions against the seventy corporations during their life careers, which have averaged about forty years, 63 per cent were rendered in the period of 1935–43, that is, during the period of the low status of businessmen.

The Federal Trade Commission Law states that a violation of the antitrust laws by a corporation shall be deemed to be, also, a violation by the officers and directors of the corporation. However, businessmen are practically never convicted as persons, and several cases have been reported, like the six per cent case against the automobile manufacturers, in which the corporation was convicted and the persons who direct the corporation were all acquitted.[9]

A second factor in the explanation of the differential implementation of the law as applied to white-collar criminals is the trend away from reliance on penal methods. This trend advanced more rapidly in the area of white-collar crimes than of other crimes because this area, due to the recency of the statutes, is least bound by precedents and also because of the status of businessmen. This trend is seen in the almost complete abandonment of the most extreme penalties of death and physical torture; in the supplanting of conventional penal methods by non-penal methods such as probation and the case-work methods which accompany probation; and in the supplementing of penal methods by non-penal methods, as in the development of case-work and educational policies in prisons. These decreases in penal methods are explained by a series of social changes: the increased power of the lower socioeconomic class upon which previously most of the penalties were inflicted; the inclusion within the scope of the penal laws of a large part of the upper socioeconomic class as illustrated by traffic regu-

[9] The question may be asked, "If business men are so influential, why did they not retain the protection of the rules of the criminal procedure?" The answer is that they lost this protection, despite their status, on the principle that "You can't eat your cake and have it, too."

lations; the increased social interaction among the classes, which has resulted in increased understanding and sympathy; the failure of penal methods to make substantial reductions in crime rates; and the weakening hold on the legal profession and others of the individualistic and hedonistic psychology which had placed great emphasis on pain in the control of behavior. To some extent overlapping those just mentioned is the fact that punishment, which was previously the chief reliance for control in the home, the school, and the church, has tended to disappear from those institutions, leaving the State without cultural support for its own penal methods.[10]

White-collar crime is similar to juvenile delinquency in respect to the differential implementation of the law. In both cases, the procedures of the criminal law are modified so that the stigma of crime will not attach to the offenders. The stigma of crime has been less completely eliminated from juvenile delinquents than from white-collar criminals because the procedures for the former are a less complete departure from conventional criminal procedures, because most juvenile delinquents come from a class with low social status, and because the juveniles have not organized to protect their good names. Since the juveniles have not been successfully freed from the stigma of crime they have been generally held to be within the scope of the theories of criminology and in fact provide a large part of the data for criminology; since the external symbols have been more successfully eliminated from white-collar crimes, white-collar crimes have generally not been included within these theories.

A third factor in the differential implementation of the law is the difference in the relation between the law and the mores in the area of white-collar crime. The laws under consideration are recent and do not have a firm foundation in public ethics or business ethics; in fact, certain rules of business ethics, such as contempt for the "price chiseler," are generally in conflict with the law. The crimes are not obvious, as are assault and battery,

10 The trend away from penal methods suggests that the penal sanction may not be a completely adequate criterion in the definition of crime.

and can be appreciated readily only by persons who are expert in the occupations in which they occur. A corporation often violates a law for a decade or longer before the administrative agency becomes aware of the violation, and in the meantime the violation may have become accepted practice in the industry. The effects of a white-collar crime upon the public are diffused over a long period of time and perhaps over millions of people, with no person suffering much at a particular time. The public agencies of communication do not express and organize the moral sentiments of the community as to white-collar crimes, in part because the crimes are complicated and not easily presented as news, but probably in greater part because these agencies of communication are owned or controlled by the businessmen who violate the laws and because these agencies are themselves frequently charged with violations of the same laws. Public opinion in regard to picking pockets would not be well organized if most of the information regarding this crime came to the public directly from the pickpockets themselves.

This third factor, if properly limited, is a valid part of the explanation of the differential implementation of the law. It tends to be exaggerated and become the complete explanation in the form of a denial that white-collar crimes involve any moral culpability whatever. On that account it is desirable to state a few reasons why this factor is not the complete explanation.

The assertion is sometimes made that white-collar crimes are merely technical violations and involve no moral culpability, i.e., violation of the mores, whatever. In fact, these white-collar crimes, like other crimes, are distributed along a continuum in which the *mala in se* are at one extreme and the *mala prohibita* at the other.[11] None of the white-collar crimes is purely arbitrary, as is the regulation that one must drive on the right side of the street, which might equally well be that one must drive on the left side. The Sherman Antitrust Law,

11 An excellent discussion of this continuum is presented by Jerome Hall, *op. cit.*, 563-69.

for instance, is regarded by many persons as an unwise law, and it may well be that some other policy would be preferable. It is questioned principally by persons who believe in a more collectivistic economic system, namely, the communists and the leaders of big business, while its support comes largely from an emotional ideology in favor of free enterprise which is held by farmers, wage-earners, small businessmen, and professional men. Therefore, as appraised by the majority of the population it is necessary for the preservation of American institutions, and its violation is a violation of strongly entrenched moral sentiments.

The sentimental reaction toward a particular white-collar crime is certainly different from that toward some other crimes. This difference is often exaggerated, especially as the reaction occurs in urban society. The characteristic reaction of the average citizen in the modern city toward burglary is apathy unless he or his immediate friends are victims or unless the case is very spectacular. The average citizen, reading in his morning paper that the home of an unknown person has been burglarized by another unknown person, has no appreciable increase in blood pressure. Fear and resentment develop in modern society primarily as the result of the accumulation of crimes as depicted in crime rates or in general descriptions, and this develops both as to white-collar crimes and other crimes.

Finally, although many laws have been enacted for the regulation of occupations other than business, such as agriculture or plumbing, the procedures used in the enforcement of those other laws are more nearly the same as the conventional criminal procedures, and law-violators in these other occupations are not so completely protected against the stigma of crime as are businessmen. The relation between the law and the mores tends to be circular. The mores are crystallized in the law, and each act of enforcement of the laws tends to re-enforce the mores. The laws regarding white-collar crime, which conceal the criminality of the behavior, have been less effective than other laws in re-enforcement of the mores.

Crime of Corporations

About twenty years ago I began to study violations of law by businessmen and have continued the study intermittently to the present day. This study was begun for the purpose of improving the general explanations of criminal behavior. The theories of crime which were then current and which are still current emphasized social and personal pathologies as the causes of crime. The social pathologies included, especially, poverty and the social conditions related to poverty, such as poor housing, lack of organized recreational facilities, the ignorance of parents, and family disorganization. The personal pathology emphasized in the earlier period was feeble-mindedness; the early theory asserted that feeble-mindedness is inherited and is the cause of both poverty and crime. At about the time I started the study of business crimes, the personal pathology which was used to explain crime was shifting from defective intelligence to defective emotions, as represented by concepts such as frustration, the inferiority complex, and the Oedipus complex.

These theories that crime is due to social and personal pathol-

Delivered to the Toynbee Club (a group composed of students majoring in sociology and of the sociology faculty) at DePauw University in the spring of 1948.

ogies had considerable support from the fact that a very large proportion of the persons arrested, convicted, and committed to prisons belong to the lower economic class.

In contrast to those theories, my theory was that criminal behavior is learned just as any other behavior is learned, and that personal and social pathologies play no essential part in the causation of crime. I believed that this thesis could be substantiated by a study of the violation of law by businessmen. Businessmen are generally not poor, are not feeble-minded, do not lack organized recreational facilities, and do not suffer from the other social and personal pathologies. If it can be shown that businessmen, without these pathologies, commit many crimes, then such pathologies cannot be used as the explanation of the crimes of other classes. The criminologists who have stated the theories of crimes get their data from personal interviews with criminals in the criminal courts, jails, and prisons, or from criminal statistics based on the facts regarding such criminals. But when businessmen commit crimes, their cases go generally before courts under equity or civil jurisdictions or before quasi-judicial commissions, and seldom before the criminal courts. Consequently, the criminologists do not come into contact with these businessmen and have not included their violations of law within general theories of criminal behavior.

I have used the term white-collar criminal to refer to a person in the upper socioeconomic class who violates the laws designed to regulate his occupation. The term white-collar is used in the sense in which it was used by President Sloan of General Motors, who wrote a book entitled *The Autobiography of a White Collar Worker*. The term is used more generally to refer to the wage-earning class which wears good clothes at work, such as clerks in stores.

I wish to report specifically on a part of my study of white-collar crimes. I selected the 70 largest industrial and commercial corporations in the United States, not including public utilities and petroleum corporations. I have attempted to collect all the records of violations of law by each of these corporations, so far as these violations have been decided officially by courts and commissions. I have included the laws regarding restraint of trade, misrepresentation in advertising, infringement of patents, copyrights, and trademarks, rebates, unfair labor practices as prohibited by the National Labor Relations Law, financial fraud, violations of war regulations, and a small miscellaneous group of other laws. The records include the life careers of the corporations, which average about 45 years, and the subsidiaries as well as the main corporations. In this search I have been limited by the available records found in a university library, and this is far from complete. I am sure that the number of crimes I shall report on tonight is far smaller than the number actually decided by courts and commissions against these corporations.

This tabulation of the crimes of the 70 largest corporations in the United States gives a total of 980 adverse decisions. Every one of the 70 corporations has a decision against it, and the average number of decisions is 14.0. Of these 70 corporations, 98 per cent are recidivists; that is, they have two or more adverse decisions. Several states have enacted habitual criminal laws, which define an habitual criminal as a person who has been convicted four times of felonies. If we use this number and do not limit the convictions to felonies, 90 per cent of the 70 largest corporations in the United States are habitual criminals. Sixty of the corporations have decisions against them for restraint of trade, 54 for infringements, 44 for unfair labor practices, 27 for misrepresentation in advertising, 26 for rebates, and 43 for miscellaneous offenses.

These decisions have been concentrated in the period since 1932. Approximately 60 per cent of them were made in the ten-year period subsequent to 1932, and only 40 per cent in the forty-year period prior to 1932. One possible explanation of this concentration is that the large corporations are committing more crimes than they did previously. My own belief is that the prosecution of large corporations has been more vigorous during the later period and that the corporations have not appreciably increased in criminality.

Of the 70 large corporations, 30 were either illegal in their origin or began illegal activities immediately after their origin; and 8 additional corporations should probably be added to the 30. That is, approximately half of the 70 corporations were either illegitimate in birth, or were infant and juvenile delinquents, as well as adult criminals.

All of the 980 decisions were decisions that these corporations violated laws. Only 159 of these 980 decisions were made by criminal courts, whereas 425 were made by courts under civil or equity jurisdiction and 361 by commissions. The most important question regarding white-collar crime is whether it is really crime. That is a difficult and somewhat technical question, and I shall not attempt to deal with it tonight since I have published a paper on that question. The general conclusion stated in that paper is that the violations of law which were attested by decisions of equity and civil courts and by administrative commissions are, with very few exceptions, crimes.

The statistics which I have presented are rather dry and may not mean much to the average student who is not a specialist in this field, but the prevalence of white-collar crimes by large corporations can be illustrated more concretely. If you consider the life of a person, you find that from the cradle to the grave he has been using articles which were sold or distributed in violation of the law. The professional criminals use the word "hot" to refer to an article which has been recently stolen. For the purpose of simplicity of statement, I wish to use this word to refer to articles manufactured by corporations, but I shall expand the meaning to include any official record without restricting it to recent times, and shall refer to a class of articles rather than articles manufactured by a particular concern. Using the word in this sense, we can say that a baby is assisted into this world with the aid of "hot" surgical instruments, rubbed with "hot" olive oil, wrapped in a "hot" blanket, weighed on "hot" scales. The father, hearing the good news, runs a "hot" flag up on his flag pole, goes to the golf course and knocks a "hot" golf ball around the course. The baby grows up, surrounded by such articles, and is finally laid to rest in a "hot" casket under a "hot" tombstone.

I now wish to describe in more detail violations of some of the specific laws and shall take first misrepresentation in advertising. Although the Pure Food and Drug Law contains a provision prohibiting misrepresentation on the labels of foods and drugs, the administrators of that law have not published regular reports including the names of the corporations which have been found to be in violation of the law. I shall therefore restrict the discussion to the misrepresentations in advertisements which have been decided on by the Federal Trade Commission.

This is one of the less important white-collar crimes, in comparison with the others. Decisions have been made in 97 cases against 26 of 70 corporations. No decisions were made against 44 of the 70 large corporations under this law. Of these 44 corporations against which no decisions were made, 27 may be classed as non-advertising corporations. That is, they do not advertise for purposes of their sales, although they may advertise for general goodwill or for the goodwill of the newspapers and journals. They sell their products to expert buyers, who cannot be influenced by advertising. It would be a waste of money for U. S. Steel to distribute pamphlets among the expert buyers of its products, claiming that its products were made from the finest ores, or with Bessemer steel imported from England, or to show a picture of a movie star in a Pullman saying, "I always select railroads which use rails made by U. S. Steel, because they are better rails," or a picture of a baseball manager saying, "I feel that my players are safer if they ride the trains on rails made by U. S. Steel, because these rails are safer." If these large corporations which do not advertise for sales purposes are eliminated, approximately 60 per cent of the large corporations which do advertise for sales purposes have decisions against them for misrepresentation in advertising.

These misrepresentations in advertising are not, in most cases, mere technical violations. The Federal Trade Commission each year makes a survey of several hundred thousand advertisements in periodicals and over the radios. From these they select about 50,000 which are questionable, and from these they pick out about 1,500 as patently false, and make adverse decisions against about 1,000 of these each year. Also, in their selection, they tend to concentrate on certain products in one year and other products in other years. About 1941, they concentrated on false advertisements of vitamins and issued desist orders against about 25 firms on this one product. The advertisements of vitamins at that time claimed with practically no qualifications that vitamins would restore vigor, aid digestion, eliminate sterility, prevent miscarriage, increase sex vigor, decrease blood pressure, reduce neuritis, reduce insomnia, stop falling hair, cure hay fever and asthma, cure alcoholism, prevent tooth decay, eliminate pimples, make chickens lay more eggs, and keep the dog in good health.

Misrepresentations fall into three principal classes. First, some advertisements are designed to sell products which are physically dangerous, with the dangers denied, minimized, or unmentioned. Most of these advertisements are in the drug and cosmetic businesses. Only 2 of the 70 large corporations have decisions against them for advertisements of this nature.

Second, some advertisements exaggerate the values of the products, and this is equivalent to giving short weights. An extreme case of advertisements of this nature was a case decided against two hoodlums in Chicago about 1930. They sold at a price of $10 a bottle of medicine to a blind man, with the claim that this would cure his blindness. When analyzed, the medicine was found to consist of two aspirins dissolved in Lake Michigan water. The hoodlums were convicted and sentenced to six months' imprisonment. The advertisements by large corporations are frequently of this class except that they are not so extreme and are not followed by convictions in criminal courts and imprisonment. Garments advertised and sold as silk or wool are almost entirely cotton. Alligator shoes not made from alligator hides, walnut furniture not made from walnut lumber, turtle-oil facial cream not made from turtle-oil, Oriental rugs not made in the Orient, Hudson seal furs not made from the skins of seals are further instances of such misrepresentation. Caskets advertised as rustproof are not rustproof, garments as mothproof when they are not mothproof, garden hose as three-ply when it is only two-ply, and radios as "all-wave reception" that do not receive all waves. Electric pads are advertised with switches for high, medium and low heat, when in fact they have only two degrees of heat. Storage eggs are sold as fresh eggs, old and re-conditioned stoves as new stoves, and worn and re-conditioned hats as new hats. Facial creams sold as skin-foods, corrective of wrinkles, do not feed the skin or correct wrinkles. Some corporations advertise that their tea is made from tender leaves, especially picked for these corporations, when in fact their tea is purchased from lots brought in by importers who sell the same tea to other firms. Cigarettes are advertised as having been made from the finest tobacco, for which the company pays 25 per cent more, but other cigarettes are also made from the "finest tobacco" for which the manufacturers pay 25 per cent more than they do for chewing tobacco.

The third class of misrepresentation overlaps the two preceding and is separated from them principally because certain advertisements do special injury to the competitors rather than to consumers. One mail-order company advertised their furnaces as containing features which no other furnaces contained when in fact the furnaces of competitors contained the same features. Consumers Research Service, which claimed to make impartial and unbiased appraisals of automobiles, was found, in fact, to be receiving payments from an automobile company for reporting that their cars were superior.

I wish to describe a few of the important cases of misrepresentation in advertising. A prominent automobile manufacturer originated the 6 per cent installment purchase plan in 1935. This plan as advertised stated that the interest rate on unpaid balances on cars purchased on the installment plan was only 6 per cent. The Federal Trade Commission, after an investigation, reported that the interest rate was actually in excess of 11 per cent and that the exaggeration in the interest rate was nearly 100 per cent. Before the Commission had ordered the pioneer firm to desist from this misrepresentation, practically all the other large automobile companies adopted the same method of taking money under false pretenses. Again, in 1936, all the important automobile companies were ordered, on two counts, to desist from misrepresentation in advertising their cars. First, they quoted a price which did not include necessary parts and accessories, the price for the car as actually equipped being 10 per cent higher than the advertised price. In addition, they added handling charges independent of transportation costs, which further increased the price required. Second, they advertised a picture of a car which was not the model actually named and priced. Again, in 1941, three of the four principal manufacturers of automobile tires were ordered to desist from misrepresentation in their advertisements of special sales prices on the Fourth of July and on Labor Day. These companies advertised prices which were reductions of 20 to 50 per cent from the regular prices. When the Federal Trade Commission investigated, it found that the 20 per cent reduction was actually only an 8 per cent reduction and the 50 per cent reduction only an 18 per cent reduction. In addition, one tire company was found to have engaged in misrepresentation in two respects. First, it advertised that with its tires a car would stop 25 per cent quicker. It did not say 25 per cent quicker than what, but the implication was 25 per cent quicker than with tires of other manufacturers, and this was not true. Second, it made claims for the greater safety of its tires on the basis of the fact that these tires were used in the Indianapolis Speedway races, whereas in fact the Speedway tires had been especially constructed, so that there was no assurance that the company's tires for regular passenger cars were safer than other tires.

When the Federal Bureau of Investigation hunts kidnappers, it tries to find everyone who is in any way accessory to the kidnapping. The Federal Trade Commission, similarly, has attempted to some degree to bring into the picture those who are accessory to misrepresentation in advertising. They have, for instance, issued desist orders to many of the advertising agencies, which prepare the advertising campaigns for the manufacturers. Though these desist orders have included many small and unimportant advertising agencies, they have included also the largest and most prominent agencies.

Also, practically all the newspapers and popular journals have participated in dissemination of false advertisements. These include publications which range from the Gannett publications at one extreme to the *Journal of the American Medical Association* at the other. Although the *Journal of the American Medical Association* claims that it does not carry advertisements which have not been checked and found to be true, it has for years carried advertisements of Philip Morris cigarettes. In earlier years the company had claimed that these cigarettes cured irritated throats and in later years claimed that they produced less irritation in the throat than other cigarettes. As proof of their truth, these advertisements cited the opinions and experiments of physicians many, if not all, of whom had received payment for their statements. Competing tobacco companies employed other physicians, who performed experiments and gave testimony which conflicted with the testimony in the *Journal of the American Medical Association.* The Philip Morris Company made a grant of $10,000 to St. Louis University to test these propositions. The Medical School insisted on complete freedom in its methods of testing and in making its report. The report was that no accurate method of testing throat irritation had been devised or of testing the effect of the substances in question, and that conflicting claims of experimenters were all bunk. The Philip Morris Company gave no publicity to that report, but their advertisements continued to appear in the *Journal of the American Medical Association.*

I do not want to take the time to go into similar detail in regard to other types of violations of law, but I shall describe a few incidents involving violations of the National Labor Relations Law. This law was enacted first in 1933 and in more developed form in 1935. It stated that collective bargaining had proved to be a desirable policy and prohibited employers from interfering with the efforts of employees to organize unions for purposes of collective bargaining. A violation of this law was declared to be an unfair labor practice. Decisions have been made against 43 of the 70 large corporations, or 60 per cent, with a total of 149 decisions. Of these 43 corporations, 72 per cent are recidivists or repeaters; 39 used interference, restraint, and coercion, 33 discriminated against union members, 34 organized company unions, 13 used labor spies, and 5 used violence. Violence has been confined largely to the steel and automobile industries. One steel corporation from 1933 to 1937 purchased 143 gas-guns, while the Police Department of Chicago purchased in the same years only 13; the steel corporation also purchased 6,714 gas shells and grenades while the Police Department purchased only 757. The corporations customarily argue that they purchase this military equipment merely to protect themselves against the violence of the unions. Doubtless the equipment is used for protective purposes, but it is also used on some occasions for aggression. I wish to report one decision of the National Labor Relations Board concerning the Ford Motor Company. Henry Ford is reported to have said in 1937, "We'll never recognize the United Automobile Workers Union or any other union." The Ford Corporation organized a service department, under the supervision of Harry Bennett, an ex-pugilist, and staffed it with 600 members equipped with guns and blackjacks. Frank Murphy, at the time governor of Michigan and previously mayor of Detroit, said, regarding this service department, "Henry Ford employs some of the worst gangsters in our city."

In 1937 the United Automobile Workers Union was attempting to organize the employees in the River Rouge plant of the Ford Motor Company. A public announcement was made that the organizers would distribute literature at this plant at a specified time. Reporters and others gathered in advance. When a reporter asked a guard what they were going to do when the organizers arrived, the guard replied, "We are going to throw them to hell out of here." The organizers arrived, went with their literature up onto an overhead pass into one of the entrances. There they were informed that they were trespassing on private property. According to many witnesses they turned quietly and started away. As they were leaving, they were attacked by the Service staff. They were beaten, knocked down, and kicked. Witnesses described this as a "terrific beating" and as "unbelievably brutal." The beating not only occurred on the overhead pass but was continued into the public highway. One man's back was broken and another's skull fractured. The cameras of reporters, who were taking pictures of the affray, were seized by the guards and the films destroyed. A reporter who was taking a picture from the highway was observed by a guard, who shouted, "Smash that camera." The reporter jumped into the automobile of another reporter, and they were chased by the guards at a speed of eighty miles an hour through the streets of Detroit until they could secure refuge in a police station. According to pre-arranged plans, women organizers arrived later to distribute literature. As they alighted from the streetcar at the entrance to the plant, they were attacked by the guards and pushed back into the cars. One woman was knocked down and kicked. While these assaults were being committed, city policemen were present and did not interfere; the Director of the Service Department was also present.

I wish next to give a few illustrations of embezzlement and violation of trust by officers of corporations. Seiberling organized the Goodyear Rubber Company and was its manager for many years. Because of financial difficulties in the corporation, he lost control of it in 1921. His successors found that Seiberling was short nearly $4,000,000 in his account with the company, that is, that he had embezzled that amount from the company. The suits which were brought resulted in a settlement by which Seiberling agreed to reimburse the company. He not only did this but also secured credit from Ohio financiers and started the Seiberling Rubber Company, which has been quite successful.

President Sloan, Mr. Raskob, and other officers of General Motors developed a plan to pay bonuses to the officers and directors of General Motors. Under this plan President Sloan secured a total payment from the corporation of $20,000,000 between 1923 and 1928. When suits were started in later years, these excessive payments prior to 1930 were not included in the suits because of the statute of limitations. The court held, however, that these officers had appropriated by fraudulent methods of calculating their bonuses approximately $4,000,000 and ordered them to repay this amount to the corporation.

George Washington Hill and other officers of the American Tobacco Company were criticized and sued for appropriating corporate funds for their enormous salaries and bonuses. One of these suits was to be tried before Judge Manton in the Federal Court in New York City. Shortly before the trial Judge Manton suggested to the attorney for the American Tobacco Company that he needed to borrow $250,000. The attorney mentioned this to the assistant to the president of the American Tobacco Company, who mentioned it to Lord and Thomas, the advertising firm for the company, and Lord and Thomas lent Judge Manton the $250,000. Judge Manton decided the case in favor of the American Tobacco Company. Probably his decision was correct, but he was convicted of receiving a bribe, the attorney for the company was disbarred from practice in federal courts, and the assistant to the president, who made the arrangements, was promoted immediately after the decision to the position of vice-president, where he was entitled to a bonus. In another suit, the American Tobacco Company paid from its own treasury $260,000 to the complainant, and also $320,000 to its law firm, and made other payments to bring the total for fixing this case to approximately a million dollars. A court later ordered the officers, against whom the suit was brought, to reimburse the corporation for these payments.

Finally, I wish to discuss the violation of the antitrust laws. Restraint of trade was prohibited by the Sherman Antitrust Law of 1890 and by several subsequent laws, and also by the laws of most of the states. Decisions that such laws were violated have been made against 60 of the 70 large corporations in 307 cases. Three motion-picture corporations stand at the top of the list for restraint of trade with 22, 21, and 21 decisions, respectively. Thus 86 per cent of the seventy corporations have decisions against them for restraint of trade, and 73 per cent of the corporations with such decisions are recidivists. Although no decisions have been made against the other 10 corporations, other evidence indicates that probably every one of them has in fact violated these laws. These decisions tend to corroborate the statement made by Walter Lippmann, "Competition has survived only where men have been unable to abolish it." Not law but expediency and practicability have determined the limits of restraint of trade. Big Business does not like competition, and it makes careful arrangements to reduce it and even eliminate it. In certain industries the negotiations among large corporations to avoid competition are very similar to international diplomacy except that they are more successful.

For competition these businessmen have substituted private collectivism. They meet together and determine what the prices shall be and how much shall be produced, and also regulate other aspects of the economic process. This is best illustrated by the trade associations, although it is not limited to them. These trade associations not only fix prices and limit production, but they have set up systems of courts with penalties for violation of their regulations. Their system of justice applies both to their own members, in which case they have a semblance of democracy, and also to non-members, in which case they resemble dictatorship and racketeering. Among 92 trade associations investigated in 1935-39, 28 had facilities for investigating or snooping on their members, 11 had provisions for fining those who violated regulations, and 18 had provisions for boycotting the offenders.

Although businessmen often complain that the antitrust law is so vague that they cannot determine whether they are violating the law or not, a very large proportion of the decisions against these 70 corporations are for making agreements to have uniform prices—that is, not to compete as to prices. This practice is clearly in violation of the antitrust law, and no one at all acquainted with its provisions and with the decisions made under it could have the least doubt that such behavior is illegal.

Also, many of the agreements limit production. Businessmen have insisted for at least seventy-five years on limiting production in order to keep prices from falling. Though many people have regarded as ridiculous the agricultural policy of killing little pigs, it is in principle the policy which industrial corporations have been using for many generations, long before it was ever applied in agriculture.

What significance do these violations of the antitrust law have? The economic system, as described by the classical economists, was a system of free competition and laissez faire, or free enterprise, as we call it today. Free competition was the regulator of the economic system. The laws of supply and demand, operating under free competition, determined prices, profits, the flow of capital, the distribution of labor, and other economic phenomena. When profits in an industry were high, other businessmen rushed into that industry in the hope of securing similar profits. This resulted in an increase in the supply of commodities, which produced a reduction in prices, and this in turn reduced profits. Thus, the excessive profits were eliminated, the prices were reduced, and the public had a larger supply of the commodity. Through this regulation by free competition, according to the classical economists, Divine Providence produced the greatest welfare of the entire society. Free competition was to be sure, a harsh regulator. Cut-throat practices were general, and in the achievement of the welfare of the total society weaker establishments were often ruined.

Because free competition regulated the economic system, governmental regulation was unnecessary. The economic system of the classical economists developed primarily because business revolted against the governmental regulations of the feudal period, which were not adapted to the changing conditions of the eighteenth century. Government kept out of business after this system was established, except as it enforced contracts, protected the public against larceny and fraud, and enforced the principles of free competition by the common-law prohibition of restraint of trade.

During the last century this economic and political system

has changed. The changes have resulted principally from the efforts of businessmen. If the word "subversive" refers to efforts to make fundamental changes in a social system, the business leaders are the most subversive influence in the United States. These business leaders have acted as individuals or in small groups, seeking preferential advantages for themselves. The primary loyalty of the businessman has been to profits, and he has willingly sacrificed the general and abstract principles of free competition and free enterprise in circumstances which promised a pecuniary advantage. Moreover, he has been in a position of power and has been able to secure these preferential advantages. Although businessmen had no intention of modifying the economic and political system, they have produced this result. The restriction of the principle of free competition has been demonstrated by the practically universal policy of restraint of trade among large corporations.

The restriction of free enterprise has also come principally from businessmen. Free enterprise means, of course, freedom from governmental regulation and governmental interference. Although businessmen have been vociferous as to the virtues of free enterprise, and have in general insisted that government keep its hands out of and off business, businessmen above all others have put pressure on the government to interfere in business. They have not done this en masse, but as individuals or as small groups endeavoring to secure advantages for themselves. These efforts of businessmen to expand the governmental regulations of business are numerous and have a wide range. One of the best illustrations is the early and continued pressure of business concerns to secure tariffs to protect them from foreign competition. Many statutes have been enacted as the result of pressure from particular business interests to protect one industry against competition from another, as illustrated by the tax on oleomargarine. Another illustration is the fair trade laws of the Federal and state governments, which prohibit retail dealers from cutting prices on trademarked articles. The Federal fair trade law was enacted in 1937. The bill was presented by Senator Tydings, as a rider to a District of Columbia appropriations bill, where it could not be discussed on its merits. The bill was prepared by the law partner of the senator, and this law partner was the attorney for the National Association of Retail Druggists. The bill was supported by many national associations of manufacturers and dealers, who were opposed to the competitive principle and to free enterprise. The bill was opposed by the Department of Justice and the Federal Trade Commission, which have been attempting to preserve the principle of free competition and free enterprise.

In fact, the interests of businessmen have changed, to a considerable extent, from efficiency in production to efficiency in public manipulation, including manipulation of the government for the attainment of preferential advantages. This attention to governmental favors has tended to produce two results: first, it has tended to pauperize business in the sense in which charity tends to pauperize poor people, and second, it has tended to corrupt government. But the most significant result of the violations of the antitrust laws by large business concerns is that these have made our system of free competition and free enterprise unworkable. We no longer have competition as a regulator of economic processes; we have not substituted efficient governmental regulation. We cannot go back to competition. We must go forward to some new system—perhaps communism, perhaps co-operativism, perhaps much more complete governmental regulation than we now have. I don't know what lies ahead of us and am not particularly concerned, but I do know that what was a fairly efficient system has been destroyed by the illegal behavior of Big Business.

Furthermore, the businessmen have practically destroyed our system of patents by the same procedures. The system of patents was authorized in our Constitution to promote the development of science and the arts. The patent system has become one of the principal methods of promoting monopoly. Not one patent in a hundred pays even the costs of registration. Patents are important for business establishments primarily because they can be used to eliminate or regulate competitors. This is illustrated by the variation in the extent to which corporations apply for patents and bring suits for infringement of patents. In industries such as steel, very few patents are secured, and very few patent-infringement suits initiated, because establishments in this country are protected from competition by the heavy capital investment. On the other hand, in industries such as the chemical industry and the manufacture of electrical equipment, new competitors can start with a very small investment. The large companies protect themselves against competition by taking out patents on every possible modification of procedure, bringing suits on every possible pretext, and granting licenses to use patents only with a highly regimented and bureaucratic control. The patent is important principally because it is a weapon for fighting competitors. This can be seen in the practice of some of the small concerns, where widespread monopoly is not threatened. The Miniature Golf Corporation secured a patent on its vacant-lot recreation and filed scores of suits against anyone who used this method without a paid license from them. The Good Humor Corporation engaged in patent litigation for more than a decade with the Popsicle Company and other manufacturers of ice-cream bars, to determine which firm had invented this contribution to science and the arts. Similarly, the Maiden-form Brassiere Company and the Snug-Fit Foundations, Inc., were before the courts for many years regarding their patented designs, each charging the other with infringement.

The general conclusion from this study of the 70 large corporations is that the ideal businessman and the large corporation are very much like the professional thief.

First, their violations of law are frequent and continued. As stated previously, 97 per cent of the large corporations are recidivists.

Second, illegal behavior by the corporations is much more prevalent than the prosecutions indicate. In other words, only a fraction of the violations of law by a particular corporation result in prosecution, and only a fraction of the corporations which violate the law are prosecuted. In general, a few corporations are prosecuted for behavior which is industry-wide.

Third, the businessman who violates laws regulating business does not lose status among his business associates. I have mentioned President Sloan of General Motors and Seiberling (previously of the Goodyear Rubber Company), and many others could be mentioned who have appropriated the funds of their own corporations fraudulently, and who have not lost status in their own corporations or in the eyes of other businessmen. Leonor F. Loree, chairman of the Kansas City Southern, knowing that his company was about to purchase stock of another railway, went into the market privately and secretly and purchased shares of this stock in advance of his corporation, and then, when the price of the stock increased, sold it at the higher price, making a profit of $150,000. This profit, of course, was made at the expense of the corporation of which he was chairman, and he could make the profit because as an officer he knew the plans of the corporation. The courts, however, determined that this profit was fraudulent, and ordered Mr. Loree to reimburse the corporation for the violation of his trust. Shortly after this decision became generally known, Mr. Loree was elected president of the New York Chamber of Commerce, perhaps in admiration of his cleverness.

Fourth, businessmen feel and express contempt for legislators, bureaucrats, courts, "snoopers," and other governmental officials and for law, as such. In this respect, also, they are akin to the professional thieves, who feel and express contempt for police, prosecutors, and judges. Both professional thieves and corporations feel contempt for government because government interferes with their behavior.

Businessmen, being like professional thieves in these four respects, are participants in organized crime. Their violations of law are not identical and haphazard, but they have definite policies of restraint of trade, of unfair labor practices, of fraud and misrepresentation.

Businessmen differ from professional thieves principally in their greater interest in status and respectability. They think of themselves as honest men, not as criminals, whereas professional thieves, when they speak honestly, admit that they are thieves. The businessman does regard himself as a law-breaker, but he thinks the laws are wrong or at least that they should not restrict him, although they may well restrict others. He does not think of himself as a criminal because he does not conform to the popular stereotype of the criminal. This popular stereotype is always taken from the lower socioeconomic class.

I have attempted to demonstrate that businessmen violate the law with great frequency, using what may be called the methods of organized crime. I have attempted in another place to demonstrate that these violations of law are really crimes. If these conclusions are correct, it is very clear that the criminal behavior of businessmen cannot be explained by poverty, in the usual sense, or by bad housing or lack of recreational facilities or feeble-mindedness or emotional instability. Business leaders are capable, emotionally balanced, and in no sense pathological. We have no reason to think that General Motors has an inferiority complex or that the Aluminum Company of America has a frustration-aggression complex or that U.S. Steel has an Oedipus complex, or that the Armour Company has a death wish or that the DuPonts desire to return to the womb. The assumption that an offender must have some such pathological distortion of the intellect or the emotions seems to me absurd, and if it is absurd regarding the crimes of businessmen, it is equally absurd regarding the crimes of persons in the lower economic class.

PART THREE

Crime and Social Organization

THE PAPERS in this section are concerned with what Sutherland tentatively called a theory of "differential group organization." This theory was designed to explain variations in crime rates rather than the criminality of specific individuals. Although Sutherland was evidently attracted to this problem and several times tried his hand at it, his ideas concerning it were not elaborately worked out. He himself was not satisfied with his own formulation and modestly suggestly that it should be called an "orientation" rather than a scientific hypothesis. Nevertheless, this theory may be as important for criminology as his ideas concerning the genesis of crime in individuals. It suggests many research leads well worthy of more systematic exploitation.

The problem of accounting for variations in crime rates is clearly different from, though related to, that of explaining the development of criminal behavior in any given individual. Involving the comparison of groups and societies, the explanation of differing crime rates is necessarily concerned with general societal conditions and with social change rather than with the social psychology of the individual person. Sutherland regarded this as an especially appropriate task for the sociologist. He repeatedly pointed out the inapplicability of current individualistic theories of crime causation to this type of problem.

Since most theories of crime causation are formulated from the standpoint of the person and neglect problems posed by variations in crime rates, Sutherland's ideas on the latter are of special importance. They represent one of the very few serious efforts to explain crime rates as a function of social organization. True to his opposition to indiscriminate multiple-factor theories and his insistence on a down-to-earth empirical approach, he attempted to formulate a general theory consistent with the available evidence.

Sutherland's article on "Crime and the Conflict Process" (1929) is an early example of his thinking on this problem. Theories of "culture conflict" were popular in the sociological literature of that time but they were usually stated in a general form and were not worked out in detail. In this article Sutherland sought to specify how the conflict between subcultures of our society influences crime rates. In the article on "Social Process in Behavior Problems" (1932) it is proposed that high crime rates in immigrant communities may be accounted for by immigrant contact with what Sutherland called the "public culture" of America coupled with relative isolation from the "private culture." This idea suggests the notion of an internally differentiated society with each of the subgroups having a culture somewhat different from that of the others. Viewed in this perspective Sutherland's reasoning can be extended to crime rates in other subgroups.

The ideas implicit in the two articles discussed above were greatly developed and explicitly formulated in the article published in 1943 on wartime crime. In it Sutherland characteristically begins with the consideration of a specific problem, in this case, wartime crime rates, and ends up formulating a general theory applicable not merely to wartime crime rates, but to crime rates in general and perhaps to other problems as well. In this article as in some of his other writing Sutherland again indicates his feeling that a narrow economic interpretation of crime does not square with the evidence.

Crime and the Conflict Process

THE LAW, theoretically, regards a crime as a particular act which is isolated from everything except the offender's intent and the law. It seems necessary in order to prove guilt to take this view of crime as an isolated act. But it is really a legal fiction, and as a matter of fact the adult courts do not carry their theory into practice at all times. In the juvenile court it is necessary, also, to prove a specific violation of legal regulations, but after this is proved, the juvenile court immediately extends its interest and activity to a great variety of other factors in the personality of the offender and the situation.

Attempts at scientific explanation, also, generally abstract crimes from everything except the law and some one factor, generally a personal or situational abnormality. Most of these explanations consist of assertions that some one factor, which by itself is really not very important as a cause of crime, is the principal cause of crime.

In opposition to these methods of the law and of many scientific explanations it seems to be desirable to attempt to describe crime as part of a process, and that process seems to be essen-

Reprinted from *The Journal of Juvenile Research*, XIII (1929), 38-48.

tially a process of conflict. It is desirable to consider the following questions: Is crime conflict? Can crime be described as the result of prior conflicts? What results when crime is met by conflict?

In the description of crime as part of a process of conflict, the following generalizations, derived from the study of many kinds of conflict, are to be regarded as basic:

(1) Conflict tends to produce either more conflict or submission and avoidance. The stronger tendency is toward more conflict. Conflict produces more conflict by developing a feeling of antagonism in the opponent, by increasing the efficiency of the efforts of the opponent, or by developing in the group to which the opponent belongs a larger feeling of sympathy and more co-operation with him. Whether increased conflict or submission is the result of conflict depends on a great variety of factors, but probably the most important is the amount of support the individual secures from the groups to which he feels allegiance.

(2) In either of these ways conflict tends to drive the participants to the logical extremes of their positions.

(3) Consequently conflict tends to isolate the participants from each other. This is seen most clearly in war, where two countries become quite incapable of understanding each other and believe all sorts of stories which later seem to them absurd. But in less degree the same thing happens in other conflicts.

The last generalization has been stated by Dr. William Allen White as follows, "No conflict can be solved on the level of that conflict." This statement may be illustrated by the Civil War. The North and South were engaged in military conflict. The North became the victor; but conflict did not cease when military victory was won. In fact it became more intense in feeling; hatred, rancor, and antagonism continued for decades. The conflict was not solved on the level of military affairs nor by the supremacy of one side over the other on the question of slavery and states' rights. Insofar as the conflict has been solved at the present time, the solution has resulted from the development of common activities on other levels on which North and South could co-operate, and especially through co-operation against a common foe. By means of this co-operation they were brought into contact again, they developed understanding and sympathy, and the conflict is consequently on the way to a solution. In general, conflicts are not ended by direct superiority of one side over the other side on the point at issue. They are settled by indirection, by amalgamation of interests, by co-operation on other points, by contacts which lead to better understanding, and then by the lapsing or forgetting of the original differences. I shall attempt to make an analysis of crime in terms of these generalizations.

Crime has been described as conflict. Count Keyserling has defined marriage as a tragic state of tension. That is neither a good joke nor a good definition of marriage, but it would be a good description of the crime situation in this country. Cartoons sometimes depict this with the worry entirely on the side of the public, while the criminal is completely carefree. The picture describes neither the habitual nor the occasional offender. Anyone who knows criminals intimately knows that few other groups are under as great a tension as the criminal groups. Frank Tannenbaum, who has had an intimate acquaintance with professional criminals, describes them thus: "The professional criminal . . . lives a life of warfare and has the psychology of the warrior. He is at war with the whole community. Except his very few friends in crime he trusts no one and fears everyone. Suspicion, fear, hatred, danger, desperation and passion are present in a more tense form in his life than in that of the average individual. He is restless, ill-humored, easily aroused, and suspicious. He lives on the brink of a deep precipice . . . and the odds are heavy against him. He therefore builds up a defensive psychology against it—a psychology of braveness, bravado, and self-justification."

It is not difficult to appreciate the fact that the crimes which receive the greatest publicity are those involving conflict. Murder, burglary, robbery, and rape are evident attacks on the person or property of individuals which also attack certain of their cultural values and call forth the antagonistic reactions of these individuals, of a part of the public, and of the State. This aspect of conflict is illustrated by the following statement made recently by the head of one of the largest pay-roll delivery companies: "My task is the problem of meeting organized murder with organized protection at every point . . . when I tell you that a few years ago I had a fine young son shot and instantly killed by an ambushed bandit, who gave no warning, no chance, you will understand that I attack this problem of beating the bandit from a viewpoint different from that of the average citizen. With me it is more than a business; it is a form of patriotic service. I regard the killing of a bandit as an outstanding service to my community, my country, and human society in general. Every man in my employ knows that I will pay $1,000 for the killing of any bandit. Also our men are instructed to take no chances with a wounded bandit." And Judge Kavanagh has described this aspect of crime in vivid terms as follows: "At this moment the country is being attacked by an army of three hundred and fifty thousand who form an invisible foe; hosts of the air, whose stroke is sudden, remorseless, and unspeakably cruel . . . In other words American soil is occupied by an invading army more formidable in size and efficiency than any that before the World War ever invaded a civilized country. It is twice the size of the Union and Confederate Armies that fought at Gettysburg."

Though this description is vivid, I doubt its accuracy as a general description of criminals. It is true that about 350,000 persons are committed to penal and reformatory institutions in the United States in a year, but relatively few of them have committed crimes of aggression against the person or property of individuals—surely no more than 20 per cent—and of these the crimes involve very small property values and very little injury to the person in at least half of the cases. Many people think principally of burglary, robbery, and murder when they think of crime; but persons convicted of those three offenses constitute a very small part of the total number handled by the police, the courts, and the reformatory and penal institutions.

About 2 per cent of the persons arrested are charged with those three offenses, 4 per cent of the persons arrested are convicted, and of this fraction 5 per cent are committed, after being sentenced, to penal or reformatory institutions. At least three fourths of the persons handled by the agencies of the law are convicted of crimes against sobriety and good order, sex morality, public health and safety, or public policy. Few of these could be described accurately as "hosts of the air, . . . remorseless and unspeakably cruel." They are intent on their own pleasures; injuries to others are incidental. They may be thoughtless and weak, and their moral codes may differ from those stated in the laws, but they do not constitute such an army as described. That is, crime when described as conflict does not necessarily mean aggressive or ruthless acts against the person or property of individuals or against standards that have been officially set by the State.

Thus crime is conflict. But it is part of a process of conflict of which law and punishment are other parts. This process begins in the community before the law is enacted, and continues in the community and in the behavior of particular offenders after punishment is inflicted. This process seems to go on somewhat as follows: A certain group of people feel that one of their values—life, property, beauty of landscape, theological doctrine—is endangered by the behavior of others. If the group is politically influential, the value important, and the danger serious, the members of the group secure the enactment of a law and thus win the co-operation of the State in the effort to protect their value. The law is a device of one party in conflict with another party, at least in modern times. Those in the other group do not appreciate so highly this value which the law was designed to protect and do the thing which before was not a crime, but which has been made a crime by the co-operation of the State. This is a continuation of the conflict which the law was designed to eliminate, but the conflict has become larger in one respect, in that the State is now involved. Punishment is another step in the same conflict. This, also, is a device used by the first group through the agency of the State in the conflict with the second group. This conflict has been described in terms of groups for the reason that almost all crimes do involve either the active participation of more than one person or the passive or active support, so that the particular individual who is before the court may be regarded as merely a representative of the group. Bootleggers are perhaps the best illustration, for it is evident that without support in the form of patronage they could not flourish; but many other criminals secure as much support from their groups as does the bootlegger from his.

It is often asserted that there is a causal relation between these three parts of the conflict process, that the number of laws and crimes has increased, that the number of punishments has decreased, and that the increase in laws and especially the decrease in punishments are the principal causes of the increase in crimes. It is probable that there has been an increase in the number of crimes, though our statistics of crime are in their infancy and cannot carry a very heavy burden of proof. Furthermore, if laws increase and behavior remains the same, crimes necessarily increase. The number of laws has certainly increased, but no one knows how many are merely laws which abolish old laws or make minor modifications in the old laws.

No one, however, can doubt that the general trend in modern civilization is away from the use of punishment. This is seen in the school, the home, and, to some extent, in the State. Professor Swift reports that a Suabian schoolmaster left the following record of his accomplishments during fifty-one years of teaching: "He had given 911,500 canings, 121,000 floggings, 209,000 *custodes*, 126,000 tips with the ruler, 10,200 boxes on the ear, 22,700 tasks by heart. It is also recorded to his credit that he had made 700 boys stand on peas, 6,000 wear the fool's cap, and 17,000 hold the rod." A survey made in 1845 of a typical school in Boston, with about 400 pupils, showed that on the average 65 whippings were administered daily. Today corporal punishment has practically disappeared from the schools. The decrease of punishments in the home is not as great as in the school, but there has certainly been a decrease in the frequency and severity of home punishments during fifty years. Similarly, there has been a trend away from punishments in the courts, as seen in the development of the juvenile court policies and in the extension of probation and some other relatively non-punitive policies to the adult court. But this is not all net decrease in punishment, for many of the cases which are now handled by these other methods would have been merely released in the earlier period without the constructive assistance now given.

Even if the trends that have been asserted are definitely proved, the causal relation between them is not certain. People who are studying the question are divided. Some contend that the decrease in punishment is the principal cause of the increase in crimes. They say that if a person gets away with something, he will try it again but that if he is caught and punished, he will not try it again. They also say that if children are punished with sufficient frequency and severity for their earlier misdeeds, they will develop a respect for authority which will keep them from crime in later years. It is in this sense that someone explained that the invention of the safety razor was the principal cause of crime. Judge Kavanagh has asserted that if Leopold and Loeb had been spanked when young, they would not have committed their horrible crimes later. I do not know whether Leopold and Loeb were spanked in childhood, though I suspect they were, but I do know that spanking in childhood has failed to prevent thousands of other persons from committing adult crimes.

On the other hand there are students of criminology who contend that the hard-boiled desperado has been produced by earlier punishments and other antagonistic efforts and conditions in the home, school, industry, and community. Dr. Miriam Van Waters summarizes her wide experience with juvenile delinquents thus: "When the delinquent attitude is studied it is shown to be a defense reaction built of habits long used in self protection. It is the natural product of a series of more or less 'trifling' experiences with adults who have confronted, mocked, insulted, hunted or set them apart. Threatening, bantering, accusing, or smashing down the personal self-respect of the child will destroy the influence of the adult, and develop hate or resistance. The punishment may concentrate attention on the forbidden thing, may build up a wall of reserve between the child and authority so that one is isolated from the other and there is a lack of sympathetic understanding and the influence of the authority is decreased, may tear down the offender's self respect which consists principally of the feeling of solidarity with his group, and lead to an assumed toughness which easily develops into real toughness. When punishment operates in this way it produces an anti-authority complex instead of the respect for authority which is desired. Professor Cooley has stated this regarding adults, 'It is more prudent to take away a man's life than to alienate his self-respect. If you let him live, leave him some reason for living well. A punished man, unless he can see his punishment as just and necessary, saves his self-respect in the only way possible, by defiance of the punitive agent and all it stands for.' "

Dr. Van Waters maintains further that when delinquents are restored to normal social life, it is by a process that re-establishes contacts with law-abiding groups, restores self-respect, and replaces a feeling of isolation with a feeling of human relationship. Benjamin Franklin showed a good deal of knowledge of human psychology when he said, "If you want the good will of a person get him to do something for you."

Thus we have conflicting views of punishment. Both are true, for punishment does produce both effects. Sometimes it develops respect for authority, sometimes opposition to authority and an anti-authority complex. No one can precisely specify the conditions under which one effect rather than the other is produced, but in a rather general and admittedly vague way it appears that punishment fails to produce submission when the offender has an important group supporting him, for the effect of punishment is produced principally, not by physical suffering but by the disapprobation of society, of which physical suffering is the symbol. To an individual the groups that count most are those with whom he feels most allied and upon whom he feels most dependent in his personal relations. When those groups do not feel or show disapprobation, the punishment is relatively ineffective. But if the individual does not have the support of the groups to which he feels allegiance, he is likely to submit. In fact, if he can sufficiently place himself in the position of those who are ordering the punishment, he may even feel relief in his suffering as an expiation.

Though there are causal relations between the parts of the conflict process, there is reason to believe that all three parts—law, crime, and punishment—are greatly affected by the fact that our civilization has become very complex, with one culture in opposition to another culture; this state of complexity and conflict has been introduced into modern life principally by the development of increased means of mobility and communication. In the simpler societies culture was uniform and harmonious, and there were little law, little crime, and little punishment. Travelers in savage communities almost always report that children are never punished. When only one pattern of behavior is presented to them, they follow that. In modern society we have no such uniformity. We have groups standing for all kinds of interests and with conflicting ideals. If an individual does not like the culture of the particular group in which he is located, he can move into another group. Thus he can find support for any behavior toward which he feels an inclination. If he wants to drink, he can find a group with which to drink. If he wants to commit burglary or robbery, he can find support for that. As a result, we find a concentration of delinquents and criminals in certain areas of the city, owing either to selective mobility or to the influence of the situation upon the inhabitants. Studies in Chicago have shown that in a square-mile area just outside the business district about 25 per cent of the boys are arrested in a year for delinquency, while in a square-mile area eight miles away from the business district about 1 per cent are arrested. It is not certain that arrests are a fair index of the frequency of delinquencies, but casual observation of the areas leads most people to place considerable confidence in the statistics. Similarly, it has been shown in a recent study of the parole system of Illinois that persons on parole from three of the state institutions are known to violate their parole about twice as frequently if they live in the area of deterioration just outside the business districts as they would if they lived in the residential districts farther out.

Because these conflicts in culture exist, the people of one culture may find it more necessary to appeal to the State to protect their values than they would if everyone within the boundaries of the State had approximately the same culture. The demand for law arises out of the conflicts in cultures; and because there is a conflict in cultures, the law is not effective as a deterrent upon the other groups that did not at first demand the law. Thus we have legal obligations without the support of generally recognized moral obligations. Liquor laws illustrate this phenomenon of legal obligation without the recognition of moral obligation, but they are unique only in that those who favor nullification constitute a larger part of the population; the principle is identical.

Conflict of cultures is also the principal reason for the inefficiency of the agencies whose duty it is to administer the law. Pressures of many kinds are placed upon the police, the courts, and the penal and reformatory institutions. These pressures are not uniform, consistent pressures in the direction of law enforcement. People of great respectability attempt to secure the release of certain offenders. People of great respectability even violate some of the laws. And, also, those who commit the most serious crimes may have some pride in the community in which they live. The newspapers reported that in a robbery in Chicago one of the victims, who was a visitor in the city, exclaimed, "Well, this is just what one might expect in Chicago." The gunman replied, "If you was a man I'd smoke you off for making wisecracks like that about our city." Further, because of cultural differentiation and isolation, most persons have no direct contact with crime, and, in consequence, are unwilling to pay taxes for the support of an adequate police program. In view of these things it is not surprising that we often find great inefficiency in the administration of the laws.

Thus back of the laws, back of the violation of laws, and back of the inefficient administration of the laws we find the complexities and conflicts in modern cultures. This same condition is a basic factor in the explanation of the increase in the frequency of punishments and the decrease in the efficacy of those punishments which are inflicted. The public feels little emotion regarding a crime when the victim is far removed; if the victim is in the same profession or the same occupation or lives in the same neighborhood, there may be an intense sympathy for him and a call for punishment of the offender. There is an interest in crime, to be sure, but it is a sporting interest. We read crime news just as we read accounts of prize fights or football games, because of the excitement, and in this sense the newspapers are one of our institutions of entertainment. There is an increasing humanitarianism in modern society which at least vaguely leads to opposition to any kind of suffering and especially to that which is arbitrarily imposed as a consistent policy. Also, there is an increased appreciation of policies of control which are based on an understanding of the processes to be controlled. In the automobile age we understand that control is ineffective unless the mechanisms are understood, and that a mere forcible expression of emotion does not produce desired results. In fact the less emotion one expends upon a stalled automobile, the more likely he is to get it started. The same view is developing to some extent in regard to human behavior. In most of the professions in which the problem is to control human behavior, definite attempts are being made to develop techniques of a similar kind, as in salesmanship, teaching, preaching, and social work.

Even if punishment could be inflicted by the State with the same frequency and physical severity as heretofore, it is improbable that the desired results would be as successfully achieved. It has been shown that punishments are most successful when the person punished has the least group support for his behavior, and least successful when the person punished has consistent support. The moder ;ocial organization gives that support to the offender. At the same time, since punishments have wholly or largely disappeared from the home, the school, and the hereafter, the State does not have the support of a general philosophy of punishment which would be necessary to produce an impression of general disapprobation of the behavior.

Consequently it seems to be desirable to attempt to develop further than heretofore the non-punitive policies, without attempting to discard the conventional policies overnight. These new policies need to be developed just as they have been developing, by a process of experimentation and measurement of results for selected groups of people. But whether the policy be punitive or non-punitive, designed to show an attitude of conflict or of conciliation and helpfulness toward the offender, it is necessary that the whole process of the offender's behavior be taken into consideration. It is possible, while retaining the isolated act as a criterion of guilt, to consider the whole person in dealing with him in connection with the act.

There is no easy solution of the problem of crime. It is rooted in the social organization and can be solved only by social reorganization. Apparently this will need to be something like the modification that took place in the public school. Fifty years ago there were many punishments and very poor behavior; behavior was not substantially modified by multiplying punishments. As soon as experts were placed in charge of the school, trained teachers developed, and curricula adapted to the needs of the pupils, the disorder almost completely disappeared, and punishments became unnecessary. Until we can do something analogous to this in society in general, we need not expect great permanent reduction in crime rates.

This paper is a preliminary attempt at an interpretation and description of law, crime, and punishment as constituting a process of conflict, subject to the principles which are found in conflicts of other kinds; in this process the reaction to conflict may be and most frequently is continued conflict, which tends to isolate the participants from each other without leading to a solution of the conflict. Though it is necessary in many cases to meet conflict with conflict, it is desirable that the State should break that process if permanent improvement is to be expected.

Social Process in Behavior Problems

Concepts in the social sciences are lacking in precision at present. This inadequacy cannot be remedied merely by reflecting about concepts. A set of perfect concepts cannot be constructed in that manner. Rather it is desirable to use some of the available concepts in research work even though these concepts are vague, to use the results of the research work for the refinement of the concepts, and then to use the refined concepts for more specific guidance in additional research work. In this way, by the combination of observations and reflection upon observations, a science may be developed in the course of time. At the present time, in my opinion, the meanings of the concepts are indefinite and their significance dubious. Consequently, it is not wise to be bound by them. They are most likely to be useful as points of departure and as frameworks within which the results of research may be organized.

"Social process" seems to be a concept of this nature. Its meaning is not clear. Sometimes it is used, especially in connection with verbal nouns in a way which adds nothing except sound, as "the process of eating" or the "process of dressing." More generally it is used as a method of explanation or interpre-

Reprinted by permission from *Publications of the American Sociological Society*, XXVI (1932), 55-61.

tation of current behavior in much the same manner that the concept of causation is used. It differs from many methods of explanation in its insistence on including a wide range of facts and a sequence of events, actions, and situations in which some order has been found by reflection.

When used as a method of explanation, it sometimes has a personal reference, sometimes an impersonal reference. When used with a personal reference, it is a collection of social mechanisms involved in the development of a pattern of behavior of a particular person. The meaning may be inferred from the the question, What is the social process by which a person develops a delinquent behavior pattern? The answer is made in terms of mechanisms such as definition of the situation, conception of one's role, or imitation. The concept when used in this sense is in contrast with the case-study method used by the social agency. In the latter procedure a particular person is studied and described in relation to his situation, and the description of his development is presented in terms of empirical facts and ends at that point. The social psychologist, on the other hand, attempts to go beyond the empirical facts as they apply to a particular person and construct a generalization regarding the mechanism of development. The concept "social process" may be contrasted, also, with the interpretation of behavior made by certain psychologists and psychiatrists in terms of particular traits or characteristics, such as feeble-mindedness or egocentrism. The interpretation in terms of social process is an attempt to go beyond the relationship between behavior and a specific characteristic and reach a generalization regarding the manner in which the specific characteristic, when present, is combined with other characteristics and situations to produce a pattern of behavior.

One of the significant conclusions derived from the study of delinquents from the point of view of social process in this sense is that the social process by which delinquent behavior develops is the same as the social process by which non-delinquent behavior develops. In either case a situation is defined, a role is conceived, or habits are formed. The variant is not in the social process but in the situation, the temperament, or something else. Consequently social process may be a valuable step in the explanation of delinquent behavior, but it does not in itself contain the explanation of delinquent behavior as contrasted with non-delinquent behavior, since the process is the same in each. The empirical facts regarding the situation must be taken into account in each case in connection with the mechanism. The mechanism is a generalization, but the empirical facts are not. Consequently generalized explanations of delinquency have not resulted from the use of social process in this manner.

The concept "social process" is sometimes used with an impersonal reference. I shall take Cooley's use of the term as an illustration, for in his general definition of the concept he presents it as having reference to impersonal changes, though in using it he often introduces personal materials. His definition of social process is that social process "is made up of functional forms or organisms working onward by a tentative method."[1] Two things are significant in this definition, namely, the unit and the method of growth. The unit is not a person, and no reference is made to wishes, emotions, attitudes, reasoning, habits, or other psychological processes of the person. The behavior is abstracted from persons for the purpose of study and is treated as integrated in behavior systems which are said to have a life of their own. Thus, a fashion, a myth, or a language is an illustration of a social form or organism which is the unit of social process. A social form is described as a system of coordinated activities, the parts of which are bound together by influences transmitted from one to another so that they form an interdependent whole which has life of its own not identical with the life of particular persons. In the second place, this social form does not grow merely as the result of rational plans of the persons involved in it, for the persons are often unconscious of the changes taking place and do not understand that the social organism is changing. The growth occurs by a tentative method, by feeling its way, by experimenting, as a means of adapting to a situation.

[1] *Social Process* (New York: Charles Scribner's Sons, 1918), p. 30.

Cooley's conception of social process in behavior problems is an application of his general theory of social process. He speaks of a degenerate process, and of the degenerate side of the social process. He states that delinquency, like everything else in life, is dependent upon a complex system of antecedents without which it could not have come to pass, and that it can be understood adequately only by tracing its history in the individual and in the group as a whole in relation to the rest of the social process. He does not, of course, attempt to include the entire universe in this interpretation. He makes an interpretation in terms of his doctrines of human nature and of social organization. He maintains that delinquency does not spring from any specific tendency in human nature, for the tendencies have no definite direction at birth either toward or away from delinquency but are guided by and take their form principally in primary groups. Conformity with social ideals can be easily achieved only if the co-operative efforts of other people are sufficient to build up and maintain an affirmative, constructive, and many-sided community life. Delinquency tends to break out whenever these better influences are relaxed. In that sense human beings are naturally depraved. These community efforts are relaxed and disorganization results when abrupt changes occur, as in the contacts of savages with western civilization through missionaries or traders, and in modern life by residential and occupational displacement. As a result of such displacement, the control of the primary group in America has been weakened, and impersonal relations have become comparatively more important.

Cooley suggests that the best way to combat delinquency is by building up constructive and many-sided social organization. The essence of his theory is that delinquency has increased in modern society and that this increase is due to the weakening by mobility of the influence of the primary group. He does not attempt to prove this hypothesis. He is merely trying to make it intelligible.

The data which have been accumulated regarding delinquency areas seem to be in accordance with Cooley's interpretation, for the explanation of the high rate of delinquency in a particular area seems to lie within that area rather than in the general culture. But if we contrast the high crime rates of the U. S. with the crime rates of Canada or England, we must take the general culture into consideration. I wish, therefore, to suggest a hypothesis by means of which it may be possible to bring together the two types of data and for that purpose to present more details regarding the delinquency areas.

Shaw and his assistants have shown that delinquency rates vary widely in different areas in a number of cities and that these variations are related to the distance of the areas from the business and industrial centers. His statistical studies show that the high rate of delinquency is related positively to economic dependency, physical deterioration of the areas, decreasing population, and recency of immigration. He finds no significant statistical relation between the delinquency rate and the proportion of broken homes within particular nativity groups or between the delinquency rate and the country of origin of immigrants. General observations indicate that the high rates of delinquency are found in areas in which the so-called constructive influences are absent or undeveloped. Collections of case studies, including long autobiographical accounts, of boys who have been reared in the same area show a great deal regarding "the spirit of the community." This may be described as a code which includes hatred of the police and the courts and belief in their general dishonesty. The code prohibits assistance to the police or courts against any member of their community and conflicts with outside standards in many respects (e.g., compulsory school laws). For want of a better term, it may be called "toughness." A boy who is reared in an area of this type becomes delinquent naturally and almost inevitably just as he assimilates the language of the area. It is almost impossible to find a boy who has been reared from early childhood in the areas of highest delinquency and who is physically capable of delinquency who is not regularly delinquent. These areas of highest delinquency are characteristically settlements of first-generation immigrants, but the delinquents are of the second generation. The problem, however, is the rate of delinquency in the area rather than the delinquency of a particular boy. The delinquency of each boy re-enforces the delinquency of each other boy, but this seems to imply that the rate of delinquency is accidental and that the high rate might be found in any area. As a matter of fact, Shaw and McKay have found a consistency and regularity in the delinquency areas of fifteen American cities which indicate that the rate, as such, is the result of an orderly process of some nature.

The following statement is suggested as a hypothesis. It has not been proved. It is not suggested as a total explanation of delinquency even in the delinquency area, and it certainly does not explain the financial crimes of the white-collar classes. It is an attempt to add a general factor to the interpretation of the high delinquency rates in the areas of first-generation immigrant settlement, where the delinquents are characteristically of the second generation of immigrants. It certainly does not apply equally to the Negro delinquency area.

The hypothesis is that the high delinquency rate is due to isolation from the private culture of America and contact with the public culture of America. The public culture is accessible to immigrants and is presented in politics, business, newspapers, sports, and other activities. The standards most frequently displayed in public activities are "easy money" and conspicuous consumption, or a luxury standard of life. These standards are in conflict with the immigrants' native standards of hard work and thrift. The immigrants see in America exaggeration (as in advertisements), misrepresentation, sharp practices, graft, grasping competition, and disregard of human beings. This immigrant group is isolated from the private culture of America as represented in the homes and neighborhoods of the older American communities. Almost the only contact that the first- and second-generation immigrants have with this private American culture is through the picture shows and newspapers, both of which give an extremely distorted view. This private culture, almost equivalent to the primary group culture, is not all "good," but it is the medium through which the older Americans secure their directions for behavior. In general, the primary group is one in which a person is in contact with the other members in so many and such intimate ways that he is easily able to put himself in the place of these others and therefore has a sympathetic human relationship with them, whereas the public and secondary relationships involve contacts which are departmentalized and therefore institutional. Though private culture is not all "good" and public culture not all "bad," a significant difference between them is present.

This conflict between the two types of culture is not confined to America. It is similarly present in many European countries. But the effect of this cultural conflict on the immigrants to America is intensified by the following conditions: First, the parents frequently bring with them heritages regarding behavior, law, and punishment which, even when not resulting in lawlessness in their native countries, easily lead to lawlessness in America. Second, the parents are not able to direct the behavior of their children or resolve the children's conflicts in standards and behavior because of the strangeness and complexity of the situation, because of the lack of help from the primary group culture of America, and because of a latent or even active antagonism toward the older Americans. This antagonism results from the epithets applied to the immigrants and their low status and from the differences between American and European customs and requirements (e.g., the age at which a child becomes a wage earner). Third, the immigrants arrive in this country with an expectation that American democracy will remove all barriers from the lower classes and entitle them to the easy money and the luxuries of the upper classes. In most of the European countries they feel absolutely barred by fixed class lines from such expectations. In America the expectation is created, but they find that they are unable to realize the expectation lawfully. Finally, the American community lacks the organization of courts, police, and private citizens for successful conflict with criminals. Consequently delinquency often proves to be a successful means of acquiring the luxuries. Young bandits, reared in the slums, often revel in dress suits, silk hats, automobiles, fine food, and similar luxuries, and have time for sports. Some criminals, of whom Terry Druggan, a Chicago "hoodlum" and "public enemy," is an illustration, often develop aesthetic tastes in regard to household equipment. Though the policy of combating crime does not eliminate crime, it is clear that certain crimes, at least, can be prevented if the prospective victims are in a position to obstruct them. In Chicago certain trade-union racketeers attempted to force a protective association upon the Hebrew meat industry, but the ruling body of rabbis were in a strategic position because of their connection with this industry and threatened a ban on the eating of all meat by the orthodox Jews. In that situation racketeering could not be developed, and the effort failed.

Wartime Crime

Any explanatory generalization regarding crime in wartime is suspect because neither war nor crime is a homogeneous entity. Wars vary widely in many respects, and the constituent elements have not been standardized, nor have their comparative weights in the total complex of war been determined. Consequently, we do not know, even approximately, how much more "war" is involved in one war than in another. Also, many social changes which occur in wars occur also in times of peace. For these reasons the effect of wars on crimes is not a good theoretical problem.

Criticism of general theories. All the special theories of criminal behavior in wartime should be regarded as invalid, inadequate, or unproved for one or more reasons. First, when one theory makes assumptions in direct conflict with the assumptions of another theory, one theory or the other must be wrong. One theory states that war produces an increase in crimes because of the emotional instability in wartime, and another states that wars produce a decrease in crimes because of an upsurge

Reprinted by permission from *American Society in Wartime*, ed. W. F. Ogburn (Chicago: University of Chicago Press, 1943), pp. 185-206. The original title was simply "Crime." The first part of this article, which cites wartime crime rates in various countries, has been omitted.

of national feeling. One states that crimes of violence increase in wartime because of the contagion of violence, and another that they decrease because of the vicarious satiation of the need for violence. The assumptions of fact are in conflict, and one of the theories must be wrong unless the statements are limited to defined areas of behavior, and this limitation is not stated.

Second, the theories which assume explicitly or implicitly that the several types of crimes increase or decrease uniformly are in conflict with the statistics of convictions and, at least, are not proved. One theory explains an assumed increase in crimes by emotional instability but makes no effort to explain why emotionally unstable people have more convictions for one type of crime and fewer convictions for another type of crime than emotionally stable people did before the war. Similarly, the theories of the diminishing role of the future or the upsurge of national feelings do not explain why convictions for some crimes increase and for others decrease.

Third, a theory of criminal behavior which is directed at individual variations is of little value in explaining the abrupt and enormous changes in conviction rates. The psychogenic theories, which explain deviate behavior in adult life by early childhood experiences, are not adapted to the explanation of these mass movements, but they should be consistent with the theories which do explain them.

Fourth, all the special theories of criminal behavior in wartime can be questioned because they fail to allow for variations in tolerance toward consummated criminal behavior. The more careful students make general criticisms of the criminal statistics, but they then proceed to use convictions as approximate indicators of criminal behavior. An adequate theory of criminal behavior must separate these two variables in the data. Also, an adequate theory should explain changes in criminal behavior and changes in the reactions toward criminal behavior in the same general terms, although not usually as applying to the same individuals. Both criminal behavior and reactions to criminal behavior are expressions of attitudes toward criminal codes and toward the concrete values which the codes are designed to protect, and generalizations which apply to one should apply also to the other.

The preceding criticisms of the theories of criminal behavior in wartime do not mean that the factors of contagion of violence, satiation of the need for violence, the diminishing role of the future, and national feeling have no effect on behavior. The criticisms mean rather that the respects in which these factors play a part have not been defined, that the relations of these factors to one another have not been determined, and that the factors have not been organized into a system of thought.

Exner's theory. If the changes in criminal behavior were separated from the changes in the reactions to criminal behavior, we should still have the problem of determining what factors and what organization of factors explain the changes in criminal behavior. In the discussion of this question I shall accept for the moment the usual assumption that convictions are an approximately accurate index of criminal behavior and consider one of the more adequate theories which makes the same assumption. This is the theory of Exner, based on his study of crime in Austria during World War I. His theory is that the scarcity of commodities explains both the increase in thefts and the decrease in sex offenses and assaults. Thefts increased because of the pressure of unsatisfied needs and the restrictions on legitimate methods of securing commodities; sex offenses and assaults decreased because the undernourished people had little surplus energy for sex offenses and assaults; included in the scarce commodities was alcohol, and the decrease in sex offenses and assaults was affected especially by the scarcity of this commodity.

This theory has the advantage of providing a unified explanation of the increases in some crimes and decreases in other crimes. Obviously it fits many of the facts, for in many ways convictions for thefts changed concomitantly with changes in economic distress. As a first approximation to an explanatory generalization it is much better than the other theories. The crucial question, as far as thefts are concerned, is, Does this theory mean that thefts would not increase in a country at war if economic distress did not increase, even though all the other changes of wartime did occur? This meaning is implied in the theory, although Exner does not state it explicitly.

When the theory is inspected from this point of view, it does not fit some of the facts. First, convictions for thefts increased in England by approximately the same percentage as in Germany and Austria, although economic distress was much less in England than in Germany and Austria. Second, thefts increased in Canada during the war, although economic distress decreased. Third, thefts by children began to increase in each of the countries immediately after the outbreak of the war, although there was little economic distress in the first months of the war. Fourth, thefts by children increased more than thefts by adults in England, Germany, and Austria, although children were probably in no greater distress than adults.

Additional shortcomings are discovered when the theory is extended beyond the data of World War I. During the present war, for example, juvenile thefts in the United States are probably increasing, although economic distress is probably decreasing. Furthermore, over long periods of time variations in convictions for theft and variations in the business cycle have a very low coefficient of correlation. Also, although the members of the white-collar class do not suffer economic distress in the sense in which those terms are used with reference to Germany and Austria during World War I, they do commit many thefts in the form of fraud.

Differential organization as an explanation. A clue to a more adequate explanation of thefts in wartime is provided by the ecological studies of crime in American cities. These studies show that crime is closely associated with poverty by residential areas, in contrast with the studies of time series, which show that crime has very little association with poverty by chronological periods. Poverty, as such, cannot be important in the causation of crime when considered in terms of geographic units and unimportant when considered in terms of chronological units. Something must be associated with poverty when it is considered geographically and not associated with poverty when it is considered chronologically. If this something can be abstracted from poverty and related directly to crime, we may be able to find a more consistent relationship. This something is probably the contacts and communications of people, for these do not change appreciably in the business cycle but do vary greatly from one residential area to another. These contacts and communications may vary independently of poverty. For this reason we find very low juvenile delinquency rates in certain segregated groups, especially in the Oriental groups in American cities, which live in poverty in areas which have high delinquency rates.

We may then ask: What other things were connected with the economic distress which Exner regarded as the cause of the increase in thefts? The following are some of these.

First, the external opportunities for thefts increased because the owners of property spent a larger part of their time away from home, because supervision in industrial and commercial establishments decreased, because the railways carried increased loads of commodities without increase in the number of guards, because a large number of persons, not selected on the basis of trustworthiness, were placed in positions of responsibility, and because the police force decreased in number and training.

Second, the efforts to train children and adults in opposition to stealing were relaxed or abandoned because parents were away from home and because schools and churches were closed or were diverted to other purposes.

Third, many persons, especially younger children, were left in complete idleness with no provision for supervised legal activities.

Fourth, many of the poor people developed increased hostility toward some property owners who were regarded as hoarders or owners of goods by other illegal methods.

Fifth, the meaning of property ownership and of property rights was confused by governmental appropriation of private property, by radical departures from the previous system of determining values and distributing property, and by general use of public property with little attention to its ownership.

Sixth, contacts with criminal patterns were increased because of the passage of large numbers of children and women from the sheltered environment of the home to the heterogeneous environment of the factory, shop, and store, because of the great increase in the mobility of people, and because persons who had been stealing previously now stole with increased frequency and thus more effectively presented the patterns of theft to the non-thieves.

Seventh, many public and private employees, especially railway employees, were in collusion with the thieves.

Eighth, many persons who were not in economic distress were engaged systematically in stealing for the black markets.

Ninth, a situation had occurred which was appropriate for theft according to the cultural definition which had been held for a long time and somewhat generally, namely, the situation in which theft is the only apparent alternative to starvation.

The first five of these changes are aspects of the breakdown of the organization for the prevention of thefts and refer primarily to those who react against prospective and consummated thefts; the last four are aspects of the organization for thefts and refer primarily to those who steal. These two groups of factors together may be called differential group organization. Many of these items may change in a country at war which has no economic distress and may result in nearly as much increase in thefts as in the country which is in economic distress.

Limitations of time prevent a similar analysis of the decrease in convictions for sex offenses and assaults, and of the factor of tolerance, which was waived for purposes of the present analysis and which is one aspect of the reaction to consummated crimes. Even if time permitted, however, a continuation of the analysis would do little more than provide additional illustrations of the possibility of organizing the multiple factors into a somewhat unified system of thought.

This system of thought may be formulated with reference to any type of crime as follows: A conviction rate is a function of two variables, namely, criminal behavior and reactions against criminal behavior; each of these is an expression of changes in group organization, and the two aspects of organization together are called differential group organization. The balance between the opposed organizations determines whether the crimes committed, the reactions against crimes, and the conviction rates increase or decrease.

In order to clarify the meaning of this proposition, a few explanations are needed. First, organization has two principal constituent elements, namely, consensus in regard to objectives and implementation for the realization of objectives. Each of these may vary independently of the other, but they usually vary together. Each of these is found in the organization for crime and the organization against crime.

Second, the phrase "differential group organization" is used here with reference to a specific behavior. Although a nation may become thoroughly disorganized and although all kinds of behavior may reflect this general disorganization, the usual change is the breakdown of organization of one kind of behavior while organization for another kind of behavior is developing.

Third, the abstract principle of differential group organization should be universally associated with these changes in conviction rates in wartime although any specific condition involved in the differential group organization may occur with greater or less frequency. The relationship between the abstract principle and the concrete conditions may be illustrated by the variations in the family conditions of delinquents. Some delinquents have cruel stepmothers and others have conscientious and religious mothers who are almost completely ignorant of the conditions of life in American cities. The abstract principle in both is that the mother is not effective in training and supervising her children; the concrete ways in which that principle appears may vary widely. This relationship between abstract principle and concrete conditions is found throughout the whole range of conditions which are related to criminal behavior in wartime.

Fourth, a statement of crime in wartime in terms of differential organization does not explain why the organizations change. The proposition is a hypothetical statement of a uniformity; it does not attempt to explain the entire chain of events preceding the criminal behavior.

I have referred to this proposed method of explaining changes in criminal behavior in wartime as a hypothesis, but "orientation" might be a better word. The explanation is obviously not a precise proposition that can be easily tested and pronounced right or wrong. Probably a precise hypothesis regarding the effect of wars upon criminal behavior cannot be stated, because this is not a precise theoretical problem.

If this orientation toward the problem of the effect of war on criminal behavior is justified, it eliminates certain other approaches. One of the theories which would be eliminated is the psychogenic theory that criminal behavior is rooted in early childhood experiences and appears in later life by a process of maturation. That theory, obviously, is not an explanation of the sudden mass movements revealed by criminal statistics. It seems necessary, however, that any theory which is to be valid in the explanation of individual differences in criminal behavior must be consistent with a theory which is valid for these mass movements in criminal behavior. Another orientation which is eliminated is one which explains crime in terms of a particular concrete condition, such as poverty. The theory advanced in this paper uses poverty as a part of the explanation, but it does so by abstracting from poverty and other concrete conditions a general principle that should be universally associated with the changes in crime rates.

*BIBLIOGRAPHY**

Exner, Franz. *Krieg und Kriminalitat in Osterreich.* Carnegie Institute for International Peace, *Economic and Social History of the World War*, ed. James T. Shotwell. Vienna, 1927.

* The following references were listed by Professor Sutherland at the end of this paper as a guide to supplementary reading on the subject of wartime crime. A general bibliography of the writings of Edwin Sutherland is included at the end of this book.

Glueck, Eleanor T. "Wartime Delinquency," *Journal of Criminal Law and Criminology*, XXXIII (July, 1942), 119–35.

Liepmann, Moritz. *Krieg und Kriminalitat in Deutschland*. Carnegie Institute for International Peace, *Economic and Social History of the World War*, ed. James T. Shotwell. Stuttgart, 1930.

Mannheim, Hermann. *Social Aspects of Crime in England between the Wars*. London, 1940.

———. *War and Crime*. London, 1941.

Reckless, Walter C. "The Impact of War on Crime, Delinquency and Prostitution," *American Journal of Sociology*, XLVIII (November, 1942), 378–86.

Rosenblum, Betty B. "The Relationship between War and Crime in the United States," *Journal of Criminal Law and Criminology*, XXX (January, 1940), 722–40.

Starke, W. *Verbrechen und Verbrecher in Preussen, 1854–78*. Berlin, 1884.

PART FOUR

Juvenile Delinquency

SUTHERLAND wrote relatively little on the subject of juvenile delinquency as such. This was partly due, no doubt, to the fact that he engaged in little original research in this field. Another reason, perhaps more significant, is that he conceived of the etiology of criminality as a unitary process. According to him, the process by which a juvenile becomes delinquent is no different from the process by which an adult becomes a criminal. Thus his analysis of delinquency was simply one aspect of his search for a general theory of causation. It is consistent with this position that he questioned the wisdom of a separate course on juvenile delinquency on the grounds, just mentioned, that the causes of delinquency could not be considered apart from the general problem of crime causation. In this respect he differed from many leading criminologists who assume that the etiologies of juvenile and adult crime are significantly different.

Although Sutherland did not regard the explanation of juvenile crime as a separate theoretical problem, he did nevertheless believe that the juvenile offender should be considered a separate and distinct penological or treatment problem. Sutherland was, indeed, a staunch supporter of the trend toward the classification, segregation, and specialized treatment of various types of offenders, including of course the juvenile offender.

The articles that follow are previously unpublished statements on the subject of juvenile delinquency. They indicate careful and thoughtful evaluation of both research and preventive efforts in this field. They again exemplify Sutherland's general orientation and his concern with the individual as a product of the social milieu. The control of delinquency is viewed basically as a problem in social organization rather than as one of treating individuals.

Prevention of Juvenile Delinquency

IN INTRODUCING this symposium on the control of behavior problems, I begin with a definition of the terms. I use the term "behavior problem" as essentially synonymous with "juvenile delinquency." This excludes, on the one hand, adult criminal behavior, and, on the other hand, deviations (such as thumb-sucking, enuresis, and bashfulness) in the behavior of children which are not appraised as invasions of the rights of the community. In the concept of "control" I include both general policies relating to the prevention of delinquency and also policies concerned with the treatment of individual delinquents for the purpose of reform. I shall state here (with as much elaboration as time permits) a series of propositions regarding the control of behavior problems.

(1) *Juvenile delinquency can be controlled.* It is not rooted in human heredity, human nature, or social organization in such a way that it cannot be eliminated or at least greatly reduced. Efforts have been made to demonstrate that delinquency is inherited, but these efforts have failed, and no significant differ-

Presented in a joint meeting of the Indiana State Teachers Association and the Indiana Academy of Social Sciences held in Indianapolis on October 27, 1945. This paper was part of a panel discussion entitled "Control of Behavior Problems"; other panel members were Mark C. Roser, Harold V. Anderson, and Floyd B. Bolton.

ence has been found between the heredity of delinquents and the heredity of non-delinquents. Negroes, to be sure, have an extraordinarily high rate of delinquency, but this can be shown to be due to the social reactions of other persons rather than to the inherited color of the skin. Even if delinquency were inherited, it could be controlled by methods of eugenics and sterilization. The studies of the causes of delinquency show conclusively, however, that delinquency is learned. The learning process, of course, is within the control of society. The individual who has learned delinquency and developed an organized set of habits or character is not readily modified, but such behavior as delinquency is much more readily modified than some other traits of personality. In any case, prevention is, in principle, easier than correction.

(2) *An efficient program for the control of delinquency must be based on knowledge of the causes of delinquency and on experiments in and training for control.* Knowledge of the causes, to be most useful, should be stated in a small number of clear-cut, interrelated general propositions, the validity of which has been established. Such propositions have not been established, but approximations to them have been, and these are useful in directing programs for control. Also, many efforts have been made to organize programs for the control of delinquency. None of these has had a very high degree of success, either in prevention or in treatment. This lack of success is due to the lack of knowledge of causes and lack of experiments and training for the experiments rather than to an inherent impossibility of control. The principal difficulty has been that everything in the universe has been regarded by some scholars as involved in the causation of delinquency and that all social institutions and other parts of the social organization seem to require changes in order that juvenile delinquency may be reduced. This conception, I believe, is fallacious; but if true, it would make control of juvenile delinquency practically impossible.

(3) *The most effective means for the control of juvenile delinquency lie almost exclusively in the local community and*

its personal groups. The family is doubtless the most important of these personal groups, but the recreational group and, for older children, the occupational group are very important. Unless the family is extraordinarily efficient, it does not keep its children from delinquency when the standards of the play groups and other groups conflict with the standards of the family. The proposition that the control of delinquency lies almost entirely in the local community is based on demonstrated knowledge regarding the causes of juvenile delinquency. The child lives his life in the personal groups within a community and in those groups acquires his standards of behavior and his conception of himself. He acquires these largely by oral definitions of the behavior which is proper and the behavior which is improper. This is illustrated by the difference between the boy delinquency rate and the girl delinquency rate. In the United States, in general, 80 per cent of the delinquency cases are boys and only 20 per cent girls. Boys and girls, in general, are equally in poverty, live equally in poor homes, have equally ignorant and inefficient parents, and are equally lacking in organized recreational facilities, with the boys having better facilities than the girls when there is a difference. Also, boys and girls are approximately equal in the proportion of those who are feeble-minded, who are not wanted at home, and who are rejected by parents, and are approximately equal in emotional disturbances. Hence they cannot differ in delinquency because of such gross situational factors. They differ rather because parents and other intimate associates define one kind of propriety for girls and another for boys, and exercise one kind of supervision over girls and another over boys.

The larger culture has some effect on the behavior of children, but this is rather incidental. Communities differ in their delinquency rates although children all over the nation read essentially the same comic strips, see the same picture shows, and listen to the same broadcasts. This indicates that these impersonal agencies of communication exert relatively little influence on children. Economic institutions have some influence, especially in relation to the distribution of wealth. Nevertheless, although juvenile delinquents are customarily concentrated in the areas of poverty in the modern city, their delinquency is not a product of their poverty as such. This is indicated by the fact that delinquency does not increase when poverty increases, in a depression, or decrease when poverty decreases, in prosperity, and actually shows a trend in the opposite direction, that is, to increase with prosperity. Further evidence is seen in the relative absence of delinquency in certain poor rural areas and in the Japanese colonies in Seattle and Honolulu, although these Japanese are quite as poor as other groups in the surrounding area.

The local community is affected in various ways by the larger culture. A great catastrophe, such as the disintegration of Germany or Austria at the end of World War I, may produce enormous increases in juvenile delinquency and adult crime, and presumably no local community can effectively counteract such general disintegration of a nation or other society. On the other hand, England, Canada, and the United States did not disintegrate at the end of the World War I and had no appreciable increase in delinquency. Unless World War II is followed, in the United States, by general disintegration of the financial, economic, political, and other social systems, we need not expect a significant excess of juvenile or adult delinquency above the prewar period.

Aside from such extraordinary catastrophes, the larger culture affects the local community primarily by mobility of population, as will be shown in the following proposition (paragraph 4). Before considering it in detail, I should like to call attention to two implications in the proposition that the local community is almost the only group which can control delinquency: First, a local community does not need to control the entire culture of a nation (which would be impossible) in order to control its delinquency rate. The things that need to be done are local and relate to personal interaction rather than to the larger institutions. Second, the state and national governments and private nationwide associations can do practically nothing to reduce delinquency except by stimulating and directing local communities to take action on their own problems. These larger organizations may keep records of the experiments made by different communities in the effort to control delinquency, and may offer suggestions; they may train personnel for such undertakings and assist in making this personnel available to any local community. But the program rests finally upon the local community and consists of alterations in the personal groups of that community.

(4) *The local community which wishes to control its delinquency must organize for that purpose.* The local community in earlier periods controlled delinquency spontaneously and without formal organization; the community was stable; the population was relatively homogeneous; and the members of the community were intimately acquainted with one another and exerted a constant and consistent pressure upon one another which produced conformity to standards without formal organization. The principal result of the changes in the larger institutions and in the material culture during the last century has been to disrupt that spontaneous control by the local community because of the heterogeneity and the rapid turnover in the population. The local community in the present period must exercise its possibility of control through formal organization.

(5) *A rise in the juvenile delinquency rate in a community disturbs that community and results in efforts to develop organization for control.* This tendency to organize against delinquency is promoted by the general practice of organizing to solve other problems. During the early years of World War II, when delinquency rates were reported to be rising, hundreds of communities initiated movements to control juvenile delinquency. Most of these efforts did not go far, and this was due to the fact that communities have not known what to do when and if they organized.

(6) *The people whose children are likely to become delinquent must be the principal participants in the local community organizations.* Many forms of organization have been tried for

the control of delinquency and for other purposes. These include local co-ordinating councils, parent-teacher associations, boys' clubs and other youth movements, and crime commissions to put pressure on police and courts for increased certainty and severity of punishments. Time does not permit a detailed appraisal of these and other community efforts to organize for the control of delinquency. The general characteristic of these organizations is that they are promoted, controlled, and directed by persons who are outside the groups which are delinquent. Crime commissions are usually composed of businessmen who regard themselves as the victims. Co-ordinating councils are composed of representatives of police departments, schools, churches, and welfare agencies. Parent-teacher associations, to be sure, are designed to include the parents of delinquents as well as other parents, but these associations seldom have any strength in the areas of a city where the delinquencies are concentrated, largely because the parents do not feel at ease with the teachers.

In contrast with such organizations, the Area Projects in Chicago have made a forthright attempt to stimulate the people whose children commit the delinquencies to organize—Polish residents of the steel mill districts in South Chicago, Italians on the lower North Side and on the West Side, Negroes on the South Side. These are the persons who organized to prevent delinquency in their own groups; the leaders in the organizations are residents of those areas and were reared there. Some stimulation and financial support came from the outside, but the people of the area decide on policies and exert the influences which control behavior. A few incidents will illustrate how these Area Projects have worked. The boys in the Italian area were stealing automobiles and accessories and selling them to the director of the public park in their neighborhood, who was the "fence." The leaders of the Area Project requested the head of the City Park system to remove this director, but their request received little attention. Then they went to the politicians and stated that they controlled the vote in their ward and would vote against the administration in the next election unless this park director were removed; the director was removed immediately and a good man substituted. Again, the scout organization had attempted on several previous occasions to organize troops in this area. These attempts had been unsuccessful, the few recruits who were secured having been ridiculed by the other boys and their uniforms torn to pieces. But when the Italian leaders passed the word along to the parents, young adults, and children that the scouts had a good program and that all the children were going to join, this area soon had a larger proportion of boys 10-12 years of age in scout troops than any other area in Chicago. Arrangements were made with the police department that any boy from this area who was arrested should be referred, without booking, to the Area Project; then his own neighbors and associates rather than an outside functionary undertook to exercise control. Persons who have been closely affiliated with the Chicago Area Projects differ in their appraisals of results, some affirming that delinquencies have declined greatly and others being at least agnostic, but all agreeing that the experiments have demonstrated that the people of deteriorated city areas can organize themselves to deal with their own problems.

(7) *People in areas with high delinquency rates must be stimulated and directed in the organization of community programs.* In the Chicago Areas Projects, Shaw and his associates made inquiries as to the most influential persons in a particular area and presented to those leaders the possibility of self-organization for control of delinquency, and the leaders and their neighbors did the rest. In the typical community, teachers, preachers, social workers, or others may be needed to initiate self-organization, but they must withdraw at an early date and not attempt to control policies, or the regular residents of the area in which the problems develop will be alienated.

(8) *The principal function of a community organization for the control of delinquency is to define delinquent behavior as undesirable.* This definition must be made by persons whom a potential delinquent values most highly and must be made ultimately in oral terms to a very great extent. This does not mean

that formal "preaching" is the essence of the program. Rather, it means that the methods which have produced a low delinquency rate for girls must be utilized in reducing the delinquency of boys. Some of the specifications of the program, both from the positive and the negative point of view, are elaborated in the following sub-points.

(*a*) Punishment has limited values but must be used as a last resort. Animal experimentation shows that behavior is controlled to some extent by punishment. Punishment of human beings is important as a control principally when it reflects the opinions of those whose opinions mean most to the children in question. If punishment is merely an expression of the opinion of policemen, judges, teachers, or other functionaries and is in conflict with the opinions of those in the child's own personal group, it is relatively impotent. This is shown by the German efforts to control the countries which they occupied during the recent war. The underground movement and sabotage flourished for years in those countries in spite of efficient detection and brutal penalties. The punishments were not effective in stopping the behavior because everyone who violated the German regulations had the approval of persons who meant more to him than the Germans did. In spite of this limited value of punishment, I see nothing that a community can do with a persistent delinquent upon whom other methods of control have failed, except to remove him temporarily or permanently from the community. Whether this is punishment or not, depends upon your definition of punishment, but it will certainly be regarded by the community as punishment.

(*b*) The program for the control of delinquency should include both policies of individual treatment and policies of general prevention. Some communities have developed behavior clinics and stopped there. This imposition of the entire load upon the shoulders of the case worker is an improper emphasis. If it were necessary to select one or the other of the two types of work, which it is not, it would be preferable to select general prevention and neglect individual delinquents. The primary task of the case worker is to modify the home and other personal groups of the delinquent, and case work customarily succeeds in proportion to the co-operation secured from those personal groups. It is more economical and more effective to develop these modifications in a community prior to the appearance of the behavior problems and, when behavior problems first make their appearance, to deal with them in such manner as to avoid definition of the child as a delinquent.

(*c*) Organized recreation is probably a necessary part of a community program for the control of delinquency, but it has been greatly overemphasized in most of the communities which have organized. Organized recreation is not provided for girls as generally as for boys, but girls are less delinquent than boys. A study of a boys' club in New York City showed that boys who participated in the club were more delinquent than other boys in the same neighborhood who did not participate in the club activities, and also that boys who participated in club activities one year and not the next year had a higher record of delinquencies during the year they were in the club than in the year they were not in the club. Despite this unfavorable record, boys' clubs and other organized recreation presumably do have some influence in impeding the development of delinquency. Their value does not consist in the modification of the attitudes of boys but in the occupation of a portion of their time in non-delinquent activities so that at least during that time, they are not engaging in delinquent activities.

(*d*) The juveniles themselves should be organized as a part of the community program; that is, the organization should not be confined to the parents of the juveniles. Some communities have stated an hypothesis as follows: Two or three generations ago children were an economic and social asset to the family and to the community, but with the lengthening of the period of compulsory education and the deferring of the period of regular occupation together with continuous unemployment, children have been forced to the conclusion that they are not wanted in the community. These communities then developed programs designed to utilize the abilities of the children with the purpose of making them feel important to the community.

During the recent war children collected paper and scrap metal and in many places, largely through the schools, have been organized to render many other services in the community.

(*e*) The function of training in relation to this total program is to prepare persons to deal in an official manner with individual delinquents, with the orientation toward organization of the personal groups with whom the problem child is associated rather than toward the solution of the problem by his own efforts, and to prepare persons to stimulate and guide the community in its self-organization. In both cases the trained personnel must function principally behind the scenes and operate by suggestion to the groups which control the behavior.

(9) *Conclusion.* The studies of the causes of juvenile delinquency indicate that delinquency is learned behavior, that it develops principally as the result of standards in the groups in which a child participates in an intimate and face-to-face manner, and that these groups are largely independent of the larger social institutions and larger culture. The local community controlled behavior in the earlier period spontaneously and without formal organization. Alterations in the larger culture have, to a considerable extent, disrupted that method of control. The local community can still control the behavior of its children but must organize for this purpose. With such organization, control still resides almost entirely in the personal groups in which children live their lives, and the formal organization must operate largely by organizing those personal groups for the definition of the behavior of children.

Juvenile Delinquency and Community Organization

THERE are areas in every American city in which criminals have a somewhat consistent culture. Shaw, who has studied delinquency in Chicago very thoroughly, reports that juvenile delinquency has been very prevalent in districts just outside the central business section for several generations, and that the rate has regularly decreased from the center of the city toward the outskirts. The interesting thing is that the juvenile delinquency rate has remained high in those areas near the Loop regardless of the nationality which lived there. Fifty or more years ago when the Irish lived there, their children were in continuous trouble over delinquencies; later the Germans and Swedes moved in, and their children were in trouble; the Austrians, Poles, and Lithuanians had the same experience; and finally the Italians and Jews. Regardless of what group lived in those slum areas, the children were delinquent; as the parents became somewhat established economically and moved into better districts, their children dropped out of the juvenile court.

A more interesting illustration is provided by the Moloccans, a religious group in Russia who somewhat resembled the Quakers in religion and behavior, and who were hard-working,

This paper, previously unpublished, is part of an address given before a meeting of the Indiana State Teachers Association in 1936.

frugal, and quiet. A group moved from Russia and settled in a poor section of Los Angeles. Of the children born in Russia, only 5 per cent ever appeared in the juvenile court of Los Angeles; of those born during the first years in Los Angeles, 40 per cent reached the juvenile court; and of those born in later years, 80 per cent reached the juvenile court. In other words, while the stock remained constant, the proportion of children who became delinquent in the city environment increased enormously.

In these areas of delinquency, just as in the professional criminal groups and in the criminal tribes of India, there is a definite philosophy of criminality and a definite organization of attitudes. Any boy who is being chased by the police may run into any home and be secreted or protected. The unforgivable sin is to "snitch" or "squeal." It is proper to steal anything that is not nailed down, provided the victim is not a friend. There is a general antagonism toward "coppers," a term which includes any agent of law-enforcement bodies. Every stranger is looked upon with suspicion and often with hostility. Various people have informed me that when they were driving a car through one of these slum areas, the boys and girls stood on the sidewalks and spat at them. The social worker is regarded as a person to be exploited to the limit. Such attitudes have prevailed in these areas for generation after generation, and the child acquires them just as he acquires the language which is current in his neighborhood.

Poverty is generally found in such areas, but it is not universal. It should also be understood that not all areas which are poor have these high delinquency rates. One of the best illustrations of the fact that delinquency is not due exclusively to poverty is provided by the Japanese children. It was found both in Seattle and in Honolulu that Japanese children from families which lived in the interior of the Japanese colony practically never appeared in the juvenile court and that Japanese children from families scattered among families of other nationalities had a very high rate of delinquency. Those in the colonies were on the average in greater poverty than those scattered among other nationalities. The principle seems to be that when the family lives in the midst of a nationality with the same culture and is supported by that group in the direction of law-abiding behavior, the family is adequate to control the children; but that when it operates alone against the conflicting standards of various national groups, it is relatively powerless. Though some parents are superior to others in their ability to control their children, group heterogeneity places a burden on parents which they are seldom able to support.

It is quite apparent that in the United States today all young people, and perhaps old ones as well, are more or less "delinquent." In various universities I have asked students to write anonymously the list of thefts committed since early childhood. Practically all of them have had thefts to report, just as all of us would have. Most of the thefts are of the kind we smile about–fruit or flowers stolen from neighbors, watermelons, "knocking down" a few pennies that were supposed to be put in the Sunday School collection or to be brought back as change from the grocery store, souvenirs from hotels and restaurants. A college student thinks it is amusing when he steals a spoon from a hotel, but in much the same sense, the young hoodlum in the slums thinks it is amusing when he steals an automobile, holds up the attendant of a filling station, or rapes a girl. The difference is not so much in the attitude with which the delinquency is started as in the length to which it progresses, and the length to which it progresses is affected decidedly by the traditions and culture of the community in which the individual lives.

Communities differ in these traditions and cultures. At one extreme we have the community with practically no delinquency; at the other we have the criminal tribes of India and the professional thieves of this country. In between these extremes, we have communities in which the standards of behavior are conflicting. It is this conflict of cultures within the community which is becoming characteristic of American life.

The variety of standards of behavior is greater in the city than in the country. This is reflected in the excessive crime rate in the city. A recent survey in Kansas showed ten times as many juvenile delinquency cases per thousand children in cities over 50,000 as in a town under 6,500. My guess is that the difference between the city and the small town is decreasing. The automobile, the picture show, the radio, and the newspaper have made the small town more nearly like the large city than it used to be. If this is true and if the trend continues, we may expect that delinquency will become an increasingly serious problem in the small town.

Because the standards of behavior presented to the child are now conflicting, it is difficult to predict the outcome in an individual case. In the interior of China fifty years ago, it was possible to predict with almost complete certainty how a boy would be behaving at the age of twenty. Life for boys had been routinized over a period of many generations, and it was almost impossible for one boy to behave differently from other boys of the same community. Consequently, behavior could be predicted. But in our society, because of the larger number of choices that must be made, it is impossible to know which boy will proceed, and which will not, from minor into more serious delinquencies.

This lack of consistency in the patterns of behavior may be called community disorganization. It is certainly one of the important factors in the developing delinquency in this country. Since it has been recognized that delinquency is promoted by this community disorganization, efforts have been made to counteract it by developing community organization. There have been two principal methods of community organization: One is an organization of representatives of agencies which deal with community problems; the other is an organization of the ordinary citizens of a neighborhood.

The first plan of organization is frequently called the local co-ordinating council. These may be co-ordinating councils to deal with all community problems or co-ordinating councils to deal with the problems of delinquency alone. The more general council is illustrated by the Committee for Social Progress in the Borough of Queens, New York City. It includes all the social agencies—Chamber of Commerce, Bar Association, Legion, League of Women Voters, and all the rest. The activities are classified as research, dissemination, co-ordination, planning, and community action. By these methods they are trying to develop social planning in the local community and to put it into action. Councils for the prevention of delinquency have sprung up in all types of communities, from large to small, East and West, North and South. They have not been promoted by any national body. They are based on the somewhat spontaneous recognition that the causes of delinquency are too varied to be attacked successfully by any one agency working alone; by coming together into a council they hope to co-ordinate their efforts so that altogether they may plan and act for the welfare of the community. Regardless of how one may feel about the social planning of our general economic and political institutions, there seems to be no need for any difference of opinion in regard to planning for the local neighborhood.

The principal problem regarding the work of these councils is that the residents of the more completely disorganized neighborhoods are suspicious of the social agencies; the residents are not represented on the school board or in the Parent Teacher Associations, the League of Women Voters, or the Chamber of Commerce. They regard most or all of these agencies with suspicion or even hatred. They are not likely to co-operate in a program for the improvement of their neighborhood if that program is imposed upon them from above, unless they regard this as an opportunity for exploitation.

Consequently, in these more disorganized communities it seems to be necessary to start with the residents rather than with the schoolteacher, the social worker, or the Chamber of Commerce. It is necessary to start with problems as the residents see them and work toward the prevention of delinquency from that point. Their program should be formulated by themselves and will, therefore, necessarily vary from one community to another. Some pressure may be exerted by a few outsiders in whom the community has confidence, but for the most part outsiders can do little except suggest and stimulate.

In both programs recreation has been emphasized. The boys' club has been emphasized especially. In general, I am in favor of the boys' clubs, but the evidence regarding their effectiveness is somewhat conflicting, as might be expected. We have an especially gratifying record of reduction of delinquency in Columbus, Indiana, after the club was started there. On the other hand, we have had a recent report from Professor Thrasher after a five-year study of the Boys' Club of New York City. He found that boys who belonged to this club had a higher rate of delinquency than boys living in the same neighborhood who did not belong to the club, and that those who attended the club for two years had a higher rate of delinquency than those who attended for only one year, and so on up. Moreover, he found that those who belonged for two years and then dropped out of the club had a lower rate of delinquency than those who continued in the club for the third year. All these things seem to indicate that the Boys' Club promoted rather than retarded delinquency.

My own impression is that in a community such as the average small town of Indiana, where the delinquency rate is not very high, almost any community development will tend to keep delinquency in check and that in the slum area of the big city, where the rate is very high, almost nothing, except extermination of the group relationships and traditions, as was done in the case of the criminal tribes of India, will succeed. In other words, delinquency is likely to become an increasingly serious problem in the small town and in the good residential areas of the city owing to the lack of community organization. Almost any kind of effort directed at the development of consistent patterns of behavior will be effective in holding back delinquency in these communities.

PART FIVE

Control of Crime: General Considerations

THE FIRST two papers in this section, written eight years apart, reflect in a striking way an important shift in the central issues that have engaged persons professionally concerned with problems of crime control. The thread of continuity between these two papers is Sutherland's insistence that the treatment and prevention of crime must keep pace with growing scientific knowledge. The earlier article includes a critique of the doctrine that crime control can be achieved through uniformity, severity, and certainty of punishment, and reviews sympathetically the trend toward individualization: a policy of treatment rather than punishment, and of adaptation of treatment to the personality, the background, and the needs of the offender.

In the years that followed the publication of this paper the philosophy of individualization, with its emphasis on the person rather than the act, enjoyed a great vogue. At the same time it became apparent to some that the person, particularly in applied penology, was often conceived in a very narrow sense, as a self-contained entity separate from his social-cultural milieu. The paper entitled "The Person and the Situation in the Treatment of Prisoners" is a criticism of this view. In particular,

Sutherland shows how the failure to appreciate the interpenetration of person and situation often leads to a sterile kind of individualization, even in prisons with relatively elaborate classification programs. He stresses that personality formation, stability, and change are dependent upon the situation; that this situation is really the community—together with its culture and social organization—in which the person participates; and that, consequently, in order to effect a change in the person one must manipulate or change the community setting.

The third paper treats of a variety of "things known about the control of crime, and, perhaps more important, some things not known." This paper, prepared as an informal talk to a lay audience, is included because it is a very late statement, hitherto unpublished, of some of Sutherland's ideas in this area. Perhaps the leading idea of this paper—which echoes the main theme of the preceding paper—is that ultimately the crime problem can be solved only on the level of the local community through changes in the social organization of the people who live in it.

The Person Versus the Act in Criminology

A CENTURY ago a crime, in the eyes of the law, was a disembodied act. The object of attention was not the person but the specific act abstracted from all other circumstances or traits of the person. This conception was manifest both in the methods of determining guilt and in the methods of determining penalties. In the trial the court could consider as pertinent evidence only that which assisted in determining whether a specific act had been performed and whether that act was in contravention of the legal rule. Intent, to be sure, was taken into consideration, but this was done because intent was deemed to be an essential part of the act. A crime was not merely an overt act; it included an intent to violate the law. Also, the penalty, though inflicted upon the person, was not determined by consideration of the person but of the public. Definite penalties were fixed in advance by legislative assemblies and were uniform for all persons convicted of violating a particular law. This uniformity was justified on the ground that it was necessary to have a definitely pre-determined penalty in order that prospective offenders might take it into their calculation of the pleasures and pains which would result from the act. The

Reprinted by permission from *The Cornell Law Quarterly*, XIV (1929), 159-67.

pride of the system was its impersonality. Theoretically it gave no consideration to social status, wealth, religion, previous behavior, or any other element or circumstance of the person. This conventional system was not, however, as consistent as described. It varied from place to place, exceptions were made for children and "lunatics," and practice often violated the theory.

This conventional system of thought and practice is still the backbone of the body of the law although there is a distinct trend away from exclusive interest in abstract acts toward the inclusion of the whole person. The modifications were not introduced by a definite statement of the new principle of personality but were defined or justified in terms of the old principle of abstract acts. Some of the modifications have been made by expansion of the concept of "intent"; many of them have been merely the legalization of methods that had been used previously without authorization.

Some of these modifications, classified logically rather than chronologically, are as follows:

(1) the habitual-offenders act,

(2) grant of greater discretion to the court to determine penalties,

(3) grant of greater discretion to administrative boards to determine penalties,

(4) grant of discretion to the court to use non-punitive methods of treatment of offenders,

(5) legislative provisions for acquiring or requiring more knowledge of personality of offenders,

(6) official methods of correcting or segregating prospective offenders prior to the commission of offenses.

An early form of the habitual-offenders act was passed in England in 1869, and several states in America borrowed this policy about 1890. These acts provided that a person who had been convicted of a specified number of felonies might or must be imprisoned for a longer period of time, up to life. The early laws did not work satisfactorily and were soon repealed or fell into comparative disuse. The principle was revived recently in New York State by a measure popularly known as the Baumes Law and has been extended to several other states. These habitual-offenders acts take into consideration so much of the person as may be revealed by the number of prior convictions of felonies. When the acts are mandatory, they definitely exclude consideration of any other aspect of personality and therefore use a mechanical criterion of personality; but they are a step in the direction of the consideration of the person since the penalty is not determined by one specific act but by three or four specific acts.

The second modification consisted in conferring upon the court greater discretion in regard to the amount of punishment to be inflicted for the violation of a particular law. In the conventional system the penalty had been definitely fixed by the legislature, and the court had little or no discretion in adjusting the penalty to the person. The modification consisted in authorizing the court to take the whole person into account and to fix the penalty between maximum and minimum limits set by the legislature. The court, to be sure, had little information regarding the offender's personality; and decisions, so far as they were adjusted to personality, were likely to be based on the appearance of the offender or upon unverified evidence which came out in the trial.

Under the third modification the legislature empowered parole boards or other administrative boards to determine within limits set by the laws or by the courts the exact amount of punishment in a particular case. In Minnesota and some other states the parole board really became the sentencing board, having complete authority within limits set by the legislature. In general this power which is given to the administrative board is taken either entirely or partly from the court which previously had it. The court, in fixing a penalty, is compelled to base a decision on scanty evidence and to base predictions entirely on the behavior prior to or very soon after the trial. The administrative board has more time to secure knowledge regarding the behavior of the offender prior to the trial and can keep him under close supervision for a considerable time while he is in prison. This means that the administrative board has a better opportunity to adjust the treatment to the particular offender.

The fourth modification instituted an important change in the conventional practice of regarding punishment as the only legal method of treatment. By probation laws the court was authorized to use non-punitive methods of treatment. Sometimes probation is regarded by offenders as less desirable than a penalty; a Minneapolis bootlegger recently, when placed on probation, requested that he be permitted to pay a fine instead. From the point of view of constitutional law, probation was justified as a suspension of penalty, but actually it meant that the laws authorized the use of either punitive or non-punitive methods in dealing with those who violated the law. Thus the court was given authority not only to vary the punishment but to eliminate punishment entirely if it seemed to be desirable in a particular case to do so. The extent to which this method is used is illustrated in Massachusetts, where for several years the number of persons on probation has been about five times as large as the number serving sentences in penal and reformatory institutions.

The fifth modification provided by legislative enactment for more adequate means of determining the nature of the person involved in the criminal case. Fingerprint bureaus were developed to assist the police, the courts, and the prisons in securing a record of the earlier career of the offender. A more complete record than found elsewhere is the one compiled by the State Commission of Probation of Massachusetts. This file in 1926 contained the names and social histories of over 750,000 persons. By a law enacted in that year the use of this central bureau was made compulsory upon courts in all cases in which persons were charged with offenses punishable by more than one year's imprisonment. In the courts of a century ago this information not only would have been useless, but its use would have been illegal. Many states have provided, also, for psychiatrists, psychologists, and social workers to assist in diagnosing the offender and recommending treatment. In a recent survey of these facilities in courts and penal institutions, Dr. Overholser reported that about 10 per cent of the courts and 36 per cent of the penal institutions from which he secured replies had the services of psychiatrists and that about 20 per cent of the courts had trained social workers other than probation officers.[1] In penal and reformatory institutions such sources of information regarding personality as were available a generation ago were called upon for assistance in determining whether an offender should be released on parole. Consequently, the examination was made shortly before his period of imprisonment so that the information might be used to direct his labor, education, recreation, and other activities while he was in prison as well as while he was on parole.

The sixth modification extended the policy of dealing through the court or other agencies with persons who showed a disposition to lawlessness even though they had not committed crimes. The feeble-minded and insane were segregated or placed under guardians by court order for the purpose, among other purposes, of preventing them from committing crimes. The juvenile court dealt under one jurisdiction with delinquent, dependent, and neglected children, and the three classes were handled thus on the theory that they equally needed the guardianship of the State in order, among other things, to be prevented from becoming criminals in adult life. The State has provided, also, child-guidance clinics, psychopathic clinics, visiting teachers, and twenty-four-hour schools for the same purpose. It is not impossible that the knowledge of personality may become sufficiently precise to justify the segregation by court order of persons who are not feeble-minded or insane but who are for other reasons so likely to become criminals that they constitute a distinct menace to society. Such persons would then be confined not because of something they had done but, as the insane are, because of something they would be likely to do in the future.

[1] Winfred Overholser, "Use of Psychiatric Facilities in Courts and Penal Institutions Throughout the United States" (1928), *Proceedings of the National Conference of Social Work*, pp. 143-150.

These modifications are developed most consistently in the juvenile court and the institutions through which it works. Great discretion is given to this court, juvenile court laws generally being blanket laws; and it has the greatest equipment of social workers, psychiatrists, and other special assistants. It is necessary, to be sure, to prove specific violation of a legal regulation in order to secure a legal basis for treating a delinquent child. But if that evidence cannot be secured, it is generally possible to adjudge the child dependent or neglected and deal with him in the same way. At any rate, once a violation has been proved, the court is free to consider everything relating to the person or his social situation that may appear to be significant, taking into account sex, age, health, mentality, emotional control, school record, recreational interests, previous behavior, the character of his home, neighborhood, and playmates, and a variety of other things. The best juvenile courts do not feel competent to deal with complicated cases without complete pictures of the personality and the circumstances of the delinquent. Developments somewhat similar in nature but less extensive are found in other specialized courts, such as domestic relations courts or morals courts.

Thus a distinct tendency to consider the whole person is evident. Guilt is still determined on the basis of specific acts, but there has been a tendency to deal officially, in advance of specific crimes, with persons who are presumed to be most likely to commit crimes. The principal modifications have been made in the methods of determining penalties, and here again the tendency is to base policies on a knowledge of the entire person rather than on consideration of abstract acts.

Few persons question the reality of this trend; many question its desirability. Some of the latter insist that crimes have increased enormously during recent generations, in which the trend has been most apparent, and assert that this chronological association is proof of a causal relation between the two variables. This is essentially a speculative problem, for the effects of policies cannot be measured accurately because of the inadequacies of criminal statistics. An analysis must be made, accordingly, in terms of general knowledge and probabilities.

In the first place it is evident that a chronological association between two variables does not prove a causal relation between them. The importation of bananas into the United States has increased during the period of increase in crime rates, but evidently the increase in the importation of bananas is not the cause of the increase in crimes. It is more probable that both the increase in importation of bananas and the increase in crime rates are the results of some underlying change. Similarly, it is probable that the increased interest in the personalities of offenders and the increase in the number of crimes are both the results of some change in general social organization and social relations. The most fundamental change in social relations is the increased mobility of people. This mobility appears to be the basic cause of the increase in crime and the increased interest in the personalities of offenders. Mobility produced crime by introducing greater variety in the patterns of behavior, by bringing into contact persons who were unknown to each other and thus making social life more anonymous, and by creating a kind of population congestion in which groups who were in contact in certain ways still remained isolated from each other. Variations from established codes were facilitated by these changes. Crime was one of these variations, science was another. Science led to the consideration of the entire personality of the offender. The conventional system was dogmatic and closed; it had a final explanation of crime and a policy in regard to it, leaving no place for research or discovery. Such a system of thought is inconsistent with science. Interest in the personality of the offender is the result of the extension of science into the field of criminology. Thus, though it cannot be definitely proved that there is no causal relation between the increased interest in personality and the increase in crime rates, both of these seem to be the results of other changes and especially of a change in mobility.

In the second place, the policy of deterrence seems to be necessarily decreasing in effectiveness in modern society. If every crime were automatically, by a law of Nature, followed immediately by extreme suffering, crime would almost entirely disappear. Persons who oppose the modifications just described do so on the assumption that the most effective method of combating crime is by approaching as closely as possible the results of this assumed law of Nature, i.e., by making punishments as uniform, certain, and severe as possible. It is necessary, however, to analyze these concepts of uniformity, certainty, and severity and to consider them in relation to modern social life.

Uniformity in the conventional system referred to the similarity of punishment for all persons who violated a particular law. That was a mechanical type of uniformity which, as has been shown, left no place for increased knowledge and which was inconsistent with the developing science of modern life. A new uniformity is being developed which consists in similarity of treatment for all offenders with a particular type of personality, regardless of the offense of which they have been convicted. The study of personality and the testing of the results of methods used tend to produce techniques that are effective in producing desired results; thus the techniques may become standardized. This uniformity is something like that which exists in medicine. One type of uniformity is decreasing, and the other increasing. But uniformity, as such, has no significance as a deterrent regardless of whether the person or the abstract act is considered as the basis. Absolute uniformity in treatment might exist without exercising the least deterrent influence. Equal rewards might be given to all persons who violated a law or who had a particular personality trait, but the uniformity would not have any deterrent value. The content of the treatment rather than its uniformity must be considered in attempting to determine the deterrent value of the conventional system in comparison with that of the modified system.

Uniformity, therefore, needs to be differentiated from certainty and severity of treatment.[2] Certainty of treatment refers to the frequency with which violations of law are followed by

[2] This problem is stated in terms of treatment rather than punishment because punishment is no longer the only method authorized by the state in dealing with those who are convicted of crime.

detection, identification, conviction, and some sort of official treatment. Severity of treatment refers to the average amount of suffering produced in those convicted by the method of treatment which is used. Uniformity, certainty, and severity are independent variables; any one of them might change in one direction while the others changed in the opposite direction.

Certainty of treatment cannot be attained in modern society, especially for robbery and burglary. Estimates have been made that not more than 3 per cent of the violations of law are followed by conviction and formal treatment. This estimate is probably too high. The certainty of treatment is probably less in the United States than in the less mobile and more homogeneous countries of western Europe, but a high degree of certainty is impossible in any complex society. In spite of great uncertainty of treatment, a very small proportion of the population commit serious crimes. A large proportion of the serious crimes are committed by a few people who violate the same laws persistently. A man who was convicted recently of burglary confessed that he had committed 174 burglaries in Minneapolis and St. Paul in one year. Two young men were caught in a robbery in Minneapolis late one night and confessed that they had committed 10 robberies earlier that same night. Thus it is not possible to depend very largely on certainty of treatment as a deterrent, and certainty must decrease as society becomes more complex unless phenomenal developments occur in the detection of criminals.

Severity of treatment is also increasingly ineffective as a deterrent. If all offenders were punished severely, the severity might be effective. But when one offender is punished severely and 99 others are not detected in their crimes, the punishment is of little value either in reforming the one who is caught or in deterring others. Moreover, social life is changing in such a way that the offender gets more support and the state less support in its policy of punishment. The one who is caught and punished severely gets both moral support and tangible assistance from the offenders who are not caught. He gets such support even if he is not punished (witness the oil scandals) whereas the state receives constantly decreasing support in a policy of punishment. A century ago punishment was used as a method of control in the home, the school, and the church. Now it has disappeared almost completely from the school and church and is fast decreasing in the home. Consequently when the state uses punishment, it does not get the support from the surrounding culture that it secured previously, and the punishment is decreasingly effective either in reforming or deterring. By the same token the offender feels less completely isolated when he is punished, and the punishment is not so clearly a symbol of social disapprobation.

Therefore, the policy of depending upon certainty and severity of treatment seems to be increasingly unwarranted. In addition, it is unable to encourage or utilize the increasing knowledge regarding offenders. The possibilities of the opposite policy are illustrated by the recent report of the committee on parole in Illinois. Professor Burgess and others classified into nine groups the persons placed on parole from the state institutions of Illinois; at one extreme the rate of violation of parole in the group was 1.5 per cent, while at the other extreme it was 76 per cent. These data suggest that a policy based on consideration of personality might be expected, if carried out consistently, to protect society from crime in three ways:

First, persons who because of mental abnormality, anti-authority complexes, or lack of appreciation of conventional values or social situations constitute the largest menace to the group would be more or less permanently segregated. Segregation would probably not reform these offenders, but it would protect the group by incapacitating them and to a slight extent by deterring others. Apparently no other policy can be used in the present state of techniques of control for a larger proportion of chronic and professional offenders and a considerable number of first offenders.

Second, a large proportion of those who have not definitely broken away from the general culture of organized society would be restored to society.

Third, the type of personality and the social situations from which crimes are most likely to issue would be isolated and dealt with in advance.

Thus protection against crime would be secured by modifying those who could be modified by available techniques, by segregating those who could not be so modified, by correcting or segregating in advance of crime those who were proved to be most likely to commit crime, and by attacking and eliminating the social situations which were most conducive to crime. Finally, such a policy would effectively demonstrate that organized society disapproved of crime, and it is disapprobation rather than punishment which tends to deter the large majority of the population from crime.

The Person and the Situation in the Treatment of Prisoners

THIS paper had its origin in a discussion last June in one of the sessions of the Committee on the Treatment of the Adult Offender, held in connection with the National Conference of Social Work in Indianapolis. At the same time some of us expressed a belief that the discussion of the treatment of the offender was confined too narrowly to case work and that this narrow view of treatment grew out of an incorrect understanding of the relation of the person and the situation, or of personality and culture. The two papers to be presented in this session and an additional paper to be presented Thursday afternoon by Mr. Saul Alinsky are developments of the ideas which were being expressed at that time.

For more than half a century individualization has been the slogan of the American Prison Association. Starting with the indeterminate sentence, individualization has lately developed in the form of classification and case work in prisons. In this latter form, individualizaton has meant that every prisoner should be studied intensively and treatment policies developed

Reprinted by permission from *The Proceedings of the Sixty-Seventh Annual Congress of the American Prison Association* (New York: American Prison Association, 1937), pp. 145-50.

to correct the defects which have been found in that particular individual.

I wish to reaffirm my adherence to the policy of individualization and at the same time to assert my belief that individualization should be reinterpreted and reorganized in order that it may become more effective. As explained and practiced, individualization is exclusively individualistic. In this way it expresses an incorrect conception of the relation of the person and the situation, or of personality and culture.

Any general policy of treatment involves certain assumptions about the personality of the criminal. Those who believe that he is a mad dog wish to have a policy of custody and punishment. Those who believe that he is a sick man wish to turn the prison into a hospital which will use medical methods of treatment. Similarly, any other general policy of treatment expresses an assumption about the personality of the offender.

It would not be possible in the time available to deal with all the intricacies of personality and culture even if I had the ability to do so. Roughly, there are two principal theories of personality. One is the subcutaneous or intra-epidermic theory. It is a theory that the personality is located within and bounded by the organism. You bring a human organism into your office, and you have a personality inside the office; you can work on this personality as you work on an organism. It is sharply distinct from the environment, the situation, or the culture. In that sense, this theory of personality is individualistic.

There are two principal subdivisions of this individualistic theory of personality. One is that the personality is fixed in heredity or early infancy and does not change thereafter, that it is not modified by the culture in which it exists, although it may select from the culture those elements which appeal to it. This is an iron law of personality development. Though it is doubtless correct in regard to certain traits, such as reaction time, it seems to be definitely incorrect in respect to general values, such as the importance of God, baseball, the State, a profit system of industry, or the law, and also incorrect in respect to more specific values, such as the relative importance of the gang leader and the judge or the mandates of the prison authorities and of the other prisoners.

A second subdivision of the individualistic theory of personality is that the person can change himself but that no one else can change him. The adherents of this theory point to persons who remain upright in the worst situations and to others who become rascals in the best situations. They insist that the person is self-sufficient and that he changes only through his own initiative. According to this view, you change someone by giving him an insight into his own behavior. This provides a basis for case work, but the work consists principally of attempts to give the offender an insight into himself, on the assumption that a professional man may be able in a few hours or even in a few minutes to provide an insight that is in conflict with the "insight" which the offender has secured in other ways and which is being re-enforced constantly by experiences outside the professional office.

The second theory of personality is that personality is not definitely distinguished from the culture and has no fixed or impervious wall which separates it from the culture, but rather that the culture runs into the person and the person into the culture continuously by a process which Dr. Plant calls psycho-osmosis. The personality may be an expression of a dominant culture or set of cultures which he has assimilated just as he has assimilated the language of his community. He may identify himself with his family, his church, his business, his political party; and to identify himself with means to be identical with. He is then an expression of the beliefs, attitudes, and feelings of each of these groups, not something distinct from them. Also, the personality may be an expression of a disorganized culture, a culture in which many aspects of life are not defined in terms of attitudes and loyalties, a culture in which behavior is impulsive. In any case, the personality and culture are not separate and distinct, and the dichotomy of personality and culture is a fallacy. Also, from the therapeutic point of view, attempts to change individuals one at a time while their groups and their culture remain unchanged is generally futile.

The policy of individualization as practiced in most penal and reformatory institutions has had a stated ambition to study each prisoner, develop a program for him as an individual, and reform him by a program adapted to what was found in studying him. This description and also the practice have frequently gone on as though the individual prisoner lived in a vacuum. Some of the professional men have made diagnoses and stopped there. They have studied an individual prisoner, made a diagnosis, written up a report which is filed and never again used, unless it be in preparation of the annual report or in a research study. When classification and case work have gone beyond diagnoses, they have very seldom touched the essential elements in the life of the prisoner. To be sure, some prisoners have been sent to one institution and others to another institution, as the Diagnostic Depot has been doing in Illinois, but although these institutions differ in the degree of comfort they provide, they differ hardly at all in respect to the types of cultures they present to the incoming prisoner. Again, the classification clinic may send some prisoners to a chair factory, others to a print shop, and still others to a quarry. But here again, it makes little difference where the prisoner works so far as the culture is concerned; he will find the same culture in the chair factory, print shop, and quarry. Even the adaptation of the individual to the occupation is narrowly limited within a prison, and the incoming prisoner is more likely to request placement in a particular occupation for extraneous reasons than because the work is adapted to his basic abilities and interests. A prisoner will tell you in confidence that there is a good "screw" there or that his pal works there or that it provides a better chance for escape. In general, the classification clinic does not have available treatment facilities that touch the important problems of prison life; nevertheless, the inadequacy of its work has frequently not been appreciated by those engaged in it.

There is an increasing realization, however, that the program needs to be reformulated. Dr. James S. Plant, director of the Essex County, New Jersey, Juvenile Clinic, says in his recent book, *Personality and the Cultural Pattern*, "Social work of any sort is only forging its own fetters so long as it accepts the ancient dichotomy of personality and culture" (p. 199). And again, "It is not sufficient to go on merely altering individuals. The purely psychiatric procedure is not only an inefficient mode of dealing with the problem but a rather futile flight from the reality of the task. We would suspect that no very real forward steps can be taken until certain pressures of the cultural pattern have been relieved" (p. 244).

Though I do not agree with all that Dr. Plant has in his book, I do agree with him on these propositions, and believe that they have implications of great significance for prison programs. In general, they mean that you cannot have great success in altering persons by direct methods, and that you have a much better prospect of success by altering situations. We cannot reform prisoners in a prison community one at a time. Those who are interested in the program of individualization must take the prison community into account and not continue to talk and act as though the individual prisoner lived in a vacuum.

When we talk about case work, we should ask ourselves, What is a case? How is it defined? Can a case be brought into an office and studied there? In the outside community the case worker seldom attempts to modify an individual without taking the family of that individual into account or, generally, without modifying that family. To some extent the case worker outside the prison gets into the occupational and recreational life of the client. But these activities are generally regarded as contributory to the adjustment of the client, considered as an isolated individual. Even this much is seldom done in the case work in prisons. But the theoretical question still remains, How is a case to be defined? Mrs. Sheffield has recently defined a case abstractly, and not in terms of a particular individual, as a "need-situation." The case extends as far as the need-situation extends. If this is a correct definition, how far does a case in prison extend? Certainly it extends much farther than the individual who can be brought into the office of the case worker.

As has been shown by Mr. Riemer, it includes the entire prison community.

How much do case workers or other professional workers in the prison know about the culture of the prison? My impression is that many of them are profoundly ignorant of it and are making no effort to become better acquainted with it. When they attempt to give a prisoner insight, they are speaking of a culture and a situation which are foreign to the prisoner, and their efforts are futile for that reason.

If this conception of personality and culture is correct, the sharp division which has been made between individualization and mass treatment is a fallacy. Mass treatment, to be sure, has generally not been treatment at all. It has been custody and economical operation of an institution, but not treatment. Most penal and reformatory institutions have been administered by persons who had relatively little interest in treatment. The treatment facilities have been looked upon with some disfavor by these administrators.

It is possible to alter the public opinion, or the culture, of an institution. Dr. Mary B. Harris, in *I Knew Them in Prison*, has shown dramatically how the whole institutional community has altered in several institutions in which she has worked. It has altered radically and suddenly. Classification clinics have had some effect, also, in altering the community spirit. I believe that these modifications in the community have been more significant than any work that has been done on particular individuals. But in addition, community methods should be developed. This will mean a greater development of group work than is contemplated in the programs of individualization. It will mean community organization in which the prisoners themselves, at least in limited ways, participate. It will mean a closer integration of the general administration and the professional group.

Finally, I believe that the prison educational system can be made the central agency for changing the prison community. This cannot be accomplished, of course, in the drab and humdrum school that is found in many of the institutions. But this school can be developed into the principal agency of public opinion in the prison community.

In general, therefore, I have in mind a policy of individualization which will not regard the prisoner as an individual in a vacuum. It will be a socialized individualization rather than an individualistic individualization. It will be individualization integrated with a general program of community treatment.

Control of Crime

I SHALL present a summary of some things known about the control of crime, and, perhaps more important, some things not known.

First, we have two very general conflicting policies for the control of crime. One is punishment. It has been believed and is still believed by many people that punishment will at the same time correct the one who commits a crime and warn others not to commit crimes. In opposition to this is the policy of treatment. Those who hold this belief assert that it is as foolish to punish a person who commits a crime as a person who has tuberculosis; both have causes for their ailments and therapeutic methods based on diagnosis of ailments should be used for control. These policies—punishment and treatment—are both used at the present time. Each of them tends to interfere with the efficiency of the other. We send criminals to prison as a punishment, and then we attempt by means of social work and educational, religious, and psychiatric methods to reform them while they are being punished. Although we use both policies, no one has an adequate definition of the area within which one policy should be used and from which the

A radio talk sponsored by the Exchange Club, Bloomington, Indiana, February 22, 1950.

other should be excluded. Over the course of a century the punishment policy has been losing ground, and the treatment policy has been gaining ground. Punishment is seldom used in the home, in the school, or the church as it was three generations ago, when sermons on hell-fire were frequent and vivid. Though the number of persons who have lost confidence in punishment is increasing, there are still many who assert with assurance that the only way we can control crime is by punishment. As a matter of fact, they can muster as much evidence for their position as can those who favor treatment policies. That is, we have two conflicting policies, each of which has some enthusiastic supporters, but neither of which can be demonstrated by logic to be superior in protecting society against crime. On this principal question, we have sentiments but no real knowledge.

Second, our system of criminal justice reflects our class values. This nation in its origin placed much emphasis on democracy and equality. Our system of criminal justice, however, shows a good many discriminations based on the class position of those who violate laws. One evidence of this is the testimony of the man who was chief of police in Milwaukee for more than thirty years in the first part of the present century. He explained that in the training of policemen in that city, great emphasis was placed on politeness and courtesy, and he added, "This emphasis on courtesy began when policemen began to come in contact with those who drove automobiles." Automobile drivers forty years ago were almost all persons of considerable wealth and social importance. They did not appreciate the sarcasm and rudeness of the patrolmen of that day and complained bitterly about it to the chief of police, who then trained the patrolmen to be polite. This had gone unnoticed when policemen came in contact principally with the poorer people. Another illustration of the class bias of the system of criminal justice is found in the new laws which have been enacted during the last fifty years for the control of businessmen. These laws deal with crimes of restraint of trade and misrepresentation in advertising. The legislators did not want respected and important businessmen treated as ordinary criminals and set up new machinery for the enforcement of these laws—a commission, with a hearing and with cease-and-desist orders. These measures avoided the stigma of crime which would have been attached to businessmen if they had been arrested by uniformed policemen, taken to regular criminal courts, and fined or imprisoned on conviction. I do not say that it is improper to deal with businessmen in this manner but that until we extend the same courtesy in our system of criminal justice to persons of the lower socioeconomic class, we cannot expect them to have much respect for law.

Third, the Federal government has been called upon to aid in the enforcement of state laws. Until two generations ago the penal code was a code of the state. In the meantime kidnapping, automobile theft, bank burglary and bank robbery, thefts from interstate commerce, and other offenses have become Federal crimes. These crimes were not written off the books of the state when added to the books of the United States. This trend is based on a belief that the Federal police systems, courts, and prisons are the most efficient. The increasing federalization and centralization of justice are consistent with trends toward Federal control in other aspects of social life. Although much opposition has been expressed to such control in certain other aspects of life, there has been relatively little opposition to it in the area of criminal justice. To some extent the trend toward centralization is found also within the state and appears in the development of state police systems, in state control of probation and parole work, and in certain other functions.

Fourth, despite these trends toward federalization and centralization, the control of crime is still primarily a problem of the local community. If the people of Bloomington, Columbus, or Kokomo are disturbed by crime, the people of Bloomington, Columbus and Kokomo must solve the problem of crime for themselves. They cannot gain much help by writing to their Congressmen, or even to the governor of their state. This is true regardless of whether we are thinking of the work of the police department, the courts, the probation departments, or the agencies for the prevention of delinquency and crime.

Fifth, we have been accustomed to expect persons in certain official positions—policemen, clergymen, teachers, social workers, recreation workers, probation officers—to determine the standards of the community, but there is a good deal of evidence that for most people standards are determined by persons of their own status, who are in intimate association with them, and that persons in official positions are relatively unimportant in this respect. An experimental program based on this principle has been in operation in Chicago for several years. The people in a particular neighborhood were assisted in developing an organization for the control of the behavior of their own children. One such organization was developed in an Italian neighborhood, with all the officers of the organization selected from Italians who were born and reared in that neighborhood; policemen, preachers, teachers, social workers, and other functionaries had practically no voice in the determination or administration of policies. Similar organizations were developed in a Polish neighborhood, a Jewish neighborhood, a Negro neighborhood. This experiment seems to me to be one of the most encouraging developments that have occurred in modern America.

Sixth, the question of what age group control policies should be focused on is still unsolved. There was great enthusiasm in the first decade of this century when the first juvenile courts were organized. People said, "At last we have attacked the problem at the proper point—in youth, before character is definitely formed; it is too late to do much when adult age is reached." But the juvenile court seemed to make little impression on the problem, and a new cry went up: "We must start earlier, in early childhood, or even infancy; it is too late by the time a child reaches the age of twelve or fourteen." And so child-guidance clinics were organized, to deal with very young children who had temper tantrums and would not eat their spinach. But still the problem continued. And now we have gone the full round and are back to the adult group again, for many assert that when a child commits a delinquency, his parents should be punished. Although this policy of punishing parents for the delinquencies of their children has met with little support from the agencies dealing with this problem, it at least calls attention to the fundamental importance of proper parental guidance. My own impression is that the most serious and damaging crime we have in the United States, considering the total number of cases and the immediate and remote effects, is family neglect. I would rank it as more serious than murder or burglary or sex attacks. However, very little is done about it, at least through the courts; the ordinary procedure is to dismiss all cases of neglect unless very immediate damage is found.

I wish to mention, finally, the problem of sex attacks because of the widespread hysteria regarding them. There has been a good deal of misrepresentation in connection with this problem, leading to confused or fanciful ideas about the seriousness and frequency of such crimes, the methods to be used in dealing with them, and the personalities of the criminals. The crucial cases, which are the headlines in the scare campaigns, are the sexual attacks on children, resulting in murders. Horrible as such crimes are, they are few—certainly less than one hundred in a year and probably not more than twenty-five in a year in the United States. No one knows whether they are increasing; they occur in every year and the statistics are not organized in such manner that anyone can tell what the trend is for the United States in general. It is certain, however, that a girl is much more likely to be murdered by her own parents than by some sex fiend—more than ten times as many girls are murdered in a year by parents as by sex attackers. The hysteria on this point has resulted in a number of states in the enactment of sexual psychopath laws. The legislature of Indiana in its last session enacted a law of this type. It provides that the person who has committed certain sex crimes and has been diagnosed by psychiatrists to be a sexual psychopath may be committed to a state hospital for the insane, and held there until he has recovered, according to psychiatrists, from his mental ailment. I am convinced that such laws are based on incorrect information and that they are dangerous in principle and useless in practice. The danger comes from the fact that no one can define or identify the sexual psychopath and that consequently no one can determine who should be committed under this law or when he should be released. These laws are a fad and a dangerous fad; inadequate as our regular criminal laws regarding sex crimes may be, they are better than this new program.

In most of the points which have been made our general ignorance as to the most effective policies is evident. Many universities have attempted to carry on organized research work on these policies, but it has been much more difficult to secure funds for such research than for research regarding atom bombs or even problems in agriculture and mechanics.

PART SIX

Control of Crime: Current Trends

NOWHERE is Sutherland's tough-minded insistence on careful and objective examination of the facts better exemplified than in his evaluation of current penological trends. He firmly refused to let his conclusions outrun the evidence or to allow himself to be swept away by currently fashionable nostrums.

The first paper in this section, published as early as 1925, is an attempt to assess the effect of the death penalty on murder rates. Sutherland's principal conclusion is that the evidence does not demonstrate that the death penalty reduces murder rates. This conclusion is based on a shrewd analysis of comparative statistics and not on any humanitarian predilections; he also asserts that it is impossible to infer from the data that those states which have abolished the death penalty in consequence enjoy lower murder rates than those which have retained it.

The paper on the sexual psychopath laws is a critique of the conception of sexual offenders as a special class of criminals who owe their criminality to a psychopathic personality and is a vigorous attack on the growing trend toward legislation which singles out these people for a special kind of treatment. Such legislation makes it possible to deprive sexual offenders of their freedom for longer and more indefinite periods than would verdicts reached according to established legal procedures.

Nobody was more convinced than Sutherland of the inadequacy of conventional methods of dealing with criminals, of the necessity of seeking alternative methods based on sound scientific knowledge, and of the desirability of adjusting treatment to the personality of the offender. In this article, however, Sutherland challenges the assumptions of fact and the popular stereotypes of the sex criminal on which the sexual-offender laws are based. Furthermore, he points out the dangers of serious injustice inherent in the rash abrogation, in the name of psychiatric treatment, of traditional legal safeguards.

The third paper is a long and carefully reasoned analysis of the decline of the prison population of England during the period 1857–1930 and of the underlying factors which have produced it. In our own country today there is great concern over our swollen prison populations, but we have been relatively slow to experiment with alternatives to imprisonment. For those who wish to utilize the experience of other countries in coping with our own problem of overcrowded prisons, perhaps the most significant conclusion of the present study is that the decline in England's prison population cannot be attributed to a general decline in criminality but is the result of the adoption of substitutes for imprisonment. It is of interest that the English Criminal Justice Act of 1948 confirmed and extended this trend away from the use of imprisonment.

Murder and the Death Penalty

MANY people have asserted that the murder rate in the United States is increasing alarmingly. They believe that the number of murders is increasing much more rapidly than the population. But if, instead of making the assertion, one tries to prove it, one finds that the task is impossible. For we have no statistics of murders, as such. We can only guess at the number of murders by considering the number of homicides or the number of persons convicted of murder. The number of homicides is considerably larger than the number of murders, for it includes, in addition to murder and manslaughter, the excusable or justifiable homicides, such as killing in self-defense when one is assaulted or the killing of a burglar by a householder or of an escaping prisoner by a policeman or prison guard. No one knows what proportion of the homicides are excusable or justifiable, though a guess that about one third of them are of this kind has been made. Thus the number of homicides is larger than the number of murders. And it is evident that some murders are not followed by convictions and that the number of

Reprinted by permission from *The Journal of Criminal Law and Criminology*, XV (1925), 522-29. Sutherland's conclusions in this paper are consistent with those of several other studies on the effect of the death penalty, notably those of Bye, Kirkpatrick, Vold, and Schuessler. See Karl F. Schuessler, "The Deterrent Influence of the Death Penalty," *The Annals of the American Academy of Political and Social Science*, CCLXXXIV (1952), 54.

convictions is therefore smaller than the number of murders. Consequently, when we learn from the statistical reports of the State of Massachusetts that one hundred homicides are committed there in a year and that twenty-five persons are convicted of murder or manslaughter there in a year, the only thing that we know about the number of murders committed is that it is somewhere between twenty-five and one hundred.

If we knew that the ratio between the number of murders committed and the number of convictions of murder or the number of homicides were constant from decade to decade, we could draw conclusions regarding changes in the murder rate from either of these other figures. But there is no possibility of knowing whether this ratio is constant, and there are many reasons for suspecting that it is not. Consequently the ordinary practice of drawing conclusions regarding changes in murder rates from the changes in homicide rates is logically invalid. But it is the only method that can be used, since we have no other statistics available.

If the assumption is granted that the ratio between homicides and murders is fairly constant from decade to decade, there is still no proof that murder is increasing appreciably in the United States in proportion to population. Superficial observers notice that the homicide rate in the United States was 2.1 per 100,000 population in 1900 and 8.4 per 100,000 population in 1922[1] and conclude from this that we have four times as many murders in proportion to population as we had a generation ago. But a more careful study of the figures shows that the conclusion is not justified. The annual reports on mortality statistics by the Bureau of the Census, from which these figures were taken, were first issued in 1900, and the procedure during the first few years was far from reliable. In 1904 the Director of the Census gave warning that the reports on homicide up to and including that year were "incorrect and absolutely misleading."[2] It was not until 1905 that the procedure

[1] Prior to the writing of this paper, the last published report of the Bureau of the Census on mortality statistics was for the year 1922.

[2] United States Bureau of the Census, Mortality Statistics, 1900–04, p. LV.

was improved sufficiently to give the statistics of homicides any value. Consequently the figures before 1905 must be discarded.

The homicide rate increased from 4.6 per 100,000 population in 1905 to 8.4 per 100,000 population in 1922. But this increase seems to have been due almost entirely to changes in the registration area from which the statistics of homicides were secured. For these figures do not refer to the entire population of the United States, but only to those cities and states in which the death records were sufficiently reliable to be accepted by the Bureau of the Census. This registration area included only 4 per cent of the population of the United States in 1905; it included 88 per cent in 1922. In 1905 it was confined almost entirely to the North Atlantic states; in 1922 it included eleven of the Southern states, with their very large Negro populations and their extremely high homicide rates. No valid conclusion regarding homicide rates in the United States in general can be drawn from a comparison of the rate in the North Atlantic states in 1905 with the rate in almost the entire United States in 1922, for the rates in the various sections differ immensely. It is necessary to compare the states in the registration area of 1905 with those same states in 1922 if one wishes to draw a valid conclusion. Such a comparison is given in Table I. This table shows that there has been a general but small increase in the homicide rate. But the last five-year period is not yet completed, and the increase is so slight that it may be due to improvements in the statistical procedure.

TABLE I. Average Annual Number of Homicides per 100,000 of Population in the Registration States as of 1905, by Five-Year Periods

YEARS	AVERAGE ANNUAL HOMICIDE RATE
1905–09	2.22
1910–14	2.83
1915–19	2.66
1920–22	2.86

The statistics of homicides may be summarized also by a comparison of the rates in the registration cities and states in 1912 and 1922: Sixty-one cities of 100,000 population or more were in the registration area from 1912 to 1922; of these twenty-nine had a lower homicide rate in 1922 than in 1912, twenty-nine had a higher rate in 1922 than in 1912, and three had the same rates in 1922 and 1912. Twenty-three states were in the registration area from 1912 to 1922; one of these had the same rate in 1922 as in 1912, eleven had a higher rate in 1922 than in 1912, and eleven had a lower rate. These figures indicate that the homicide rates were practically the same at the end as at the beginning of the decade.

Such statistics do not prove that murder is not increasing. Murder may be increasing while homicides are remaining constant. But there is no way of proving that murder is increasing.

Nevertheless we have approximately ten times as many homicides in the United States as in England in proportion to population and possibly ten times as many murders (although this estimate is, of course, subject to the reservations expressed in the foregoing discussion). The principal reason for the difference between the United States and England is that the populations differ in composition. The United States has a homicide rate about ten times as high as England's for the same reason that Florida has a homicide rate about twenty-two times as high as that of Vermont (although this difference is not entirely due to the presence of Negroes in Florida). The homicide rate of whites in the registration area of the United States in 1922 was 5.6, of all colored, 34.7. The homicide rate of Chinese in the registration area was 155.6 in 1921. Among the industrial policyholders of the Metropolitan Life Insurance Company only tuberculosis and pneumonia rank higher than homicide as a cause of death among young-adult Negro males.

The colored people in the United States have a very high death rate by homicide partly because they are the victims of race riots, but principally because they kill each other in individual or group quarrels. This seems to be true, also, of some of the Italian groups and of some other immigrant groups. According to the police report, forty-one Negroes were murdered in Chicago in the year 1921–22, and of these thirty-three were murdered by other Negroes; and sixty-seven of seventy-one Italians who were murdered were murdered by other Italians. In Washington, D. C., in the period 1915–19, eighty of eighty-seven Negroes who were murdered were murdered by other Negroes. The names of the victims of murder or manslaughter (taking as a sample only those whose names begin with the letter S) and of those indicted for these murders in Massachusetts in 1922 were as follows:

VICTIM	PERSON (OR PERSONS) INDICTED
Hagop Sarkisian	John Bedrosian
Michael Scarpone	Joseph Simboli, Luigi de Padova, Guiseppe [*sic*] Anzardo
Guiseppi [*sic*] Simboli	Stefano Militello, Antonio Bianco
Carlo Simscalchi	Guiseppe [*sic*] Parisi
Frank E. Small	Albert W. Bartless (alias)
Frederico Spirito	Biagno Visella

This list of names is fairly typical of those that have appeared in the reports of the Attorney General of Massachusetts during the last generation. It is not wise to place much dependence on names as an indication of nationality, but when taken with the other evidence, they lead to the conclusion that a good many of the homicides in these foreign groups are due to the acts of other members of the same foreign group. Some of these groups bring with them to this country a special code of violence and belong to societies such as the Camorra or the tongs in which killing is a common practice. There is evidence that the children of Italian immigrants do not commit the crimes of violence characteristic of their parents more frequently than do the native-born of native parentage.[3] And all of these groups are to a large extent outside of American culture, not in contact with Americans, isolated in the midst of our society. Not even the Negroes have come into real contact

[3] See *Journal of Applied Sociology*, IX (1924), 54.

with American culture. England has practically no Negroes, Chinese, Italians, or Mexicans. If we could exclude from our statistics the killings of such persons in riots and the killings of such persons by other members of their own groups, we should probably have a homicide rate higher than that of England, to be sure, but certainly much less than ten times as high.

Other things than the difference in the composition of the population need to be taken into consideration in explaining the higher homicide rate of the United States, but there is no good evidence that the difference in the penalties for murder is of great significance. It is a fact that the death penalty is used frequently in England and that the homicide rate is low. But it is a fact, also, that the death penalty is used frequently in the Southern states and that the homicide rate there is high. There is no proof of causal connection in either case.

The evidence regarding the correlation between the death penalty and the homicide rate in the United States is, in brief, as follows: The homicide rate is almost exactly twice as high in the states that have retained the death penalty as in those that have abolished the death penalty. The average homicide rate in 1922 in the North Central states that had retained the death penalty was 7.7, as contrasted with a rate of 4.4 in the North Central states that had abolished the death penalty. The median homicide rate in 1922 in cities of 100,000 population or more in states that retained the death penalty was 8.1, as contrasted with a rate of 6.5 in cities in states that had abolished the death penalty; and if the comparison is restricted to cities in the North Central states, the figures are 11.8 and 3.1 respectively. In every such comparison that can be made within the United States it is found that the homicide rate is lower in the cities and states in which the death penalty has been discontinued. But this does not prove that the homicide rate is lower *because* the death penalty has been abolished. These cities and states differ from each other in many other respects and especially in the composition of the population. It is probable that the death penalty has been abolished because the homicide rate was low rather than that the homicide rates are low because the death penalty has been abolished. And the homicide rates vary widely from city to city within the same state and from year to year within the same city though the laws remain the same. In Ohio, for instance, where capital punishment is practiced, the homicide rate for 1920 was 19.5 in Akron, 6.0 in Cincinnati, and 5.2 in Dayton; but in 1922 it was 5.3 in Akron, 16.5 in Cincinnati, and 12.4 in Dayton. In Michigan, where the death penalty is no longer in use, the homicide rate in 1920 was 2.2 in Grand Rapids and 13.7 in Detroit; in 1922 it was 1.4 in Grand Rapids and 8.7 in Detroit. Thus legislation regarding the death penalty seems to make no significant difference in the homicide rates.

Some people have made much of the fact that certain states, such as Missouri, Oregon, and Washington, after abolishing the death penalty, have restored it, being convinced that murder increased when the possibility of receiving the death penalty was removed. But the homicide statistics, inadequate as they are as a measure of murder rates, give no good basis for such a conclusion. In Missouri the homicide rate was very much higher in 1917, the year in which the death penalty was abolished, than it had been in 1916; and the homicide rate decreased in Missouri in 1919 and 1920, after the death penalty was restored. But the homicide rate in 1918, the only complete calendar year in which the death penalty was illegal, was almost exactly the same as in the years 1916 and 1921, when the death penalty was legal. Moreover, the changes in the rates in Missouri were typical of the changes in the other states in which no changes in legislation were made during this period. In exactly half of these other registration states the homicide rate was higher in 1917 than in 1916; and it was higher in 1918 than it was in 1920 in 48 per cent of these other states. The direction and the extent of the changes in the homicide rates of Missouri from 1916 to 1921 were almost identical, year by year, with those of Ohio, though no changes were made in the death-penalty laws of Ohio during this period. That leads one to believe that the changes in the homicide rates of Missouri would have been practically the same if no changes had been made in the death-penalty laws of that state in 1917 and 1919.

The assertions regarding homicide rates in Oregon and Washington are similarly lacking in proof. The homicide rate in Washington was lower from 1913 to 1919, when the death penalty was not in use, than it had been previously; but the rate was still lower after 1919, when the death penalty was restored. In Oregon the homicide rate was lower during the period when the death penalty was illegal than after the restoration of the death penalty in 1920. There is no evidence that murder will increase if the death penalty is abolished or decrease if it is restored.

But the death penalty is sometimes not used even if it is legal. The death penalty was legal in Kansas until 1907 but was not inflicted once between 1876 and 1907. In Massachusetts about fifty persons are convicted in an average biennium of murder or manslaughter, and about one of them is executed. But it is quite impossible to prove that the actual use of the death penalty is a more effective deterrent than the other penalties for murder. If one studies small areas, such as a city, the number of executions is so small and varies so much that no assertion regarding the relation between murder rates and executions is justified. And if one studies a larger area, there are so many differences in the composition of the population and in other factors that no case can be made out regarding the relation between executions and the murder rates.

Thus the conclusion is that there is no evidence of a significant relation between the murder rate and the possibility or practice of using the death penalty as a punishment for murder. There may be such a significant relation, but it cannot be demonstrated. Most people who hold such a belief have not tried to verify it. It seems to them to be merely a matter of common sense. One assumes that one would be deterred more effectively by the death penalty than by anything else and concludes that those who commit murder would be deterred more effectively if the death penalty were fairly certain. One may be mistaken, however, even in regard to oneself in this process of rationalization, and it is certainly a mistake to assume that persons who commit murder have the same motives and the same mental processes and social situations as those who prescribe for them. We are slowly learning that common sense is not an adequate basis for policies of social control. We are substituting for it the policy of science, which is an understanding of the nature of the processes one wishes to control. In the fields in which we have made the most wonderful progress we have abandoned prejudice and common sense and substituted science. The best prospect for the control of crime, similarly, is to study as scientifically as possible those who commit crimes and the situations in which the criminal attitudes are developed. This means a great deal more than a classification of the offenders as feeble-minded, insane, or psychopathic. It is necessary to understand the physiological and social processes that underlie the criminalistic attitudes. If such studies could be made in a large number of cases, we would know much more than we now know about why people commit murder, and we would then have a basis for policies that would deter people from committing murder. The death penalty might be found useful for this purpose, but if so, it would not be an appeal to ignorance or common sense or magic; the decision to use it would be based on a thorough understanding of the situation and of the processes concerned.

The problem of the death penalty is important primarily because it is an issue on which those who wish to act on the basis of prejudice, magic, and common sense confront those who wish to act on the basis of a scientific understanding of the processes at work in the causation of crime. Some "sentimentalists," to be sure, oppose the death penalty because lives are taken. But the number of persons who are legally executed is not more than a hundred a year; and even if all who are convicted of murder in the first degree were executed, the number would probably not exceed six or seven hundred a year. This total is only a very small fraction of the number of lives lost in automobile accidents, and one is tempted to recommend that those who are interested in saving lives would do well to concern themselves with the problem of reducing such accidents.

Of far greater relevance in this paper is the importance of insisting that in any attempt to solve the problem of crime there must be a scientific study of those who commit the crimes.

The Sexual Psychopath Laws

In recent years several states have made an effort to protect the public from "sexual psychopaths" ("persons with criminal propensities to the commission of sex offenses") by authorizing their commitment to mental institutions.[1] Implicit in these laws is an ideology which has been made explicit in an extensive popular literature.[2] This ideology contains the following propositions:

(1) Women and children are in great danger in American society because serious sex crimes are very prevalent and are increasing more rapidly than any other type of crime. J. Edgar

Reprinted by permission from *The Journal of Criminal Law and Criminology*, XL (1950), 543-54.

[1] Among these states are the following: California (Welfare and Inst. Code, §§5500-5516, 1939); Illinois (Rev. Stats. ch. 38, §§820-825, 1938); Massachusetts (Laws ann., ch. 123A, §§1-6, 1947); Michigan (Stats. ann., ch. 25, §28.967, 1939); Minnesota (Stats., §§52609-52611, 1945).

In 1948 the Federal Congress passed a sexual psychopath statute for the District of Columbia. Act of June 9, 1948, H.R. 6071, 1 U.S. Code. Cong. Serv. (80th cong., 2nd sess.) 361.

[2] J. Edgar Hoover, "How Safe is Your Daughter?" *American Magazine*, CXLIV (1947), 32-33; David G. Wittels, "What Can We Do About Sex Crimes?" *Saturday Evening Post*, CCXXI (1948), 30 ff.; C. J. Dutton, "Can We End Sex Crimes?" *Christian Century*, LIV (1937), 1594-95; F. C. Waldrup, "Murder as a Sex Practice," *American Mercury*, LXVI (1948), 144-58; Charles Harris, "A New Report on Sex Crimes," *Coronet*, XXII (1947), 3-9.

Hoover wrote, "The most rapidly increasing type of crime is that perpetrated by degenerate sex offenders. . . . [It] is taking its toll at the rate of a criminal assault every 43 minutes, day and night, in the United States."

(2) Practically all of these serious sex crimes are committed by "degenerates," "sex fiends," or "sexual psychopaths." Wittels wrote, "Most of the so-called sex killers are psychopathic personalities. . . . No one knows or can even closely estimate how many such creatures there are, but at least tens of thousands of them are loose in the country today."

(3) These sexual psychopaths continue to commit serious sex crimes throughout life because they have no control over their sexual impulses; they have a mental malady and are not responsible for their behavior.

(4) A sexual psychopath can be identified with a high degree of precision even before he has committed any sex crimes.

(5) A society which punishes sex criminals, even with severe penalties, and then releases them to prey again upon women and children is failing in its duty.

(6) Laws should be enacted to segregate such persons, preferably before but at least after their sex crimes, and to keep them confined as irresponsible patients until their malady has been completely and permanently cured.

(7) Since sexual psychopathy is a mental malady, the professional advice as to the diagnosis, the treatment, and the release of patients as cured should come exclusively from psychiatrists.

All of these propositions, which are implicit in the laws and explicit in the popular literature, are either false or questionable. Some of the errors in these propositions will be indicated.

HOW GREAT IS THE DANGER?

Sex crimes are generally divided for statistical purposes into three categories, namely, prostitution, rape, and other sex offenses. In the discussions of the present problem, prostitution is disregarded and only rape and other sex crimes are considered. Other sex crimes include indecencies with children (generally not involving intercourse), sodomy and other perversions, indecent exposure or exhibitionism, and incest.[3] The cases of rape, which are estimated to number about 18,000 a year in the United States, are customarily used as an indication of the extent of the danger to women and children. This idea needs to be examined.

Rapes are divided into two categories, namely, forcible and statutory. The latter is sexual intercourse regardless of force with a female below the age of consent; the age of consent is now generally sixteen or eighteen. It is impossible to determine at present how many rapes are forcible. The Federal Bureau of Investigation reports that approximately 50 per cent of all rapes known to the police of the United States are forcible rapes. But only 18 per cent of the convictions of rape in New York City in the decade 1930–39 were forcible rape. Because of these and other variations, the statistics of rape are very unreliable. The Committee which prepared the plans for the uniform crime reports that are now collected by the Federal Bureau of Investigation hesitated for some time before including rape as one of the crimes to be reported. The hesitation was due to the belief that the statistics of rape would be less reliable than any other criminal statistics. On the one hand, females frequently conceal the fact of forcible rape rather than undergo the shame of publicity. On the other hand, charges of forcible rape are often made without justification by some females for purposes of blackmail and by others who, having engaged voluntarily in intercourse and having been discovered, are attempting to protect their reputations. Physicians have testified again and again that forcible rape is practically impossible unless the female has been rendered nearly unconscious by drugs or injury; many cases reported as forcible rape have

[3] Certain psychiatrists regard almost all crimes as sex crimes; even theft, through its connection with the Oedipus Complex, is regarded as symbolic incest. Others regard crimes which have any unusually horrible features as sex crimes, as illustrated by the English murderer who drank the blood of his victims. None of the sexual psychopath laws makes explicit reference to this broad conception of sex crime.

certainly involved nothing more than passive resistance. Finally, statutory rape is frequently a legal technicality (with the female in fact a prostitute, taking the initiative in the intercourse); and this becomes increasingly probable as the age of consent increases. In any case it is absurd to include all cases of statutory rape as cases of criminal assault by degenerates; as is indicated in the preliminary reports of the Kinsey investigation of the sex behavior of the female, millions of cases of statutory rape occur annually in the average state.

Since the statistics of rape are useless as an indication of the extent of the danger of serious crimes, another method has been used. A tabulation has been made of all murders of females reported in the *New York Times* for the years 1930, 1935, and 1940, and of the murders which were reported as involving rape. In those three years 324 females were reported to have been murdered, 110 in New York City, 32 elsewhere in New York State, 56 in New Jersey, and 126 in other parts of the United States. Only 17 of the 324 murders of females were reported as involving rape or suspicion of rape. This is an average of 5.7 cases of rape-murder per year in the United States as reported in this newspaper. Of these 17 cases of rape-murder, two were reported in 1930, eleven in 1935, and four in 1940. Only 39 of the total were murders of children, and of these, twelve were reported as rape-murders—two in 1930, six in 1935, and four in 1940.

Of the 324 murders of females, 102 were reported to have been committed by husbands of the victims, 37 by fathers or other close relatives, and 49 by lovers or suitors. Thus nearly 60 per cent of the murders of females were committed by relatives or other intimate associates. Only 10 per cent were committed in connection with other crimes, and all the rape-murders reported were in that group. The danger of murder by a relative or other intimate associate is very much greater than the danger of murder by an unknown sex fiend. In fact, in one of the three years as many females were reported to have been murdered by policemen—two cases, both involving drunkenness on the part of the policemen—as by the so-called sex fiends. Also, 25 per cent of the persons who murdered females committed suicide.

Although these newspaper reports are certainly not a complete record of all rape-murders, they probably include a larger proportion of such crimes than of other murders. The number of rape-murders per year is certainly greater than 5.7, but it is doubtful whether it is greater than 100, and it may be no more than 25. This is certainly a far cry from Wittels' estimate that tens of thousands of sex killers are abroad in the nation.[4]

"Other sex offenses" are generally misdemeanors. Exhibitionism and homosexuality are the most prevalent of these. Hundreds of homosexuals can be found in any large city. Few of them are arrested because their perversions are generally limited to their own kind and constitute little danger to the rest of society. Many of these perverts have good standing in society. Nearly four thousand homosexuals were discharged from the armed forces; they exceeded the average in intelligence and education, and were generally "law-abiding and hard working."[5] The Kinsey investigation indicated that of the males studied more than fifty per cent who had arrived at middle age had had some homosexual experience in their lifetimes.

ARE THE SERIOUS SEX CRIMES COMMITTED BY DEGENERATES?

The popular literature identifies sex crimes and degeneracy. Wittels writes regarding sexual psychopaths, "Such creatures, neither sane nor insane, are responsible for most sex crimes." And Hoover uses the word "degenerate" to refer to the persons who commit the 18,000 rapes a year. When it is remem-

[4] Harris reported that Los Angeles had 24 "sex murders" in 1946. The Department of Police of Los Angeles reports that 17 of these were lovers' quarrels and that only five were rape-murders—letter from Thad F. Brown, Deputy Chief Commander, Detective Bureau, October 27, 1949.

[5] "Homosexuals in Uniform," *Newsweek*, XXIX (1947), 54. See also George W. Henry, "Psychogenic Factors in Overt Homosexuality," *American Journal of Psychiatry*, XCIII (1937), 889-903.

bered that at least half of these rapes, perhaps more than three fourths, are statutory rape, and that millions of cases of statutory rape occur which are not reported to the police, the identification of sex crimes with psychopathy or degeneracy is absurd. The reasoning is not based on factual evidence but on the circular and fallacious argument that only degenerates can commit serious sex crimes and that persons who commit serious sex crimes are therefore degenerates. Further evidence on this point will appear in subsequent paragraphs.

HOW PERSISTENT ARE SEX OFFENDERS?

The sexual psychopath laws are based on a belief that persons who commit serious sex crimes have no control over their sexual impulses and will repeat their crimes again and again regardless of punishment or other experiences. A few cases of this kind, to be sure, are reported. The question is whether sex offenders differ from other offenders in their rate of recidivism. Three types of evidence indicate that sex offenders have a low rate of recidivism when they are compared with other offenders.

The Federal Bureau of Investigation reports on twenty-five types of crimes, indicating the proportion of persons arrested in a year who have had previous criminal records. The drug addicts have the largest proportion of previous convictions and stand first in recidivism in the list of twenty-five types of crimes; larceny is second, vagrancy third, drunkenness fourth, and burglary fifth. Rape, on the other hand, is nineteenth—almost at the bottom of the list and "other sex offenses" ties for seventeenth.[6] Moreover, the previous criminal records in the rankings above include all types of former crimes. If the previous record is restricted to sex crimes, we find, for instance, that of 1,447 males arrested in 1937 for rape only 5.3 per cent

[6] These ranks differ slightly from year to year. The ranks reported above are for the year 1937, which was a typical pre-war year; they refer to the male sex only.

had previous convictions of rape. This is a much lower rate of recidivism in the same type of crime than the average for all other crimes.

The New York City Committee for the Study of Sex Offenses concluded from its study that sex offenders tend to be first offenders as compared with those who commit other crimes. In a study of all sex offenders in New York City in the decade 1930–39 this Committee found only six recidivists who had been convicted twice of sex felonies and none more than twice. It found that of 555 persons convicted of sex crimes in 1930, only 31 or 5.5 per cent, were convicted of sex crimes, either felonies or misdemeanors, during the next twelve years; two were convicted three times each, four twice, and the others only once.[7] The sex offenders with the highest rate of recidivism have generally been the exhibitionists and not the persons who commit violent sex crimes.

The third type of evidence as to the rate of recidivism of sex offenders is provided in a special study of juvenile delinquents before the juvenile court of New York City. Of 108 boys accused of sex offenses only, three had subsequent appearances for delinquencies, and none of these delinquencies was a sex offense; of 148 boys with miscellaneous offenses (including sex offenses combined with other offenses) 109 had subsequent criminal records.[8]

These three types of evidence demonstrate that if specialized procedures based on recidivism are to be provided, the sex offenders should be almost the last group for consideration. The rebuttal may be made to the preceding argument that even if the number of serious sex crimes is small and is not increasing and even if those who commit serious sex crimes are seldom recidivists, yet some sex offenders do persist in sex crimes, and these, who are called sexual psychopaths, constitute a serious danger to women and children. This raises the fundamental

[7] New York, *Report of Mayor's Committee for the Study of Sex Offenses*, pp. 92-95.

[8] L. J. Doshay, *The Boy Sex Offender* (New York, 1943), Chs. 9-12.

question of the definition and identification of the sexual psychopath.

WHO IS A SEXUAL PSYCHOPATH?

The laws which have been enacted regarding sexual psychopaths generally contain two elements in their definitions of sexual psychopaths. The first of these is an overt act[9] and the second is a particular state of mind. The mental state is variously defined. The law of the District of Columbia defines it as "lack of power to control his sexual impulses." The laws of Minnesota and Wisconsin define it as "emotional instability or impulsiveness of behavior, or lack of customary standards of good judgment, or failure to appreciate the consequences of his acts, or a combination of such conditions."

The relation of the overt act to the mental state is defined in the several laws in two different ways. In the first definition the mental state is to be determined from the overt sex crimes. The law of Massachusetts defines sexual psychopaths as "those persons who by an habitual course of misconduct in sexual matters have evidenced an utter lack of power to control their sexual impulses." And the law of the District of Columbia says, "The term 'sexual psychopath' means a person, not insane, who by a course of repeated misconduct in sexual matters has evidenced such lack of power to control his sexual impulses as to be dangerous to other persons." Such definitions state explicitly that anyone who commits several serious sex crimes is a sexual psychopath; a fingerprint record is the only evidence needed for diagnosing an offender as a psychopath, and the services of psychiatrists are not needed.

This identification of a habitual sex offender as a sexual psychopath has no more justification than the identification of any other habitual offender as a psychopath, such as one who repeatedly steals, violates the antitrust law, or lies about his golf score. The psychiatrists would almost unanimously object to this definition. They do, however, often accept an equally mechanical definition which is not stated in the laws. This is

9 In some laws "propensity to sex crimes" is substituted for the overt act.

the proposition that the human being has a normal course of development in sexual behavior, with the following stages appearing successively from infancy onward: polymorphous perverse, narcissistic, homosexual, and heterosexual. According to this proposition a person's sexual behavior, without reference to anything else, will reveal the general stage of development of his personality, and his personality can be diagnosed from his sexual behavior. Homosexuality, for instance, is regarded as evidence of the arrest of personal development in the preadolescent period and exhibitionism as regression to infancy, and both are regarded as pathologies of personality.[10] The absurdity of this theory should be evident to anyone who has an acquaintance with the variations in sexual behavior and sexual codes throughout the history of mankind; practically all of the present sex crimes have been approved behavior for adults in some society or other. Similarly, within our society deviant forms of sexual behavior prevail in sub-groups. The manner in which juveniles are inducted into the cultures of these sub-groups in the toilets of schools, playgrounds, and dormitories, as well as in other places, has been shown in many research reports on juvenile sex behavior.[11]

The second definition of the relation of the overt act to the mental state makes these two elements co-ordinate. According to this conception the sexual psychopath is a person whose misconduct consists wholly or partially of violations of the sex code but whose personality can be diagnosed as psychopathic independently of his sexual behavior. However, the Minnesota statute, which makes these two elements co-ordinate, has been upheld in the Supreme Court on the argument that the psychopathic state is to be revealed by the overt sexual behavior.[12]

10 This idea is stated with few qualifications by Beatrice Pollens, *The Sexual Criminal* (New York), 1938, Ch. 3.

11 Esther Richards, "Dispensary Contacts with Delinquent Trends in Children: Twenty-nine Cases of Abnormal Sex Trends in Children," *Mental Hygiene*, IX (1925), 314-39; Raymond W. Waggoner and D. A. Boyd, "Juvenile Aberrant Behavior," *American Journal of Orthopsychiatry*, XI (1941), 275-91.

12 *State ex rel Pearson v. Probate Court of Ramsay County et al.*, 205 Minn. 545, 287 N.W. 297 (1939), 309 US 270 (1940).

This interpretation of the law makes the second definition identical with the first, and the law becomes merely an habitual sex-offenders act.

Wittels makes the unqualified statement that "Psychopathic personality can easily be detected early in life by any psychiatrist."[13] Any person at all familiar with psychiatric literature knows that scores of psychiatrists have deplored the use of this concept because of its lack of definite criteria. The vagueness of the term is indicated by the fact that under the administration of one psychiatrist 98 per cent of the inmates admitted to the state prison of Illinois were diagnosed as psychopathic personalities, while in similar institutions with other psychiatrists not more than five per cent were so diagnosed. Of the sex offenders diagnosed by the Psychiatric Clinic of the Court of General Sessions in New York City, 15.8 per cent were reported to be psychopathic, while of sex offenders diagnosed by psychiatrists in Bellevue Hospital in New York City 52.9 per cent were diagnosed as psychopathic.[14]

The most careful investigations of the concept of the psychopath have been made by Cason. He found 202 terms which have been used as more or less synonymous with the term "psychopath."[15] He condensed these into 54 traits which are generally held to characterize the psychopath. From 101 psychopathic inmates of the Psychopathic Unit in the Federal Medical Center at Springfield, Missouri, he selected two groups—the 23 least psychopathic and the 29 most psychopathic—on the basis of the number of times that their behavior had been characterized as psychopathic. He found that 46 of the 54 traits had no statistical significance in the differentiation of the most psy-

[13] The terms "psychopath," "psychopathic personality," and "constitutional psychopathic inferior" are used somewhat interchangeably, although the last mentioned is being abandoned because of its connotation regarding the biological constitution.

[14] Jack Frosch and Walter Bromberg, "The Sex Offender—A Psychiatric Study," *American Journal of Orthopsychiatry*, IX (1939), 761-76; B. Apfelberg, C. Sugar, and A. Z. Pfeffer, "A Psychiatric Study of 250 Sex Offenders," *American Journal of Psychiatry*, C (1944), 762-70.

[15] Hulsey Cason, "The Psychopath and the Psychopathic," *Journal of Criminal Psychopathology*, IV (1943), 522-527.

chopathic from the least psychopathic and that of the eight remaining traits six were just barely significant. With the exception of intolerance and making threats, the traits which are generally regarded as being most characteristic of psychopaths were less useful for the purpose of classification than the fact that a person was born in the East or that he had engaged in farming or that he had violated the Dyer Act against automobile theft. In general, Cason concluded that the saint is at one extreme and the psychopath at the other, and that a person can be diagnosed as a psychopath "if he has a reasonable number of these symptoms in a fairly pronounced form."[16] This appears to equate the psychopath and the sinner.

Also, Cason and Pescor analyzed the records of 500 prisoners in the Medical Center who had been diagnosed as psychopathic and compared them with the records of all Federal prisoners. They found that the psychopathic prisoners were very much concentrated in the age group 20–29 in comparison with federal prisoners and with the civilian population. This is extremely significant, for it indicates either that people cease to be psychopathic after they pass the age of thirty or else that psychopathic persons cease to commit Federal crimes. Moreover, 63 per cent of those prisoners who had been discharged for an average of 19.2 months had no subsequent criminal record with the Federal Bureau of Investigation; of those who had some supervision after release 71 per cent had no subsequent criminal records. Also, 39 per cent of the psychopaths were reported to have been as obedient and well-behaved as children, and an additional 22 per cent as obedient but inclined to get into mischief or trouble.[17]

The conclusion from this analysis of the concept of the sex-

[16] Hulsey Cason, "The Symptoms of the Psychopath," *Public Health Reports*, LXI (1946), 1833-53. See also "The Characteristics of the Psychopath," *American Journal of Psychiatry*, C (1944), 762-70.

[17] Hulsey Cason and M. J. Pescor, "A Statistical Study of 500 Psychopathic Prisoners," *Public Health Reports*, LXI (1946), 557-74. See also, by the same authors, "A Comparative Study of Recidivists and Non-Recidivists among Psychopathic Federal Offenders," *Journal of Criminal Law and Criminology*, XXXVII (1946), 236-38.

ual psychopath is that it is too vague for judicial or administrative use either in committing him to an institution or in releasing him as "completely and permanently cured." According to the laws of most of the states the court must rely on two psychiatrists for decisions as to sexual psychopathy. The psychiatrists have no diagnostic instruments or criteria by which to arrive at demonstrable conclusions on this question; they are expected to make expert judgments on questions on which neither they nor others are qualified to speak as experts. The criterion of "irresistible impulse" which is implicit in the laws cannot be applied in practice.[18]

The inadequacy of the concept of sexual psychopath has been recognized by leading psychiatrists and others. Dr. Winfred Overholser, superintendent of St. Elizabeth's Hospital, stated, "Before the law can be expected to recognize this group (sexual psychopaths) as calling for specialized treatment, it will be necessary for psychiatrists to come to a better agreement on the deliminitations of the group."[19] Similarly, Dr. A. Warren Stearns, a psychiatrist who was at one time director of the Massachusetts Department of Correction, stated regarding sexual crimes, "The definition of these crimes and the classification of the persons who commit them present very serious administrative problems. For the present it is perhaps wiser to administer existing laws carefully."[20] The British Joint Commission on Sex Offenses stated, "Owing to the difficulties of legal and medical definition, it is not practicable to press effectively at this stage for special provisions for the detention and treatment, as such, of convicted persons suspected of abnormal mentality who are not certifiable either as insane or as mentally defective."[21]

[18] Jess Spirer, "The Psychology of Irresistible Impulse," *Journal of Criminal Law and Criminology*, XXXIII (1943), 457-62.

[19] "Legal and Administrative Aspects," *Mental Hygiene*, XXII (1938), 20-24.

[20] "Sexual Crime," *Journal of the Maine Medical Association*, XXXVII (1946), 249 ff.

[21] Quoted by I. S. Wile, "Society and the Sex Offender," *Survey Graphic*, XXVI (1937), 569-72.

The lack of precision in the concept of the sexual psychopath is especially dangerous in view of the emotions which are aroused by sexual crimes. In the hysteria which results many crimes are committed in the name of justice. The hysteria is illustrated by the fact that during a so-called wave of sex murders in California nearly a dozen men confessed to one sex murder which had been committed by one and only one man. The crimes committed in the name of justice are illustrated by the case of James Montgomery. He was convicted of rape in 1924 and held in the state prison of Illinois until 1949, when the decision against him was reversed on the ground that the evidence in the medical report that no rape had been committed was suppressed in the original trial.[22] The dangers of this law, moreover, threaten every person. It is not necessary in many states that a person be convicted of a sexual crime; it is sufficient to diagnose his personality. Also, in many states the state's attorney *or any other person* may ask for an investigation as to the sexual psychopathy of any person. According to the laws of at least one of these states the person who has been investigated and found not to be a sexual psychopath may not bring suit for damages against the person who initiated the investigation, regardless of the injury that he has suffered.[23] Furthermore, a person who is found to be a sexual psychopath may be confined, as irresponsible, in a state hospital and may also be punished, as responsible, by confinement in a state prison.

Although these sexual psychopath laws are dangerous in principle, they are of little importance in practice. They are never used in some states and seldom used in the others. Only 16 persons were confined under this law in Illinois during the ten years after its enactment.[24] The number of cases under the Minnesota law decreased from about 35 in the first year after its enactment to about 10 per year at the end of the ten-year period; moreover, most of those confined under this law were

[22] *Time*, LIV (1949), 14-15.

[23] Wis. Stats. (1947) ch. 51.37(7).

[24] Newton Minow, "The Illinois Proposal to Confine Sexually Dangerous Persons," *Journal of Criminal Law and Criminology*, XL (1949), 186-87.

charged with homosexuality and were released after a few months.[25] During the first four years under the Michigan law of 1939, 99 persons were committed as sexual psychopaths, and of these 29 were released on parole or by court order by the end of that period.

Several reasons have been suggested for the failure to use these laws. One is that the laws were passed in a period of panic and were forgotten after the emotion was relieved by this action. A second reason is that the state has no facilities for the care and custody of sexual psychopaths; the state hospitals are already crowded with psychotic patients. A third reason is that the prosecutor and judge, anxious to make records as vigorous and aggressive defenders of the community, favor the most severe penalty available and are unwilling to look upon serious sex criminals as patients. They use the sexual psychopath laws only when their evidence is so weak that conviction under the criminal law is improbable. Finally, it is reported that defense attorneys have learned that they can stop the proceedings under this law by advising their clients to refuse to talk to the psychiatrists, since the psychiatrists can make no diagnosis if those who are being investigated refuse to talk. Threats of contempt of court have been made in such cases, and the law of the District of Columbia explicitly provides that refusal to talk to the psychiatrist is contempt of court. Aside from the fact, however, that a person can better afford to be punished for contempt of court than to be confined for an indeterminate period as a sexual psychopath, a psychiatric diagnosis made under threat of punishment can have no validity from a medical point of view.

In view of the slight use which has been made of these laws, their effect on sex crimes should not be expected to be appreciable. The reports of the Federal Bureau of Investigation show that in the four states which enacted sexual psychopath laws in 1938–39—California, Illinois, Michigan, and Minnesota—the trend in rape rates was the same after the enactment of the laws

[25] Minnesota, *Annual Reports of Bureau of Criminal Apprehension.*

as it was in adjoining states which had not enacted such laws. These statistics have little significance in view of the slight relation between rape and the crimes for which persons may be confined under the sexual psychopath laws, but no other evidence of the effects of these laws is available.

Certain psychiatrists have stated that they are interested in the sexual psychopath laws principally as a precedent; they believe that all or practically all criminals are psychopathic, that all should be treated as patients, and that psychiatrists should have a monopoly on professional advice to the courts. These laws are dangerous precisely from this point of view; they could be passed over in silence otherwise, as a product of hysteria. The question is whether psychiatrists have a monopoly on knowledge of human personality and human behavior which warrants their nomination as "the experts" in the diagnosis and treatment of criminals.

Other disciplines, such as psychology, social work, and sociology, require as much training as does psychiatry, and have points of view, hypotheses, and techniques which should be used, together with those of psychiatry, in the diagnosis and treatment of sex offenders and other offenders. At many points the theories of one of these disciplines are in conflict with the theories of the other disciplines, and one theory has as much scientific validity as the other. Moreover, the question of importance is not whether an offender has a low I.Q. or unstable emotions, but how this trait is related to the violation of the law and to a process of rehabilitation. There is no more reason for turning over to the psychiatrist the complete supervision of a criminal who is found to be psychopathic than for turning over to the dentist the complete supervision of a criminal who is found to have dental cavities. If the official agencies of the state are to use professional advice, the advisors should represent all the branches of knowledge and should be on an equal footing.

The Decreasing Prison Population of England

PRISONS are being demolished and sold in England because the supply of prisoners is not large enough to fill them. The number of prisoners in custody in England in 1930 was less than half the number in 1857, though the population of England was twice as large. This decrease was not a direct result of a reduction in the general crime rate, but rather of changes in penal policies. An analysis of the reasons for this decrease should be useful in the attempts to revise the penal policies of the United States, where the prison population has been increasing and where overcrowding of prisons is a chronic evil even though many huge prisons have been constructed.

The English system at present consists of four types of prisons under the control of the prison commission. The first are the local prisons, of which there were twenty-nine in 1931. These were under the control of county and other local governments until 1877, when they were transferred to the central government. Offenders convicted of less serious crimes either on indictment or summarily may receive sentences of imprisonment in local prisons of two years or less. In this respect the local prisons are somewhat similar to the houses of correction and the county penitentiaries in the United States. The second

Reprinted by permission from *The Journal of Criminal Law and Criminology*, XXIV (1934), 880-900.

type is the convict prison, to which offenders may be committed on sentences of penal servitude (as contrasted with sentences of imprisonment in local prisons) after conviction and indictment. In 1931 there were five convict prisons in England, three of which were merely departments in local prisons and two of which were independent of any other establishment. The convict prisons are somewhat similar to the state and Federal prisons in the United States. The third type of prison is the Borstal Institution for offenders sixteen to twenty years of age. The Borstal policy started unofficially in 1902, but sentences to Borstal Institutions were first officially authorized in 1908. In 1931 England had seven Borstal Institutions; one of these was a department in a local prison, one was a department in a convict prison, and five were independently located. Borstal Institutions are somewhat similar to the state and Federal reformatories in the United States. The fourth type of prison is the preventive detention prison, authorized in 1908 for habitual criminals. Persons who, after three previous convictions of crime and proof of habitual criminality, are again sentenced to penal servitude may at the same time be sentenced to an additional period in a preventive detention prison, to begin at the end of the term of penal servitude. England has two preventive detention prisons, both of which are departments in local prisons.

In addition, the courts may send offenders to other institutions which are not in the prison system. Juvenile delinquents may be sent to reformatory schools, industrial schools, and places of detention. Also, certain types of offenders may be committed by order of the court to institutions for the insane, to institutions for mental defectives, and to police cells.

THE DECREASE IN CONVICT PRISONS

The number of persons committed to convict prisons decreased rather consistently from 2,841 in 1857 to 536 in 1930.[1] The annual commitment rate per 100,000 of population de-

[1] The statistics used throughout this paper are from the official annual reports of Great Britain: Criminal Statistics of England and Wales; Reports of the Commissioners of Prisons and the Directors of Convict Prisons.

creased from 13.5 in 1857–64 to 2.46 in 1895–99, increased slightly through the period 1905–09, and then in 1915–19 dropped to 1.25, where it has remained approximately constant to the present time.[2] This trend is shown on Chart I. What is the explanation of the continuous decrease from 1857 to 1900 and of the abrupt decrease about 1907? It is essentially that neither of these decreases resulted directly from a reduction in crime but that both were due to partial substitution of other policies for sentences to convict prisons.

The number of sentences to convict prisons decreased principally because the courts preferred to send criminals to local prisons. The substitution of local prisons for convict prisons can be shown by taking the crimes of robbery, burglary, and housebreaking as illustrations. In 1857 the number of persons convicted of these crimes came to 1,419; 40.0 per cent were committed to convict prisons and 59.1 per cent to local prisons. In 1894, the number convicted was 1,137, of whom 6.2 per cent were sentenced to convict prisons and 76.4 per cent to local prisons. The percentage sentenced to convict prisons decreased 24.2 points while the percentage sentenced to local prisons increased 17.3 points.

This partial substitution of local prisons for convict prisons was part of a general movement away from the more severe penalties. In 1827 the general policy in England was to impose a death penalty upon all persons convicted of the more serious crimes and then to commute it to transportation to a penal colony for terms varying from seven years to life. As opposition to this policy increased, prisoners were sentenced instead to convict prisons, and by 1850 this practice had become general for serious crimes. Then the terms in convict prisons were shortened, from an average of 7.6 years in 1857 to 6.5 in 1880, to 5.3 in 1893, and to 3.8 in 1930. The minimum sentence in convict prisons was 5 years during most of the period prior to 1891, when it was reduced to 3 years. A sentence which was less than that minimum automatically became a sentence to a local prison. Especially before the reduction of the minimum

[2] For the rates of commitment to convict prisons see Table A at the end of this paper.

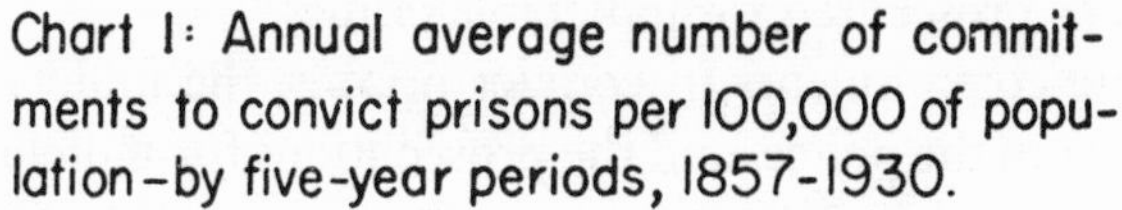
Chart I: Annual average number of commitments to convict prisons per 100,000 of population—by five-year periods, 1857-1930.

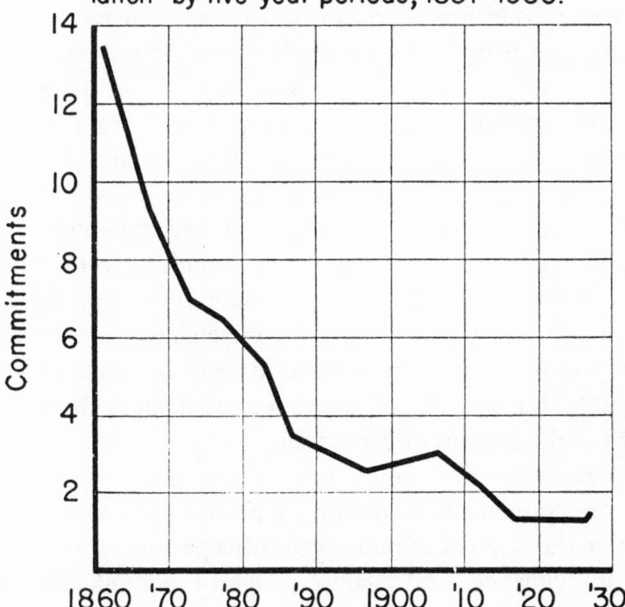

term to 3 years in 1891, the courts sentenced many criminals to local prisons in order to avoid the long terms required in the convict prisons. The rate of commitments to convict prisons increased slightly after this minimum was lowered. This substitution of local-prison for convict-prison sentences was the main factor in reducing the convict-prison population.

It is possible, in addition, that criminals were occasionally kept out of convict prisons by the substitution of reformatory and industrial schools, which were started in 1854, and by the use of probation and recognizances, which were authorized by laws of 1879 and 1887.

The decrease in commitments to convict prisons prior to 1900 was not to a very great extent the direct effect of a reduction in the number of crimes committed. This is indicated by the two measures of crime that are available—the number of indictable crimes known to the police and the number of persons prosecuted for indictable crimes.[3]

The commitments to convict prisons, the indictable crimes known to the police, and the prosecutions for indictable crimes all decreased consistently from 1857 to 1900. The rate of commitments, however, decreased much more than did the indexes of crime. The number of crimes known to the police per 100,000 of population decreased 43 per cent from 1857 to 1900, the prosecutions, 41 per cent, and the commitments, 81 per cent (see Table A at the end of this paper).

Table I shows that, in 1857–64, 30.1 per thousand of the crimes known to the police resulted in commitments to convict prisons, in 1895–99, only 9.7 per thousand; in 1857–64, 48.8 per thousand of the prosecutions for indictable crimes resulted in sentences to convict prisons and in 1895–99, only 15.0 per thousand.[4] Thus the commitments decreased about three times as much as the indexes of crimes did.

The decrease in the crime rate is seen to be even less important if the commitments to convict prisons are considered in relation to the types of crimes—against the person, against property with violence, and against property without violence. These three components differ in the extent to which they result in penal servitude, and they have changed since 1857 at different rates. Crimes against property without violence, which constitute about 80 per cent of all indictable crimes, least frequently result in penal servitude. Of crimes known to the police, those against property without violence decreased 48.6 per cent from 1857–1900, those against the person decreased 11.1 per cent, and those against property with violence only 2.7 per cent. Thus, the decrease in the general crime rate was due almost entirely to the decrease in crimes against property

[3] For a discussion of the comparative reliability of these two indexes, see National Commission on Law Observance and Enforcement, *No. 3, Report on Criminal Statistics*, 1931; Thorsten Sellin, "The Basis of a Crime Index," *Journal of Criminal Law and Criminology*, XXII (1931), 335-56; Audrey M. Davis, "Criminal Statistics and the National Commission's Report," *Journal of Criminal Law and Criminology*, XXII (1931), 357-74.

[4] These ratios are computed from Table A at the end of this article. See p. 224.

without violence, for which criminals are seldom sent to convict prisons, while crimes against the person and against property with violence, for which sentences to penal servitude are relatively more frequent, hardly decreased at all. The conclusion is that the decrease in the crime rate did not directly affect the commitments to convict prisons very decidedly.

The psychological effect of this decreasing crime rate, however, was probably important. The feeling of security engendered by a constantly decreasing crime rate may have made the courts feel inclined to avoid the more severe penalties and

TABLE I. Annual Average Number of Persons Committed to Convict Prisons per 1,000 Indictable Crimes Known to the Police and per 1,000 Prosecutions for Indictable Crimes—by five-year periods, 1857–1930[a]

	COMMITMENTS TO CONVICT PRISONS	
YEARS	*Per 1,000 Indictable Crimes Known to Police*	*Per 1,000 Prosecutions for Indictable Crimes*
1857–64	30.1	48.8
1865–69	20.6	32.9
1870–74	19.2	30.3
1875–79	18.5	30.6
1880–84	14.8	23.4
1885–89	10.9	16.6
1890–94	10.0	14.9
1895–99	9.7	15.0
1900–04	10.8	15.9
1905–09	10.7	16.7
1910–14	8.4	12.9
1915–19	4.9	7.3
1920–24	4.6	8.3
1925–29	3.7	7.5
1930	3.6	8.3

[a] Since persons can be sentenced to penal servitude only if tried on indictments and since many persons prosecuted for indictable crimes are not tried on indictments, the number of prosecutions on indictments would be preferable in some respects to the number of prosecutions for indictable crimes as a crime index for the purposes of the present analysis. During the period under consideration, however, the summary procedures for trying indictable crimes developed a great deal. Because of these procedural changes the more inclusive prosecutions for indictable crimes have been used.

therefore to impose sentences of imprisonment or even probation rather than sentences of penal servitude.

The apparently abrupt decrease, about 1907, in the commitments to convict prisons was really spread over the period from 1907 to about 1915, with the number of commitments dropping steadily from 1,182 in 1908 to 815 in 1913, 591 in 1914, and 351 in 1915. Since 1915 the annual average commitments have been 477, with comparatively little variation from the average. How was this decrease of about 500 in the annual commitments produced? The answer is found principally in three changes in penal provisions and policies.

The first was the Borstal Institution, officially authorized in 1908. The number of offenders received in Borstal Institutions was 171 in 1909, 426 in 1910, and 515 in 1912. Since 1912 the trend has been evenly upward, with a low point in 1915 and high points of 780 in 1920 and 774 in 1930. Thus the annual commitments to Borstal Institutions increased from zero to about 500 during the period when the annual commitments to convict prisons decreased by about 500, and these changes are certainly related. The principal question is whether the inmates of Borstal Institutions would have been sentenced to local prisons or to convict prisons if Borstal Institutions had not existed. In 1907, before the Borstal sentences were authorized, there were 270 young men of the age group 16–20 in Borstal classes in local prisons and 150 in Borstal classes in convict prisons. This indicates that more than half the members of Borstal classes were in local prisons. Arguments were presented, however, that this special training should be concentrated on the young prisoners who had long terms, and these arguments were effective in the formal organization of the Borstal policy of sentencing young offenders. Thus at first this system was intended primarily as a substitute for convict prisons for young offenders. In later years, however, the prison commissioners and others have been attempting to induce the courts to substitute Borstal sentences for sentences of imprisonment in local prisons. Consequently, though the Borstal Institution when first authorized was primarily a substitute for the convict prison, it is at present much less completely so.

The second innovation that reduced commitments to convict prisons in the period 1908–15 was probation. The laws of 1879 and 1887 had authorized probation, recognizances, and discharges after proof of guilt but without formal conviction, sometimes including orders to make restitution or pay costs. These provisions were extended by the probation law of 1909. The number of persons granted probation[5] after conviction on indictment increased from 13.9 per cent of all so convicted in 1908 to 26.1 per cent in 1930, while the number sentenced to convict prisons decreased from 10.1 per cent of all so convicted in 1908 to 7.6 per cent in 1930. Thus, probation increased during the period in which commitments to convict prisons decreased while persons granted probation by courts which might have sentenced them to penal servitude increased in numbers.

A third element in the reduction of the convict prison population was the preventive detention prison (authorized in 1908) for habitual criminals. The first prisoners were received in 1911, after the completion of their terms of penal servitude. The maximum number of receptions in any year was 113, in 1912. Since that date, the number has decreased to 25 in 1930. No group has been enthusiastic about the results of this policy, and consequently the number of commitments has decreased. The policy did, especially in the earlier years, keep some criminals out of convict prisons.

The decrease in commitments to convict prisons after 1908 cannot be explained adequately by a decreasing crime rate. The two indexes of crime–indictable crimes known to the police, and the number of persons prosecuted for indictable crimes–run parallel from 1900 to the end of the War,* both showing slight decreases after 1905, but diverge sharply at the end of the War. The number of crimes known to the police increased rapidly after the War until it is now 47 per cent more in pro-

[5] The term "probation" is used generally in this analysis to include all of these non-institutional methods of disposing of cases after conviction or proof of guilt. This does some violence to the concept of probation, but in most respects the distinction between probationary supervision, recognizances, and discharges after proof of guilt is not important for purposes of this analysis; in addition the distinction is not very strict in practice.

* I.e., World War I.

portion to population than in 1915–19. On the other hand, the number of prosecutions for indictable crimes continued to decrease after the War and now is 6 per cent less in proportion to population than in 1915–19. The "true" trend is probably between these two indexes, for the crimes known to the police may show a fictitious increase owing to the more complete reporting of crimes, whereas prosecutions have probably decreased in proportion to crimes actually committed because of the greater mobility of the population, which has made detection, apprehension, and securing of evidence more difficult. Certainly, the increase of 47 per cent in the crimes known to the police or of, say, 15 or 20 per cent in the "true" index of crimes could not explain the decrease in commitments to convict prisons. Also, the number of prosecutions for indictable crimes, which is probably a less reliable index of crimes committed, cannot explain the decrease in commitments to convict prisons. For the commitments decreased twice as much in the period 1905–14 as did the prosecutions. Furthermore, the decrease in prosecutions occurred almost entirely in crimes against property without violence, which seldom result in sentences of penal servitude. The number of prosecutions for crimes against property without violence per 100,000 of population decreased 14.9 per cent between the period 1900–09 and 1930 while prosecutions for crimes against property with violence increased 38.8 per cent and crimes against the person increased 22.2 per cent. The annual number prosecuted for robbery, burglary, and housebreaking decreased 16.8 per cent between the period 1905–09 and 1930, while the number of persons committed to convict prisons for these crimes decreased 53.0 per cent. For these reasons, it appears that the changes in the number of crimes committed do not provide a direct explanation of the decreases in the convict prison population.

It is probable that during this period, as during the earlier period, the psychological effect of the crime rate has been significant. Since decisions regarding dispositions are made by courts, and since the attitudes of the courts are determined by the number of prosecutions rather than by the number of crimes known to the police, and since the rate of prosecutions has decreased steadily, the sense of security, even if not justified, tends toward a continued use of relatively moderate alternatives to penal servitude. During the last few years, however, the severity of sentences seems to have been increasing slightly.

In summary, the commitments to convict prisons decreased during the period 1857–1900 principally because local prisons were used as a substitute for the long terms required in convict prisons. Commitments to convict prisons decreased in the period 1908–15 and remained constant thereafter principally because of the emergence of three new policies in 1908 and 1909. These are represented by the development of the Borstal Institutions and by the use of probation and preventive detention. Crime rates probably exerted a slight effect on this decrease in the period 1857–1900 and in the first part of the period 1905–30, but had no direct effect in the latter part of the period 1905–30, when, if the crimes known to the police are taken as a criterion, they tended to increase rather than decrease the number of commitments to convict prisons. The reduction in the rate of prosecutions did produce a feeling of security which was significant in the choice of the alternatives to penal servitude.

THE DECREASE IN COMMITMENTS TO LOCAL PRISONS

The general trend in the rate of commitments to local prisons is shown in Chart II.[6] The most striking thing in this chart is the rapid decrease from 529.1 per 100,000 of population in 1905–09 to 112.3 in 1915–19. This reduction appears to be a continuation of a reduction which began in 1880 and was interrupted in the decade 1900–09. At any rate, the annual commitments dropped from 197,023 in 1904 to 37,531 in 1930, and the primary problem is that of determining what produced this reduction of approximately 150,000 in annual commitments shortly before the War.

[6] This chart is based on the last column in Table A.

The essence of the following explanation is that this reduction resulted from the development of probation and of facilities for the payment of fines and, to a slight extent, of new institutions, and in addition was profoundly affected by the reduction of intoxication and allied offenses, although not by changes in the general crime rates.

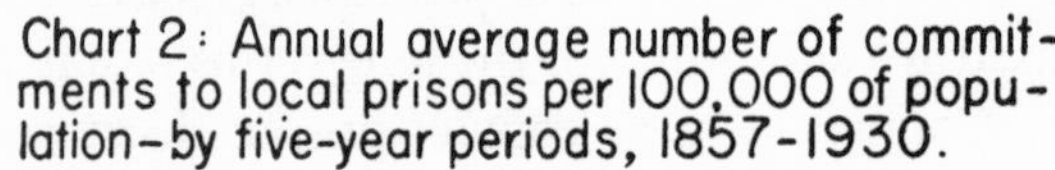
Chart 2: Annual average number of commitments to local prisons per 100,000 of population—by five-year periods, 1857-1930.

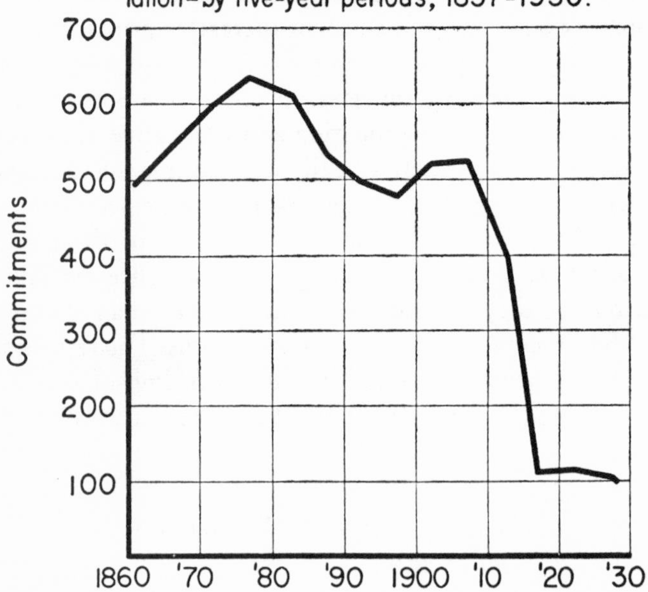

The analysis of this decrease is facilitated by dividing commitments to local prisons into commitments for indictable crimes and commitments for non-indictable crimes, and by subdividing each of these into commitments without option of fines and commitments in default of payment of fines. This analysis is confined to the period since 1904 because the statistical reports did not show these subdivisions prior to 1904. The decreases and increases in the several methods of disposition are presented in Table II[7] (p. 211), which shows that while the

[7] Further statistics for the years between 1904 and 1930 are given in Tables B and C at the end of this paper.

number committed to local prisons in each of these classes decreased, the number placed on probation and the number who paid fines increased.

(1) *The Effect of Probation.* Probation has been principally an alternative to commitment to local prisons without option of fines. It has been used both for persons charged with indictable crimes and for persons charged with non-indictable crimes, but it has increased more for the former than for the latter group, and its significance for the two groups is somewhat different.

TABLE II. Number of Persons Convicted or Found Guilty and the Several Dispositions in Such Cases in 1904 and 1930 by Indictable and Non-Indictable Crimes

	INDICTABLE CRIMES			NON-INDICTABLE CRIMES		
Dispositions	*1904*	*1930*	*Change*	*1904*	*1930*	*Change*
Local prisons:						
Default	3,524	945	−2,579	104,031	11,552	−92,479
No option	26,103	13,357	−12,746	63,365	11,677	−51,688
Other prisons	1,100	1,745	+645	469	1,535	+1,066
Probation	9,498	28,501	+19,003	48,359	69,621	+21,262
Fines paid	11,011	11,478	+467	435,518	473,217	+37,699
Whipping	2,382	130	−2,252	3	0	−3
Death	28	14	−14	......	......	....
Total	53,646	56,170	+2,524	651,745	567,602	−84,143

For indictable crimes the number committed to local prisons without option of fines was 12,746 less in 1930 than in 1904, while the number granted probation was 19,003 more. Probation for indictable crimes increased steadily throughout this period. In 1904, 17.7 per cent of all persons convicted or found guilty of indictable crimes were granted probation; in 1930, 50.7 per cent. This increase in the use of probation was confined almost entirely to probation in the narrower sense, while recognizances remained practically constant and discharges after proof of guilt increased slightly and at the expense of discharges without proof of guilt.

For non-indictable crimes the situation is somewhat different. Commitments to local prisons without option of fines were 51,688 fewer in 1930 than in 1904, while grants of probation were 21,262 more. This shows that probation may account for a part of the decrease in prison commitments of this type, but at best, it accounts for less than half of the decrease. Furthermore, its influence was confined largely to the period 1908–15, for grants of probation were made in 1904 to 7.4 per cent of the persons convicted or found guilty of non-indictable crimes, were increased to 11.4 per cent in 1910–14, and thereafter remained approximately constant. Also, probation in most of these non-indictable cases was nothing more than a discharge after proof of guilt; 78 per cent of the grants of probation were of this nature in 1908 and 82 per cent in 1930. In general, probation, though of some importance, is not a sufficient explanation of the decrease in commitments to local prisons without option of fines for non-indictable offenses. The additional factor in the explanation is the decrease in drunkenness and of allied offenses, which are to be discussed later.

(2) *Fines*. The decrease in commitments to local prisons in default of fines is explained to a very considerable extent by improved arrangements for the paying of fines. The annual average number of persons fined in the period 1905–09 was 498,958, of whom 19.6 per cent were committed to prisons in default of payment, whereas in 1930 the number fined was 496,139, of whom only 2 per cent were committed to prison in default. For indictable crimes the decrease in commitments to prison in default of fines was small in absolute number, though large as a percentage. A small part of this decrease was due to the increased number who paid fines, the rest to the increased use of probation, Borstal sentences, and other institutions.

For non-indictable offenses the decrease in commitments in default of fines is very much larger, and this decrease is approximately equal to the increase in the percentage who paid fines. In 1905–09, 15.7 per cent of all dispositions were commitments to prison in default of fines; this percentage decreased slightly to 12.9 per cent in 1910–14 and then in 1915–19 dropped abruptly to 2.9 per cent, where it remained approximately constant thereafter. Also, 65.6 per cent of all dispositions for non-indictable offenses in 1905–09 were fines paid; this percentage increased slightly to 67.3 in 1910–14 and then increased abruptly to 82.6 per cent in 1915–19, remaining approximately constant thereafter. Why did the number committed to prison for default decrease while the number who paid fines increased?

The percentage of persons sentenced to pay fines who are committed to prisons in default of payment is certainly affected to some extent by the general economic conditions. This percentage fluctuated within narrow limits during the period 1893–1913, when it decreased very abruptly. Improvements in economic conditions during the War undoubtedly assisted in reducing this percentage, but there was no appreciable increase in the percentage after the War, when economic conditions become more difficult. Consequently the variations in income seem to explain only the narrower fluctuations and do not explain the decided change from one level to another.

The immediate and important explanation of this substitution of fines paid for commitments in default of fines is found in the Act of 1914, which provided that a court of summary jurisdiction, when imposing a fine, must grant the offender time in which to pay the fine unless the offender were able to pay the fine outright or had no fixed abode within the jurisdiction of the court, or unless the court for other specific reasons decided that time should not be granted. The effect of this law was probably significant and immediate, as is shown in Table III (p. 216), but unfortunately it cannot be demonstrated clearly because statistics of the total number of persons who received time in which to pay fines are not available. The only available statistics on this point are provided in a special study of the Birmingham prison, in which commitments in 1913 were compared with commitments in 1915 in order to measure the effect of the Act of 1914. This study showed that of the persons fined, 11.9 per cent more stayed out of prison in 1915 than in 1913, although approximately one third of those who stayed out of prison did so because they were "lost sight of," while two thirds paid their fines either within the alloted time or immediately after arrest.[8] If this percentage is representative of the entire country from 1915 to the present date, the law of 1914 has reduced the annual commitments in default of fine by about 60,000. There is little basis for this assumption, however. The only thing which can be shown from the available statistics is that the number committed in default of fine to whom time had not been granted for payment of fines decreased from 97,859 in 1905–09 to 8,063 in 1930, or from 19.6 per cent of fines imposed to 1.6 per cent, while the number committed in default after allowance of time to pay the fine increased from none in 1905–09 to 4,434 in 1930, or to about 1 per cent of the total number fined in 1930. The number committed in default of fine to whom time had been allowed for payment of fines is increasing slightly, and this increase is probably due to the granting of time to a larger proportion of the number fined, though this cannot be determined from the available statistics. There seems to be no doubt, however, that this law has kept many thousands of offenders out of prison.

(3) *Decrease in Drunkenness.* At several points in the preceding analysis it was apparent that changes in penal policies did not adequately explain the decreases in the commitments to local prisons, especially for non-indictable offenses. An additional factor is the great decrease in drunkenness and allied offenses, such as assaults, sleeping out, begging, general vagrancy, and prostitution. Prosecutions for these offenses, in general, have been decreasing since 1880, with a more rapid decrease after 1900, an abrupt decrease at the beginning of the War, and no increase subsequent to the war.[9] The number

[8] Report of Commissioners of Prisons, 1916-17, p. 7.

[9] See Great Britain, Royal Commission on Licensing, 1932, and George B. Wilson, "A statistical review of the variations during the last twenty years in the consumption of intoxicating drinks in the United Kingdom," *Journal of Royal Statistical Society*, LXXV (1912), 183-247.

of prosecutions for intoxication decreased from 626.4 per 100,000 of population in 1900–09 to 147.2 in 1930. Other available statistics regarding the liquor traffic agree with the statistics of prosecutions. The number of places licensed to sell intoxicating drinks decreased from 38.73 per 10,000 of population in 1904 to 28.66 in 1930; the per capita consumption of beer decreased from 31.56 gallons in 1900 to 16.42 in 1929, and of spirits from 1.12 gallons to 0.28; and the number of deaths certified as due to cirrhosis of the liver decreased from 3,996 to 1,656. This decrease seems to have been due to education, to the methods of regulating the liquor traffic, and to the social-insurance policies.

Corresponding with this decrease in intoxication, the number sentenced for intoxication to terms of imprisonment without option to fines decreased from 7,764 in 1905 to 1,933 in 1930, though the ratio of this penalty to all penalties for intoxication remained nearly constant, being 3.6 per cent of all penalties in 1905 and 3.2 per cent in 1930, as shown in Table IV (p. 217). The number committed to prison in default of fines decreased very much more, from 61,360 in 1905 to 6,660 in 1930. This was a decrease from 28.5 per cent of all dispositions for intoxication in 1905 to 10.9 per cent in 1930; and while this decrease was occurring, the percentage of fines paid and of grants of probation increased by an approximately equal amount. Consequently at least two factors were operating, one being the decrease in the amount of intoxication, the other the change in the methods of dealing with persons prosecuted for intoxication. The relative importance of these factors can be indicated roughly by comparing two hypothetical situations. If the number of prosecutions had been the same in 1930 as in 1905, with the methods actually used in 1930 applied, the number of commitments to prison in default of fine would have been 16,394 greater than the actual number of commitments. On the other hand, if the methods of disposition used in 1905 were assumed to be operative in 1930 for the number actually prosecuted for intoxication, the number committed to prison in default of fine would have been 10,690 more than the number

TABLE III. Annual Average Number of Persons Fined and Number and Percentage of Those Fined Who Were Disposed of in Specified Ways–tabulation by five-year periods, 1905–1930

				IMPRISONMENT IN DEFAULT OF PAYMENT					
		PAID FINES		TOTAL		WITHOUT ALLOWANCE OF TIME		AFTER ALLOWANCE OF TIME	
Years	*Total Fined*	*No.*	*% of Those Fined*	*No.*	*% of Those Fined*	*No.*	*% of Those Fined*	*No.*	*% of Those Fined*
1905–09	498,958	401,099	80.4	97,859	19.6	97,859	19.6	0	0.0
1910–14	465,092	389,648	83.8	75,444	16.2	75,139	16.1	305[a]	0.1
1915–19	394,913	382,660	96.9	12,253	3.1	10,620	2.7	1,633	0.4
1920–24	446,524	431,467	96.6	15,057	3.4	12,487	2.8	2,570	0.6
1925–29	490,790	476,948	97.2	13,842	2.8	9,783	1.9	4,059	0.9
1930	496,139	483,642	97.5	12,497	2.5	8,063	1.6	4,434	0.9

[a] For 1914 only.

actually committed. These figures indicate that the decrease in the number of prosecutions was somewhat more important in decreasing the number of persons committed to prison for intoxication than the change in methods of disposing of cases of intoxication.

TABLE IV. Number Convicted of Intoxication and Per Cent of Those Convicted Who Were Disposed of in Various Ways—tabulation by selected years

		PER CENT OF THOSE CONVICTED WHO			
Year	*Number Convicted*[a]	*Paid Fines*	*Were in Prison in Default*	*Were in Prison without Option*	*Were on Probation and Recognizance*
1905	215,458	62.3	28.5	3.6	5.6
1909	178,377	60.7	29.2	3.6	6.5
1913	198,665	66.5	23.1	3.1	7.3
1922	81,541	79.7	10.2	3.0	7.1
1930	60,876	74.0	10.9	3.2	10.8

[a] Including the cases in which the charge was proved and an order issued without conviction.

While intoxication has decreased immensely since 1905, some other non-indictable offenses have increased. Of these the most important is the group of highway violations. The rate of prosecutions for traffic violations has increased consistently since 1857, with an increased acceleration after 1890 and a very abrupt rise beginning immediately after the War. The number of prosecutions for traffic violations per 100,000 of population increased from 144.2 in 1900–09 to 693.0 in 1930. While there were 152,132 fewer prosecutions for intoxication per year in 1930 than in 1900–09, there were 229,717 more prosecutions for traffic violations. But although the increase in traffic violations is greater than the decrease in intoxication, the penalties for traffic violations are quite different from the penalties for intoxication. Specifically, traffic violations seldom result in commitment to prison. In fact, in spite of the great increase in prosecutions for traffic offenses, the number of persons sentenced for traffic offenses to terms of imprisonment in default of fines decreased from 4,790 in 1905 to 687 in 1930. It is possible that the Act of 1914 accounts for a part of this decrease, but changes in the types of traffic offenses and of the economic status of offenders also play a part. Consequently, in general, a considerable part of the reduction in commitments to prison is due to the decrease in intoxication, and this decrease has not been offset by increases in the other important types of non-indictable crimes.

(4) *The Effect of the General Crime Rate.* The indexes of indictable crimes—crimes known to the police and prosecutions for indictable crimes—are not closely correlated with commitments to local prisons for indictable crimes. The number of indictable crimes known to the police decreased slightly between the periods 1905–09 and 1915–19 and then increased slightly. Consequently, there has been an increasing divergence between these two variables, as is seen in the fact that 31.9 per cent of the indictable crimes known to the police resulted in commitments to local prisons in 1904, and in 1930 only 9.7 per cent, as is shown in Table V. Therefore commitments to local prisons for indictable crimes decreased in spite of, rather than because of, the increase in the number of indictable crimes known to the police. Nearly the same conclusion can be reached regarding the relation between prosecutions for indictable crimes and commitments to local prisons for indictable crimes. The prosecutions decreased very slightly prior to the War and thereafter remained nearly constant. In 1904, 49.0 per cent of the prosecutions for indictable crimes resulted in commitments to local prisons; in 1915–19 the percentage decreased to 20.7 and thereafter did not change much, being 22.3 in 1930.

For non-indictable offenses the only index is the number of prosecutions, and such prosecutions are not at all reliable as an index of the changes in the number of offenses committed. Taking them for what they are worth, one sees that they do not show a close correlation with variations in commitments

TABLE V. Per Cent of Crimes Known and of Prosecutions for Indictable Crimes Resulting in Commitments to Local Prisons and Per Cent of Prosecutions for Non-Indictable Crimes Resulting in Commitments to Local Prisons—tabulation by five-year periods, 1904–30

	NO. OF COMMITMENTS TO LOCAL PRISONS FOR INDICTABLE CRIMES		NO. OF COMMITMENTS TO LOCAL PRISONS FOR NON-INDICTABLE CRIMES
Years	*Per 100 Crimes Known to Police*	*Per 100 Prosecutions*	*Per 100 Prosecutions*
1904	31.9	49.0	22.4
1905–09	29.6	46.3	22.3
1910–14	23.8	36.6	18.7
1915–19	14.1	20.7	5.3
1920–24	14.6	26.6	5.2
1925–29	11.1	22.1	4.0
1930	9.7	22.3	3.8

to local prisons for non-indictable offenses. The rate of prosecutions for non-indictable offenses decreased slowly prior to the War and then increased slowly, but not up to the prewar level. Commitments to local prisons for non-indictable offenses, on the other hand, decreased slowly prior to the War, then dropped abruptly to about one fourth the previous rate, and have remained approximately constant at the level of the War period up the present date. In 1904, 22.4 per cent of the prosecutions for non-indictable offenses resulted in commitment to local prisons, in 1930 only 3.8 per cent. Consequently the conclusion can be reached that changes in the general crime rates had little direct influence on the rate of commitments to local prisons but that the decrease in the number of prosecutions has had some influence in inducing courts to refrain from sentences of imprisonment and to use other methods of disposing of cases.

(5) *Commitments to Other Types of Institutions.* In addition to the factors previously described, the development of other types of institutional sentences has had some influence in decreasing commitments to local prisons. In the following sec-

tion an analysis will be made of the trends in the commitments to these other institutions, and this will show that the net increase from 1904–1930 in the number committed to these other institutions was about 1,500 and that this could have reduced the annual commitments to local prisons by about more than 1,500 a year, which is comparatively insignificant in view of the total decrease of 150,000 in the commitments to local prisons.

In summary, the general argument regarding the decrease in the number of local prisons from 1904 to 1930 is that the number of commitments to local prisons without option of fines decreased principally because of the development of probation. Probation had real significance as a method of dealing with persons found guilty of non-indictable offenses and was principally a substitute for discharge without finding of guilt. Commitments to local prisons in default of fines decreased partly because the Act of 1914 gave offenders time to pay fines as an alternative to being imprisoned immediately in default of payment and partly because of the decrease in drunkenness. Also, the development of new institutional penalties had a slight significance in decreasing the number of commitments to local prisons. Changes in the general crime rate had very little direct effect but probably had an indirect effect, because the feeling of security resulting from a constant or decreasing number of prosecutions tends towards leniency.

COMMITMENTS TO OTHER INSTITUTIONS

Descriptions and explanations of the trends in convict prisons, local prisons, Borstal Institutions, and preventive detention prisons have been presented in the preceding sections. Somewhat similar trends may be found in other institutions which receive offenders from the courts.

During 1930, 61 persons were received in the special institutions for the criminal insane at Broadmoor and 99 in local asylums. The number of commitments of the criminal insane per 100,000 of population increased from 0.60 in 1893–94 to 0.67 in 1910–14, when it dropped to 0.43 in the War years and to 0.40 in 1930. This number was too small to produce any appreciable effect on the number of commitments to other institutions.

Special classes for mentally defective offenders have been provided for many years, but the courts first received specific authority to commit offenders to institutions for the mentally defective in 1913. The number so committed increased from 27 in 1914 to 281 in 1930. These persons are generally held in the institutions for comparatively short periods, being released under supervision if they respond to training. This policy may explain in part the small decrease in the receptions in institutions for the criminal insane after 1914 but, because of the small numbers involved, the policy had a very slight effect on the number committed to other institutions.

Two reformatories for inebriates were authorized by an act of 1899. Offenders who were troublesome in private reformatories might be committed to these state reformatories by court order. The annual average number of commitments was 268 in 1900–04 and 293 in 1910–14, but thereafter these institutions were practically abandoned. Even at the high point of reception in these reformatories, the commitments were so few that they produced no appreciable effect on the number of persons sentenced to imprisonment because of intoxication.

The courts, by authority of an act of 1914, have used police cells as a method of institutional punishment. This penalty is used principally for vagrancy and for simple larceny, and the terms of imprisonment are comparatively short. The annual average number of commitments increased from 183 in 1917–19 to 1,537 in 1930. This method of punishment has to a slight extent reduced the number of commitments to local prisons.

Reformatory schools for delinquent children[10] were authorized in 1854. They are used principally for children 14 to 16 years of age found guilty or convicted of indictable crimes. The institutions are privately managed but are under the supervision of the Home Office. The annual average number of commitments (about 1,200) remained nearly constant in absolute

[10] See Myers, E. D., "England's Industrial and Reformatory Schools," *Social Forces*, XI (1933), 373-78.

numbers from 1860 to 1910–14. The number increased in the War years to 1,616 and then decreased to 724 in 1924, and has decreased slightly more since that date. In general the rate has shown a slightly downward trend in proportion to population, and this trend has been decidedly accelerated since the War.

Industrial schools for dependent, neglected, and delinquent children up to the age of fourteen were started in 1854. These schools are also under private management and are also supervised by the Home Office. In their early history they were used principally for dependent children, but at present they are used principally for younger delinquents. In 1893–94, 469 children were sent to industrial schools for punishable offenses, and the number has remained approximately constant except in the War years, when it increased to 1,363.

By authority of an Act of 1909, children under sixteen who are found guilty of punishable offenses may be sentenced by the court for terms not exceeding one month to the places used by the police to detain children who are awaiting trial. The annual average number sentenced to these places of detention decreased from 195 in 1910–13 to 14 in 1925–29 and to 5 in 1930. Thus this form of incarceration has been practically abandoned.

In addition to the persons committed as previously described, many non-criminal prisoners are committed to local prisons for debt and other reasons.[11] In 1930, 13,276 non-criminal prisoners were committed to local prisons, of whom 13,002 were debtor prisoners. Of the debtor prisoners committed by order of the courts of summary jurisdiction, 29 per cent were committed for non-payment of bastardy orders, 48 per cent for failure to provide family maintenance, and 23 per cent for failure to pay taxes. The significant thing is that whereas the criminal prisoners have decreased very greatly in number, the non-criminal prisoners have decreased hardly at all. The number committed as debtor prisoners in 1893 was 7.8 per cent of all commitments to local prisons; in 1930, 25.5 per cent.

In general, these other institutions can be neglected in the

[11] See Sara Margery Fry, "Debtor Prisoners," *The Magistrate*, October-November, 1932.

explanation of the decrease in commitments to the prisons. Several of them, in fact, show the same downward trend which is evident in the commitments to institutions in the regular prison system, and this is true especially of the reformatories for inebriates and reformatory schools, places of detention, and to a very slight extent of the institutions for the criminal insane.

CONCLUSION AND SUMMARY

The general positive conclusion from the preceding analysis is that the reduction in the prison population of England is due to two factors: first, to the development of probation and the practice of providing time in which to pay fines; second, to the reduction in intoxication. The general negative conclusion is that the reduction was not a direct effect of changes in crime rates, though a constant or a decreasing crime rate facilitates the substitution of other measures for imprisonment, because of the feeling of security engendered by a rate of that nature.

Among the underlying factors which have produced the changes described, the crime rate and improvements in education and economic conditions are certainly important.[12] In addition the Howard Association has been constantly pressing for the reduction of particular groups of prisoners and has been very influential. Recently this association has been working for the reduction in the number of debtor prisoners, of young offenders, and of short-term offenders. The prison commission and the prison officers are, in general, engaged in this work for a lifetime and develop professional interests, abilities, and attitudes. In addition, the prisons are all under one central management, so that policies can be organized, experiments controlled, and results determined. Furthermore, this reduction in the prison population appears as part of a great social movement which has been under way in England and other countries for at least a century. In England transportation to penal colonies has been abandoned, and sentences to the death penalty and

12 For a general analysis of the crime rate in England in relation to social and economic conditions, see S. K. Ruck, "The Increase of Crime in England," *Political Quarterly*, III (1932), 206-25.

to whipping and flogging have been almost entirely eliminated. Also, punishments in prison for violation of prison regulations have been greatly reduced. In convict prisons in 1902–07, 37.4 per cent of the male prisoners were punished; in 1930, only 13.4 per cent. In local prisons the percentage punished decreased from 12.8 per cent in 1913–14 to 4.3 per cent in 1930. The severity of prison punishments has also decreased. Even the use of the lock-up for individuals awaiting trial has been greatly reduced. In 1893, 56 per cent of the prosecutions were initiated by summons rather than by arrest, and this increased to 77.1 in 1930. Even when the offender was charged with an indictable crime, the summons was used in 22.5 per cent of the cases in 1930 as compared with 8 per cent in 1893. The movement toward a reduction of the prison population has also taken place in Scotland and Ireland and in Sweden, Germany, and other continental countries, presumably spreading wherever the crime rates do not produce a feeling of insecurity.

TABLE A. Annual Average Number of Indictable Crimes Known to the Police, of Persons Prosecuted for Indictable Crimes, and of Commitments to Convict Prisons and Local Prisons, Per 100,000 of Population–tabulation by five-year periods

			COMMITMENTS TO	
Years	*Crimes Known to Police*	*Prosecution for Indictable Crimes*	*Convict Prisons*	*Local Prisons*
1857–64	448.75	276.61	13.50	494.80
1865–69	442.56	277.40	9.12	547.82
1870–74	366.43	232.10	7.04	593.88
1875–79	357.35	216.00	6.62	626.32
1880–84	367.50	231.63	5.43	611.64
1885–89	312.29	204.78	3.40	545.81
1890–94	284.93	191.05	2.86	498.84
1895–99	255.02	163.84	2.46	480.96
1900–04	255.87	172.71	2.76	524.86
1905–09	285.72	182.82	3.05	529.08
1910–14	269.56	175.11	2.27	396.49
1915–19	251.00	171.50	1.25	112.33
1920–24	279.99	154.25	1.28	117.31
1925–29	324.87	162.89	1.22	102.98
1930	369.37	160.90	1.34	95.08

TABLE B. Annual Average Number of Penalties Imposed for Indictable Crimes—tabulation by five-year periods, 1905–30

Penalty	*1904*	*1905–09*	*1910–14*	*1915–19*	*1920–24*	*1925–29*	*1930*
Total convicted or found guilty	53,646	55,562	55,257	50,418	49,749	56,540	56,170
Death	28	27	27	21	23	23	14
Convict prison	918	1,056	828	428	498	491	532
Local prison							
Default of crime	3,524	2,819	1,993	442	846	1,059	945
No option	26,103	26,579	21,332	11,514	14,782	13,129	13,357
Borstal Instns.	.....	171[a]	492	458	539	590	720
Police cells	.....	.....	.....	44	89	143	205
Instns. for the insane	182	184	190	117	120	120	123
Instns. for mental defectives	.....	.....	4	46	91	152	165
Fines paid	11,011	9,512	9,393	14,254[b]	11,414[c]	13,999	11,478
Probation, etc.	9,498	13,128	19,071	19,696	20,796	26,563	28,501
Whipping, flogging	2,382	2,086	1,927	3,398[b]	551[c]	271	130

[a] 1909 only. [b] 1917-19 only. [c] 1922-24 only.

TABLE C. Annual Average Number of Penalties Imposed for Non-Indictable Crimes—tabulation by five-year periods, 1905–30

Penalty	*1904*	*1905–09*	*1910–14*	*1915–19*	*1920–24*	*1925–29*	*1930*
Total convicted or found guilty	651,745	600,384	569,316	398,191	500,673	556,597	567,604
Local prison							
Default of crime	104,031	94,041	73,452	11,811	14,211	12,783	11,552
No option	63,367	59,549	47,072	14,286	15,023	13,571	11,677
Borstal Instns.	......	......	9	28	38	37	54
Police cells	......	......	......	138	742	1,096	1,332
Instns. for the insane	51	42	50	16	24	22	33
Instns. for mental defectives	......	......	4	31	59	91	116
Reformatories for inebriates	418	376	293	35	2	......	......
Fines paid	435,518	395,404	383,273	328,723	417,509	466,912	473,219
Probation	48,359	50,969	65,152	43,058	53,057	62,085	69,021
Whipping, flogging	3	3	11	45	8	......	......

PART SEVEN

Methods and Techniques

The importance that Sutherland attached to the abstract hypothesis as an element in scientific method is clear from his writings on differential association. Of equal importance in his methodology, although not as prominently featured, was thorough familiarity with the facts to be explained. This current in Sutherland's thinking stands out especially in the articles in this section. They clearly demonstrate his opposition to mere abstract theorizing not properly grounded in the significant empirical data.

The first paper, previously unpublished, was written within the framework of the controversy which surrounded the Michael and Adler assessment of twentieth-century American criminology. Along with their criticism, Michael and Adler recommended that a research institute of criminology be established and that it be staffed by a logician, a mathematical statistician, an econometrician, other specialists in methodology, and one criminologist, preferably with no research experience. Sutherland's faith in the inductive method is plainly revealed by the manner in which he greeted this bizarre proposal. This faith is also manifested in his article on the prisoner as a source of criminological data, advocating as it does careful study of the individual prisoner from diverse points of view.

While recognizing the selected nature of prison populations, Sutherland felt that much could be learned about the processes of criminal behavior from the study of prison inmates, just as much has been learned about disease from the study of hospital patients. The third and final selection is a practical demonstration of Sutherland's belief that the methodological problems of criminology cannot be solved by technical experts alone. He felt that statistical experts, for example, could doubtless contribute in many ways to the improvement of criminal statistics, but that fundamentally the burden is on those persons most familiar with the difficulties involved in defining, measuring, and sampling crime. In this paper Sutherland and Van Vechten investigated the inconsistencies in the public records and the causes thereof.

Except for these papers and his critical reviews, Sutherland did relatively little writing on the subject of method, most of it during a brief period when he held a research professorship at the University of Chicago. This occupational circumstance perhaps explains his momentary concern with methodological matters. His long-run, dominant interest, however, was not in methodological issues, but rather in building a valid explanation of crime. For this reason, his opinions as to a proper methodology should carry at least as much weight as those of specialists in logic and method who have never engaged in criminological research.

The Michael-Adler Report

In many of its specific criticisms of research studies in criminology the Michael-Adler Report is entirely justified. These studies are often based on inadequate and biased samples, and many have other defects. The Report recognized, however, that not all criminological research is open to criticism in regard to specific techniques. It praises the specific techniques used in the studies by Lund, Goring, Burgess, Shaw, Slawson, Dorothy Thomas, Ogburn, Glueck, and others. It also passes over without criticism specific techniques in many other studies. The criticisms and recommendations of the Report are based on general logical considerations rather than on the spe-

The Michael-Adler Report on criminology and criminal justice, published in 1932 under the title "Crime, Law, and Social Science," was prepared for the Bureau of Social Hygiene of New York City under the auspices of the School of Law of Columbia University. It recommended an institute to be concerned with "such research as may be necessary to lay the foundations of a science of criminology," with special reference to the problem of causation; and with "empirical studies of the administration of the criminal law." Following this distinction between crime causation and crime control, two separate divisions were proposed: a division of criminology and a division of criminal justice. The staff of the former was to consist of a logician, a mathematician, a statistician, a theoretical physicist, an experimental physicist, a mathematical economist, a psychometrist, and a criminologist who preferably had not engaged in criminological research. The staff of the division of crimi-

cific questions of reliability and technique. The present appraisal of the Report is therefore directed primarily at these general logical considerations, and questions of the specific reliability of data and of findings are neglected.

The general argument of the Michael-Adler Report is as follows:

(1) *Criminological research has been futile.*

(2) *The reason for the futility of research in criminology is the incompetence of criminologists in science.*

---

nal justice was to consist of students in the fields of legal philosophy and jurisprudence, the history of law and legal institutions, comparative law, criminal law and the administrative code, and of specialists in police work, prosecution, and the treatment of criminals.

The Bureau of Social Hygiene submitted the Report to the Social Science Research Council indicating that it would be most interesting and helpful to have an expression of the views of the Council. The Council in order to secure thorough consideration of the Report created a large committee of twenty-one persons; fourteen of these represented as nearly as possible the staff positions of the proposed institute, and seven were persons engaged in criminological research. These persons were requested to organize their opinions around three questions: (1) Is it your opinion that criminological research of the kind which has been and is now being done, should not be continued? (2) Is it your opinion that useful theories of crime causation are more likely to emerge from the direct and immediate attempt to construct such theories, as advocated in the Report, or from the continued use of established methods of criminological research, assuming normal continuation of improvement in these methods? (3) Is it your opinion that the staff proposed for the institute is more likely to achieve significant results in the study of crime causation than a staff made up of the best of present criminologists? It is of interest that of the eighteen who replied, only one supported the conclusions of the Report on the first two points, and that only one supported the conclusions of the Report as to the last two points. In all other cases, where the questions were directly answered, the conclusions of the report were opposed on all these points, with minor qualifications in several instances.

Sutherland's statement was written shortly after the Report appeared and is largely negative. It is therefore of interest to notice that in the previously unpublished paper entitled, "Development of the Hypothesis of Differential Association," Sutherland candidly admits that after his first reaction of emotional antagonism had worn off, he was greatly influenced by the Report. In informal discussions he often agreed that the negative evaluations of criminological research in the Michael-Adler volume were essentially correct, and in the article mentioned, he states that the Report exerted an important influence upon him in turning his attention to abstract generalization.

(3) *The current methods of criminological research should be abandoned, and scientists should be imported into criminology from other fields.*

Each of these propositions is analyzed and criticized in the following discussion:

(1) *The authors conclude that criminological research has been futile.* The criteria by which this judgment is reached are stated variously, but they agree in the finding that the research has not produced adequate explanations of crime:

> It is our thesis that criminological research has not yet achieved a single definite conclusion. [p. 123]
>
> The body of knowledge called criminology does not contain a single scientific proposition. [p. 77]
>
> The work of criminologists has not yet resulted in scientific knowledge of the phenomena of crime. [p. 73]
>
> In short, (1) common sense knowledge is by itself inadequate to cope with the practical problem of controlling crime, and (2) the descriptive knowledge yielded by criminological research does not supplement common sense so as to compensate for its inadequacy. It is for these reasons that we recommend that criminological research of the kind which has been and is being used should not be continued. [p. 415]

If these statements mean what they seem to mean, they are not true, for criminology has achieved some definite conclusions, some scientific propositions, and a body of scientific knowledge. The summary of criminological research which is presented in the Report provides sufficient evidence of such achievements.[1]

The statements quoted do not mean, however, what they seem to mean. They are tied together by a system of interlock-

[1] The Report does not summarize the studies which bear on a particular topic (e.g., broken home, psychopathic make-up, age, or economic conditions). The only topic on which a summary appears is mental defectiveness, and that study had been made in advance of the survey by other persons than the authors of the Report. Consequently the authors do not know how definite the conclusions are on any particular factor in relation to crime causation.

ing definitions in such a way that a "definite conclusion" in criminology involves and presupposes a complete and full explanation of crime. A "conclusion" is differentiated from the "finding" of a research study and is made identical with a "scientific proposition" (p. 86). A "scientific proposition" in turn must be not only a generalization, based on determinate evidence, but also a statistical relationship between all significant variables and a member of a set of related propositions each of which has characteristics similar to the one in question. Consequently the criticism that criminology has produced no "definite conclusion" and no scientific propositions means that it has not produced a complete explanation of crime, and the last statement quoted means that criminology must continue to be futile in the future unless the method recommended in the Report is adopted. No other alternative, such as the improvement of present methods in the line of their own growth and development, is recognized as a possible means of arriving at a more complete explanation of crime.

The judgment that criminological research of the current type is futile because it has not yet achieved a complete explanation of crime is clearly unwarranted. First, theoretical knowledge in the form of propositions is not the only kind of useful knowledge. Anatomy is a type of science which has almost no theoretical knowledge and which is nevertheless very useful. Similarly, some of the descriptive information in criminology is directly useful in the solution of problems. For instance, the knowledge that foreign-born persons have no more than their quota of criminal convictions and the further knowledge of the relative standing of different national groups in this respect are useful in planning immigration policies.

Second, it is unwarranted and unjust to apply the criteria of well-established sciences to the theoretical achievements of a very young discipline. Aside from a small number of ephemeral and rationalistic explanations of crime, serious research work in criminology has been confined almost entirely to the last sixty or seventy years. The Michael-Adler Report criticizes this research because the theories preceeding from it are mere speculations and because the knowledge is mere description, saying, in effect, that the theories which would pull together all the descriptive knowledge have not yet been stated. This is, of course, true, but it is to be expected in a young science. Theories are stated as speculations. Research results in descriptive information which is not contained within the theories. New theories are stated on the basis of the new descriptive knowledge, and research again results in knowledge which cannot be fitted into the theories. If the staff of the proposed institute were engaged in this work and if they used the same methods of research, their results would proceed along the same lines, and it is doubtful that the gap between theory and fact would be closed any more rapidly.

Third, the proper criterion of the value of criminological research is the extent to which it makes possible further research leading to a complete explanation of crime. If this criterion were used, the question would be asked, Has criminology shown a healthy growth? The answer to this question must be secured from a historical survey of criminological research. The Report contains no such historical survey and consequently does not furnish a proper basis for judging the value of criminological research. It is not possible in this appraisal of the Report to present such a survey, but it is possible to point out that, though the full explanation of crime has not been achieved, the fields of ignorance regarding the causes of crime have been diminished. Criminals and non-criminals have been compared on many traits, and some differences have been established in fairly definite fashion. The differences between criminals and non-criminals in respect to physical characteristics, mental abilities, temperamental characteristics, psychopathic make-up, home circumstances, neighborhood situations, and economic situations have been discovered and described with some approximation to accuracy. The differences between crime rates in England and America, in America at present and America fifty years ago, in city and country, and in the different parts of a city have been roughly determined, as have the differences between the crime rates of males and females, Negroes and whites, and immigrants and their children. The relation of age to the beginning and ending of criminality has also been roughly indicated. None of these studies, to be sure, has succeeded in establishing precise differences, but all together they result in a pushing inward of the areas of ignorance toward what is presumably a central principle of causation. Consequently, the possibility of discovering an adequate hypothesis for the explanation is far better now than it was thirty or sixty years ago, and if research in criminology continues along the lines of its recent development, the chances will be still better ten or twenty years from now than at present. In fact, there are several indications that we are approaching the time when a central principle of causation will be discovered. This principle will be immensely valuable, of course, as a means of promoting and directing research, but such discoveries do not come frequently in any science, least of all to those who merely sit down and think about them. Thinking is necessary, but it must be related to accumulated data.

Criminology contains an expanding body of definite conclusions and of scientific propositions, in the sense in which these words are usually employed. Many hypotheses have been stated, tested, and discarded or modified. Others have been stated and are still in the process of being tested. New problems have been formulated, new sources of information made available, new agencies for the collection of information set up, and new techniques of observation developed. There is also much information which, though it does not result in statistical conclusions, provides important cues for subsequent research. Of particular importance in this area is the intensive study of individual case histories.

Because the authors of the Report have failed to recognize the growth of criminology, they would hardly seem qualified to recommend that current criminological research should be abandoned because it is inadequate to solve the problem of crime. Certainly criminological research has not solved the problem of crime. Also, criminological research, if continued just as at present, would be no more adequate. But criminological research cannot possibly remain unchanged. Criminology has been changing and growing during the last fifty years, and its growth will inevitably continue. Having failed to recognize this growth, the authors of the Report are not competent to predict the future of criminology, and their prediction is meaningless. But even if it did mean something, it would be the author's personal judgment and as such worth no more than the opposite prediction of any two of dozens of other persons much better acquainted than Michael and Adler are with the literature and methods of criminological research.

The conclusion of this analysis of the judgment that criminological research is futile is that the judgment is unwarranted and that the authors of the Report have set up an impossible and unjustifiable criterion for determining the value of such research.

(2) *The explanation of the futility of criminological research, as given in the Report, is that criminology is not a science and that criminologists are not competent as scientists.* The unscientific character of criminology is explained by saying that psychology and sociology are unscientific and by emphasizing that criminology is dependent on these two. The authors assert that until the concepts and methods and propositions of these sciences are developed, no one will be able to do scientific work in criminology (not even logicians, mathematicians, or physicists). This interpretation should have led, but did not, to the recommendation that an institute of criminology would not be advisable until scientific work in criminology had become possible. Oddly enough, however, the authors go on to say that one of the values of such an institute would be its contribution to psychology and sociology (pp. 438–40).

This view of the logical dependence of criminology upon psychology and sociology is to some extent accurate: If theoretical tools and equipment had been perfected in psychology and sociology, research in criminology would have been greatly facilitated. But if research in each specific field were postponed until general sciences of psychology and sociology were perfected, it would be postponed for eternity. For the methods of these general sciences are most likely to be perfected through intensive research in criminology and in other specific fields, and the contributions of these various specific studies will interact in and facilitate the development of general methods in the social sciences.

The second interpretation of the failure of criminological research is in terms of the training of criminologists; the defects may be remedied, it is said, by changing the personnel; scientific work in criminology will thereby be made possible. This interpretation leads logically to a recommendation that an institute of criminology be established, whereas the other leads to no such recommendation.

Scientific method, according to the Report, consists in the "proper co-operation of theoretical analysis, observation, and inference" (p. 86). The methods of criminology, psychology, and sociology are characterized as "raw empiricism," which is defined as "an exclusive emphasis upon observation to the total neglect of the abstractions of analysis" (p. 88). Raw empiricism is explained as an extreme reaction against the extreme rationalism of the earlier centuries. The thesis of the authors is that reason should be reinstated to its proper position in scientific method. "Proper position" is not defined specifically, but the dominant thought of the Report seems to be a kind of extreme rationalism which was long ago discarded as futile. This aspect of the Report is seen clearly in the statement that "a science must exist before it can grow [p. 83]," which apparently means that a science can be originated merely by sitting down and thinking about it and that concepts can be defined scientifically in advance of observations.

All sciences, except for a few late offshoots of mature sciences, have begun as common-sense knowledge with concepts defined in common-sense terms and have grown by the interplay of theory and observation (as the Report states on page 83); the precision of definitions of concepts, of formulation of problems, and of findings is an outgrowth of the previous work. In a young science concepts cannot be defined scientifically. The concepts can be defined scientifically only in sciences which have already become mature. The development of concepts in physics or in any other mature science is abundant evidence of this conclusion.

The criticism that criminology is raw empiricism is justified to some extent. This is not reprehensible, for a very great deal of exploratory research and descriptive knowledge is essential to the development of a science, as the Report agrees (pp. 75 and 83). It may be noted, also, that psychometrics, of which the Report speaks most favorably, has practically no etiological theory and in that respect is the rawest type of raw empiricism in psychology.

The principal types of research on crime causation have been directed by theory, either in the form of speculative systems of thought (as such systems must be when a science is constructed on the principle that "a science must exist before it can grow"), of specific hypotheses, or of concepts. There has been an abundance of theories in criminology. This is due largely to the conflicts of different disciplines in this field. There have been the theories of hedonistic psychologists, of socialists, Italian positivists, French social psychologists, mental-testers, psychiatrists, psychoanalysts, ecologists, and many others. Each of these theories consists of a set of hypothetical compendent propositions having etiological significance. The procedure recommended in the Report has been followed many times. People have sat down and formulated theories of crime causation on the basis of the knowledge available to them. They have then tested these theories by observations; and the results of this testing have been used in the formulation of new theories, which again have been tested. These procedures are in the best tradition of scientific method, and to characterize such work as raw empiricism is therefore entirely unjustified. This point will be elaborated, since the principal criticism of criminological research is that it has resulted merely in statistical generalizations, that these have no etiological significance, and that what is needed is the development of a theory which will direct research.

Goring, working under the direction of Karl Pearson in England, made a study of English convicts which resulted in the finding that criminals do not differ significantly from non-criminals in the physical characteristics which were measured. The authors of the Michael-Adler Report characterize this finding as a mere statistical generalization, of no etiological significance, and refer to the study as raw empiricism. The correct statement of the situation is quite different.

The Italian positivists about 1875 developed a theory which contained the following hypothetical propositions: (*a*) Criminals differ from non-criminals in certain physical characteristics; (*b*) the peculiar characteristics which differentiate criminals from non-criminals resemble those of savages and of modern degenerates of the epileptoid type; (*c*) this resemblance is evidence that criminals are a reversion to an earlier and lower biological type of mankind; (*d*) criminality is therefore an inborn and biologically determined characteristic which (*e*) can be eliminated only by limiting the freedom of those who have such characteristics. This theory was used in the direction of research work. People began to believe the theory. Social policies were based on it. Then a rival theory, which explained crime in terms of imitation, developed in France. The controversy between the two schools became acute. The crucial point of controversy was the alleged difference between criminals and non-criminals in physical characteristics. Goring made his study to answer that question. His conclusion that there was no significant difference in the physical characteristics of criminals and non-criminals was immensely important and had great relevance both for theories of criminality and social policy. The significant point here is not whether Goring's finding was valid, but whether his study was raw empiricism. The conclusion that it may not properly be called raw empiricism and that its findings were not etiologically insignificant applies also to dozens of earlier research studies of the same type.

Zeleny has recently reported that the ratio of mental defectives among criminals and non-criminals is about 125 to 100[2]

[2] L. D. Zeleny, "Feeble-mindedness and criminal conduct," *American Journal of Sociology*, XXXVIII (1933), 547-63.

(correction having been made for variations in the methods of grading mental tests). This finding, similarly, would be characterized as a mere statistical generalization without etiological significance, but here again a knowledge of the historical antecedents of the study gives an entirely different interpretation.

For many decades opinions regarding the relation between crime and mental defectiveness have been expressed. Goring's positive conclusion supported that opinion. About twenty years ago this opinion was expressed as a theory with the following propositions: (*a*) Criminals are almost always feeble-minded; Goddard asserted that the ratio of mental defectives among criminals and non-criminals was about 15,000 to 100; (*b*) feeble-minded persons become criminals because they cannot foresee and appreciate the consequences of their acts; (*c*) feeble-mindedness is inherited as a unit characteristic in accordance with Mendelian principles; and (*d*) crime can be prevented adequately only by preventing the propagation of the feeble-minded.

This theory aroused great interest. Practical policies based on this theory were formulated and to some extent put into operation. Hundreds of mental tests of criminals were made over a period of twenty years. The results indicated that the reported difference between criminals and non-criminals is in a ratio of about 125 to 100 (rather than 15,000 to 100) and have yielded the conclusion that feeble-mindedness is not of great etiological significance in crime. This research was directed by a theory, as were hundreds of earlier studies on the same problem. These studies have not enabled anyone to explain why people commit crimes, but the studies do meet the requirements of scientific methods as outlined in the Report and do not warrant the use of any such epithet as "raw empiricism." The studies grew out of theoretical problems and were directed toward the solution of etiological problems.

A third illustration of the error made in the Report is furnished by the recent investigations of the ecological distribution of juvenile delinquents. Shaw has found that in each of fifteen American cities which were studied the rate of delinquency in an area decreased as the distance of the area from the center of the city increased. This finding is also characterized in the Report as a mere statistical generalization, without significance from the standpoint of etiology or social control. As a matter of fact, the statistical generalization is merely one element in a general theory of the causation of juvenile delinquency. The theory includes generalizations regarding the direction of growth of population in city areas, the characteristics of the various areas, and the relation of behavior to these characteristics.

Six propositions concerning delinquency were made: (*a*) Delinquency is not scattered evenly over a city but is concentrated in certain areas; (*b*) the areas of high delinquency are near the center of the city, those of low delinquency near the outskirts; (*c*) the areas of high delinquency are characterized by great mobility of population; (*d*) this mobility thwarts the exercise of neighborhood control over its members; (*e*) delinquency is thus a product of the social disorganization in the neighborhood situation; and (*f*) can be reduced by developing neighborhood organization. These studies have been repeated in other places by other authors, and the method has aroused much interest. There have been at least five attempts to develop programs dealing with the neighborhood as a unit rather than with the individual in isolation from his groups. The research does not provide any final answer to the question of crime causation, but the method is directed by a theory, is of significance from the standpoint of etiology and social control, and results in a finding which is not a mere statistical generalization.

Many other general theories of criminality might be similarly demonstrated. The statistical generalizations which the Report analyzes are, in general, not divorced from theories, and the method is not raw empiricism. The authors' assertion to the contrary can be explained only by assuming that they know very little about criminological research. They had practically no knowledge of criminology at the time they started work on the survey, and the advisory committee which worked with them during the first year of the survey (but not during the second and third years) was not consulted regarding the argument presented in the Report until the Report was in print. At that time the errors could not be corrected.

The failure of criminological research to produce a full and completely satisfactory explanation of crime is explained by the authors as being due to the incompetence of criminologists as scientists. The fallacy in this argument has already been commented on. It has also been noted that the backwardness of criminological research is inevitable in a youthful science and is in some measure attributable to the fact that psychology and sociology are relatively undeveloped as sciences.

Of equal relevance here are the difficulties that beset any attempt to conduct research in the field of criminology. Research in this field cannot be carried on in laboratories, as it can in physics, chemistry, and even psychology, and little progress can be made by working in libraries. Field studies are essential for progress in criminology. This means contacts with institutions for delinquents or with neighborhoods in which delinquents reside or with individual delinquents. Such contacts cannot be made easily. The studies are slow, difficult, and expensive. Funds have seldom been available for persons in academic positions, either as students or teachers, to make such studies. Consequently a large part of the academic research work in criminology has been confined to libraries. Studies in the field have been confined principally to records which were inadequate or to a very small number of cases. Graduate students who start field studies in a community for the purpose of writing dissertations leave the community when their studies are completed and have to make new contacts in some other place. Teachers have a teaching load with confines them to the campus most of the time and have no funds with which to make large-scale consecutive studies.

Some research has been done under the direction of persons in administrative positions in penal and reformatory institutions. Within the last two decades a small number of persons with technical training for the study of human behavior have secured positions, generally as psychologists or psychiatrists, in such institutions and have had first-hand contact with criminals. Some of these specialists are producing research studies that are significant, but they also are burdened with administrative duties and have had little time for research.

It is, therefore, very significant that practically all the important research studies in criminology which have been made in this country by persons in academic or administrative positions have been subsidized. One of the most continuous, large-scale, and productive research programs in criminology is found in Chicago. It has been subsidized by grants from national and local foundations. Good cooperation between academic and public agencies has been secured. The program has been pursued continuously for ten years. Studies by Thrasher, Shaw, McKay, Landesco, Lashley, and others have resulted. This work is an illustration of what may be accomplished in criminology by persons who are not logicians, mathematicians, or physicists. It is also an illustration, on a small scale, of what may be expected from an institute of criminology.

It may be indicated at this point that the statement in the Report that millions of dollars have been wasted in the criminological research of the past is entirely unsupported by evidence. Expenditures in the United States for research in criminology probably amount at most to a few hundred thousand dollars if the crime-commission studies which are not directed at crime causation are excluded. It is surprising in view of the importance of this problem in social life that funds have not been available, for it is the lack of funds and equipment (together with the fact that serious research has been in progress for a relatively short period of time) that has prevented the production of a larger body of significant knowledge.

(3) *The recommendation that current methods of criminological research should be abandoned and the research turned over to the suggested staff of logicians, mathematicians, physicists, and other scientists is quite unjustified, as the preceding analysis shows.* A detailed discussion of the recommendation is therefore unnecessary. The following discussion is limited to

three relatively unimportant aspects of the recommendation.

First, the ordinary graduate student in the social sciences has had some preparation in logic, mathematics, and psychometrics and some knowledge of the physical sciences. These students do not become specialists, but they acquire an acquaintance with the methods. If the knowledge of these methods had any promise of working wonders in the social sciences, the wonders should have been already worked.

Second, specialists in the physical and biological sciences have attempted at various times to make applications of their methods to the data of social life. The results have almost always been very unfortunate. The methods of the physical and biological sciences were developed in relation to the data of those fields, and the methods of the social sciences must be developed in relation to the problems in social behavior. There is no evidence that members of the physical and biological sciences are intellectually more competent than members of the social sciences. They have a larger body of demonstrated knowledge which confines and directs their work and their inferences. When they get away from their own data, they are quite as biased and fallible as other persons. To demonstrate this nothing more is needed than a ten-minute conversation with a physicist on a political problem.

Third, the methods that the suggested staff would use in an institute, if established, are not outlined in any respect. The essential characteristic of their method, as defined in the Report, would be the reinstatement of reason in research. But it is possible to reason only about things you know something about. The staff would know practically nothing about crime and would have to adopt either of two procedures. They might attempt to construct a theory of criminality out of their common-sense knowledge. (It is possible that a theory so constructed would, because of our cultural heritage, turn out to be a form of psychological hedonism.) Or they might attempt to make a survey of the studies that had been made and build up a theory out of the accumulations of previous research work. It is highly probable that in spite of the injunction of the authors of the Report the staff would in the course of a few years become acquainted with the problems, methods, and sources of information that had been the concern of criminologists in previous years, and that they would end up doing, less efficiently, the very kind of research that, in the opinion of the authors, should be abandoned. There would be no other conceivable procedure for them to follow. They would have the advantage of funds, equipment, and leisure for research and would make significant contributions in the course of time, but there would be presumably a period of from five to ten years that would be wasted while they were becoming acquainted with the results of the previous research and were trying to secure some competence in the types of research needed.

Conclusion: I shall summarize the foregoing analysis by presenting it in the form of answers to the three questions which have been asked.

Q. "Is it your opinion that criminological research of the kind which has been and is now being done should not be continued?"

A. The Report appraises criminological research as futile because it has not produced a full and complete explanation of crime. This is an unwarranted criterion to use in judging the value of the work which has been done in a discipline in which serious research work has been conducted under great difficulties for not more than sixty or seventy years. The criterion that should have been used is the extent to which the research is effective in stimulating and directing subsequent research. The authors make no analysis of this sort and are therefore not in a position to evaluate the research which has been done. My impression is that criminological research has shown a very healthy growth under existing conditions and will eventually lead to the discovery of a central principle of causation at some time in the future.

There have been certain shortcomings in criminological research, but these are not explained by saying that criminologists are incompetent as scientists. The correct explanation of the failure of criminological research to develop a larger body of scientific knowledge is the short time which has elapsed since serious research began, the lack of funds and equipment and leisure, and the multiplicity of conflicting theories in this field (socialist, biological, psychiatric, psychoanalytic, etc.) which has diverted some of the effort to partisan propaganda.

Q. "It it your opinion that useful theories of crime causation are more likely to emerge from the direct and immediate attempt to construct such theories, as advocated in the Report, or from the continued use of established methods of criminological research, assuming normal continuation of improvement in these methods?"

A. I find it difficult to answer this question by the choice of either alternative. Both types of work are being undertaken constantly. Some persons are spending more effort on one type of work, some on the other. Those who are engaged in research work are constantly searching, in my opinion, for general theories. I have had the feeling that two things might be done to advantage in the development of new theories. The first is that some person or persons might make a survey of the theories which have been stated and of the factual data in relation to those theories, for the purpose of determining more precisely than we now can just where we stand with reference to these various theories. The second would be a series of conferences among the representatives of the various disciplines dealing with problems of delinquency (sociologists, psychologists, psychiatrists, psychoanalysts, and others) for the purpose of developing acquaintance with the method, points of view, and techniques used in the various approaches. Such contacts would be conducive to the development of better rounded theories of criminality. I should not like to see criminological research stopped for this purpose, however, and it seems to be quite unnecessary that this should be done. Research and the development of theories have been going on together for several decades, and there is no reason why one should stop in order that the other may develop.

Q. "Is it your opinion that the staff proposed for the institute is more likely to achieve significant results in the study of crime causation than a staff made up of the best of present criminologists?"

A. It is my opinion that a staff constituted as suggested in the Report would be very greatly hampered both by their ignorance of the subject matter of criminology and by their own methods if they attempted to carry on research in the field of criminology. At best they would be compelled to construct their theories out of the data accumulated for them by criminologists previously engaged in research, and they would be less competent to construct such theories than the criminologists themselves. I believe that it might be well to have on the staff of the institute a person who had a wide acquaintance with the methods of the biological sciences (rather than the physical sciences, which are more distantly related to the social sciences) for advisory purposes, provided he were not in a position to dictate procedures.

My general reaction to the Report is that its condemnation of criminology as a science that has failed in its early years to produce the results that have been achieved in the mature sciences is unwarranted and that an attempt is being made to reinstate an extreme rationalism which has already been tried in all the social sciences and has been found to be unproductive. The authors are in effect recommending that we abandon an infant which is showing a healthy growth and adopt a mummy which has been dead for more than a century.

The Prison as a Criminological Laboratory

Among students of criminology it is now accepted as a commonplace that it is necessary to understand the criminal in order to deal successfully with the problem of crime. Dr. William A. White has illustrated this point by an analogy, as follows:

> If the Department of Agriculture is called upon to eliminate some insect pest from the land that is upsetting its agricultural projects by destroying crops, the first thing it does is to make an exceedingly careful and meticulous survey of the life history of the insects that it wants to wipe out.[1]

Successful methods of dealing with the problem of crime are either accidental or are based upon adequate knowledge of the processes by which criminality develops. The failure of most of the methods of dealing with criminals is explained by the obsolete *a priori* theories of behavior upon which the methods are

Reprinted by permission from *The Annals of the American Academy of Political and Social Science*, CLVII (September, 1931), 1-6. This volume, carrying the title *Prisons of Tomorrow*, was edited by Professor Sutherland and Professor Thorsten Sellin. In their Foreword, which is still timely, the editors allude to "the riots and disturbances which in recent years occurred in our prisons" and offer the volume "in the hope that it may stimulate thought by its presentation of problems which require solution."

1 "Prisons as Laboratories for Personality Study," *Mental Hygiene Bulletin*, VI (1928), 1, 3.

based. Improvements in the methods of dealing with criminals are likely to be the outgrowth of more adequate knowledge regarding the criminals upon whom the methods are used.

This knowledge of the processes by which criminality develops may be secured in part by a study of the relation between changes in crime rates and changes in other impersonal phenomena, in part by a comparison of criminals and non-criminals in respect to particular traits or conditions, in part by intensive case histories of criminals, and in part by observation of the results of experimental methods of control. At the present time, no one of these approaches to the problem has attained sufficient success to justify the assertion that any one approach should be used in preference to the others. They should all be continued in the hope that one or more of them may throw light upon this problem.

STUDY OF IMPRISONED CRIMINALS

All of these methods except the measurement of crime rates in relation to other phenomena may be applied at any point in the procedures of criminal justice, but there are many obvious advantages to applying them in prison. Here the study of the criminal may be continued over a relatively long period of time. The prisoner is always accessible in a physical sense, whereas in other circumstances it is often impossible to have a physical access to the criminal. Consequently experimental methods of control can be tried in prison and the results observed. Furthermore, the prisoner is generally willing to co-operate in a wholehearted manner when he is approached sympathetically. In some of the prisons of Illinois an approach in the name of science has been especially successful; the prisoner is easily persuaded that because of his experiences he can make a contribution to science. The statements of the criminal who has been convicted are more likely to be reliable than are the statements of the same person before his guilt has been established. In certain respects the attitudes and the mental abilities of the prisoner are adapted to study at this time. Many prisoners have mentioned in their autobiographies the extraordinary vividness, clarity, and strength of their memories of the events and scenes of pre-prison life. This has been explained as being due to the absence of sensory and ideational distractions for the prisoner, to the contrast between prison life and outside life, and to the fact that his memories turn generally to his own career and his own personality.[2]

OBSTACLES TO PRISON STUDIES

There are two difficulties confronting the study of criminals in prison, but neither of these is insuperable. First, prisoners are a selected group of criminals. Not all criminals are committed to prison, and those who are committed are likely to differ from those outside of prison in respect to mentality, economic status, emotional stability, race, nativity, nationality, and other items. Consequently, unless data regarding prisoners are corrected, they cannot be used statistically as a means of drawing conclusions regarding criminals. It is possible, nevertheless, to make studies of prisoners which will throw light on the processes by which criminality develops. Even if intelligent criminals are less likely to be imprisoned than feeble-minded ones, it is possible to find some intelligent criminals in prison, and a study of them will result, not in a statistical conclusion regarding the importance of intelligence as a factor in the causation of crime, but in a description of the process by which intelligent persons become criminals. Feeble-minded criminals can be studied in a similar manner. Again, "organized criminals" are less likely than others to be committed to prison, but even Al Capone has been incarcerated once, and most of his lieutenants and many other gangsters and racketeers have served prison terms.

Comparable studies are conducted in medical clinics. It is not necessary that the proportion of persons with typhoid fever who appear in the clinic should be the same as the proportion of persons with scarlet fever in order that the physicians in the

[2] Michael Hernett, "Die Gedankenwelt im Kerker," *Blätter für Gefängniskunde*, LIX (1928), 10-24.

clinic may make studies of the patients. If each prisoner is regarded as a representative of a "species" of criminals, he can be studied as such, even though some species may not be represented in prison in proportion to their crimes. Consequently the fact that prisoners are a selected group of criminals makes it necessary to be cautious regarding the conclusions that are drawn from the data, but does not preclude the practice of collecting data.

A second difficulty in the use of the prison as a "laboratory" is that the prisoner is not in his "natural habitat." It has been asserted that a criminal can no more be understood in prison than a lion can be understood in a cage. The point of this argument is that the criminal should be studied "in the open." This may be admitted, but it does not follow that he should not also be studied in prison. Access to the criminal who is not in confinement is extremely difficult. The basic studies need to be made at a point where the criminal is accessible, and these may be supplemented by occasional analyses of those who are less easily accessible. Aside from that, this argument seems to be relatively unimportant. The habitat which is significant is found in the interpretations of the criminal, and he carries his interpretations with him. In addition, it is desirable to study the prisoner in relation to his prison environment.

Consequently, in spite of the limitations, the prison has decided advantages as a place in which to study the criminal. This is especially true in regard to the older, more difficult, and more dangerous criminals.

OBJECTIVES OF RESEARCH

Assuming that it is desirable to use prisons as laboratories for the study of criminals, one must be clear about the objectives of the investigations. These should provide information which will be immediately useful for administrative purposes and which will contribute to a theory of criminal behavior and hence to more general control of the crime problem. Such data are desirable for administrative purposes in several respects. It is important that prisoners should be classified, and the classification should be based on the characteristics of the prisoners. Assignment to tasks, to recreation, to school, and to other prison activities should be based on a knowledge of the prisoners, as should the length of the period of confinement.

These assignments and dispositions are rather formal and are perhaps relatively unimportant. It is highly important, however, that the prison administration which is concerned with improvement in the behavior of criminals should be intimately acquainted with the attitudes of prisoners. The whole prison regime should be based on such knowledge. Very little information of this nature has been secured, but studies in Illinois and Massachusetts indicate that it can be secured and that it is likely to be much more significant than the knowledge which results merely in formal classification and assignments. Mr. Henry Field has made most interesting studies of the prisoners' attitudes in relation to the institutional program for promoting successful adjustments,[3] and Clifford Shaw is securing similar information from the autobiographies of prisoners.

Another objective is to acquire knowledge regarding the processes by which criminality develops, in order to make possible the development of experimental projects for preventing crime and for organizing substitutes for imprisonment. In these ways the prison should provide the information which will tend to eliminate the prison. Even though the study of prisoners may in certain respects interfere with the program of the prison, it should be continued because of the prospective value of solving the crime problem.

The ideal is to develop knowledge which is useful at the same time for administrative purposes and for purposes of broader control. It is probable, however, that the two objectives will not coincide exactly. Knowledge which is found useful for ad-

[3] Henry E. Field, "The Attitudes of Prisoners as a Factor in Rehabilitation," *The Annals of the American Academy of Political and Social Science*, CLVII (1931), 150-63.

ministrative purposes may seem to have no general significance, and vice versa. From both points of view, however, it is important to understand the criminal; and there seems to be no theoretical reason to believe that the two kinds of knowledge cannot be made to concur.

VALUE OF EXPERIMENTATION

It is not necessary or desirable that knowledge of the processes which produce criminality should be absolutely complete and final before it is used for purposes of control. Information which is available at a particular time should be used for the direction of experimental methods of control. These efforts will add to the understanding of criminalistic processes, and this additional understanding will contribute to the subsequent efforts at control. The relationship between knowledge and control has been stated by John Dewey as follows:

> It is a complete error to suppose that efforts at social control depend upon the prior existence of a social science. The reverse is the case. The building up of a social science, that is, of a body of knowledge in which facts are ascertained in their significant relations, is dependent upon putting social planning into effect. . . . Physical science did not develop because inquirers had piled up a mass of facts about observed phenomena. It came into being when men intentionally experimented, on the basis of ideas and hypotheses, with observed phenomena to modify them and disclose new observations. This process is self-corrective and self-developing. Imperfect and even wrong hypotheses, when *acted upon*, brought to light significant phenomena which made improved ideas and improved experimentations possible. The change from a passive and accumulative attitude into an active and productive one is the secret revealed by the progress of physical inquiry. Men obtained knowledge of natural energies by trying deliberately to control the conditions of their operation. The result was knowledge, and then control on a larger scale by the application of what was learned.[4]

[4] "Social Science and Social Control," *The New Republic*, LXVII (1931), 276-77.

TYPES OF "PRISON LABORATORIES"

Knowledge about criminals is inevitably acquired in every prison and is inevitably used for purposes of control. The typical prison is one in which this information is acquired casually and is utilized in a haphazard manner. Departures from this procedure appear to be of three kinds, and each of these may be regarded an attempt to use the prison as a laboratory.

First, in some prisons specialists have been added to the staff for the purpose of making studies of the prisoners. The institution in other respects remains as it was previously, or, at best, the study of criminals results only in a rough and formal classification of prisoners. This is the situation in general in prisons which have developed laboratories or clinics. These specialists ordinarily represent one discipline or technique, and their studies are unilinear and particularistic. Thus, in the prison clinics in most of the European countries the biological interest has been dominant and represents a new school of criminology. The Society of Criminal Biology is an outgrowth of and a means of extending this interest. The schedules used for studying prisoners, to be sure, include space for social data, but the latter are of the most formal kind.[5]

Somewhat analogous developments have appeared in American prisons, where psychologists give mental tests to prisoners and psychiatrists make diagnoses of various psychopathies. Dr. Winfred Overholser found in 1928 that 8 per cent of the prisons surveyed by him had full-time psychologists and 23 per cent, part-time psychologists; and that 11 per cent had full-time psychiatrists and 24 per cent, part-time psychiatrists.[6] The data acquired by these specialists are used to some extent in the

[5] A good summary of the developments in the European prisons is given by Thorsten Sellin, in "Prison Tendencies in Europe," *Proceedings National Conference of Social Work*, 1930, pp. 118-32. A more detailed description of the prison clinics of Europe is given by Werner Petrilka, *Personlichkeitsforschung und Differenzierung im Strafvollzug* (Hamburg, 1930). See review by W. Healy in *Journal of Criminal Law and Criminology*, May, 1931.

[6] "Psychiatric Service in Penal and Reformatory Institutions and Criminal Courts in the United States," *Mental Hygiene*, XII (1928), 801-38.

more formal activities of the institution, but in general the prison continues very much as it was before the specialists were added to the staff. Moreover, because the data are acquired by specialists and are of an atomistic character, they have not been highly significant for purposes of understanding criminal behavior in general.

Second, the institution adds to itself staff specialists of different kinds whose techniques supplement each other. Working co-operatively these specialists develop a more complete and better rounded knowledge of the prisoner than is generally obtained.[7] This group of specialists, however, is relatively external to the administrative system, and in most respects the functions of the institution remain unchanged. The primary difference between this type of prison laboratory and the first type is that the studies in the second are not so completely under the dominance of one specialized interest and that consequently the work can more properly be called clinical.

This system is illustrated in the prisons of Illinois. In each prison a unit, composed of one or more psychiatrists, psychologists, and sociologists, working under the direction of the state criminologist, is making studies of prisoners. The resulting knowledge is used at present to a very slight extent by the parole board for purposes of classification and disposition, but it does not greatly affect the institutional policies. One very interesting part of the work of this unit is the collection of autobiographies of prisoners under the direction of the sociologist. Clifford R. Shaw has published two of these autobiographies, which seem to have great significance both for immediate administrative purposes and for a theory of criminal behavior and a general policy of control.[8]

A third type of prison laboratory, which is generally not recognized as such, is found in the prison in which the staff, without any or much assistance from psychological, psychia-

[7] An excellent description of the function of the different specialists in clinical study is given by Louis Wirth, "Clinical Sociology," *American Journal of Sociology*, XXVII (1931), 49-66.

[8] *The Jack-Roller* (Chicago: University of Chicago Press, 1930); *The Natural History of a Delinquent Career* (Chicago: University of Chicago Press, 1931).

tric, or sociological specialists, conscientiously attempts to acquire knowledge regarding each prisoner and to utilize this knowledge for purposes of immediate control. The prison in this case is an experimental institution, though it is not directed by scientific specialists. The Borstal Institutions of England illustrate this development. Every member of the staff is expected to become acquainted with the prisoners, to make appraisals of them, and to contribute his findings to a joint institutional program that includes both the prisoners and the administration. Since the members of the staff retain their positions for many years and are under the guidance of inspectors and directors who have even wider experience, the entire staff acquire an expert competence though they do not act as representatives of the scientific disciplines. The scientific specialists are not entirely lacking in the Borstal Institutions, but they play a part which is relatively small and are, in general, called in only for advice in regard to psychopathic or defective prisoners.

The Massachusetts State Prison Colony is a similar experiment. The whole institution is an experiment from the point of view of architecture, discipline, government, occupations, recreation, and personal relations. It is recognized as an experiment, and an organized effort is being made to observe the procedures and the results. The scientific specialists play a very unimportant part in the institution. Dependence is placed primarily upon the regular members of the staff. A prison of this nature becomes a criminological laboratory. In prisons of the first two types, a criminological laboratory or clinic is set up in the institution, but the prison in other respects remains approximately the same as it was previously.

A fourth type of prison laboratory would be one which combined the features of the third and the second. The scientific specialists would become essential parts of the staff and would work with the entire staff to develop the whole prison as an experiment. Judging from meager reports, I would say that the experimental prison in Moscow is somewhat of this nature. The Massachusetts Prison Colony is perhaps not far from this type, and in one of the Illinois institutions a similar approach is being used.

This seems to be the ideal type, but the ideal is difficult to attain. Legislation and public opinion tend to hold the prison in its beaten path and prevent experimentation. Adequately trained specialists are difficult to secure, and competent members of the regular staff are not numerous. Provisions for training psychologists, psychiatrists, and sociologists for clinical work are inadequate. No effective method of training the regular members of the prison staff or filling the positions with persons who are suitably trained has been developed, though progress is being made in both respects. It must be expected that the process of turning the prison into an experimental laboratory will be slow; perhaps when the time for change is at hand, an adequate supply of staff personnel will be available.

PROGRAM FOR THE FUTURE

The staff personnel would regard the entire prison as an experiment and would utilize their knowledge of the prisoners for the purpose of directing this experiment. Scientific specialists would play a part in the institution—not, at least at first, by making routine studies of all prisoners, but by assisting the regular staff when intensive studies of difficult or crucial cases were desired, and by studies designed to contribute to the generalized knowledge of criminality. Perhaps certain routine observations might be made by these specialists in all cases, but they would not direct the entire procedure. In the first place, intensive and specialized study is very expensive and would require a large staff of specialists who are not now available. In the second place, some of the national leaders in the field of juvenile delinquency have become very pessimistic in regard to the value of the work done by specialists.

The primary contribution of the experimental prison would be to demonstrate how prisoners could be controlled in the direction of better behavior adjustment. Ultimately, it might be expected that a knowledge of the formation of criminal habits would be acquired, and that this general knowledge would contribute to broader programs for the prevention of crime.

The Reliability of Criminal Statistics [1]

THE SOCIAL information contained in police records and prison records is generally based on the unverified statements of the prisoners. Notwithstanding the lack of verification these records are used as data in many extensive and expensive research projects and are the most general source of statistical information regarding the social characteristics of criminals. These statistics are sometimes important in the formation and development of social policies and of theories of criminality. If the social information in such records is unreliable, the conclusions drawn from them are necessarily unreliable, also. Furthermore, from the administrative point of view, the work of collecting, compiling, and publishing this information is not justified unless the data are fairly reliable.

Two attempts have been made to determine the extent to

Reprinted by permission from the *Journal of Criminal Law and Criminology*, XXV (1934), 10-19. The article was written in collaboration with C. C. Van Vechten, Jr.

1 This study was made possible by a grant from the Social Science Research Committee of the University of Chicago, and by the hearty co-operation of the Chicago Police Department, the Illinois Institute for Juvenile Research, the Illinois State Penitentiary at Joliet, the Illinois State Reformatory at Pontiac, the Illinois State School for Boys at St. Charles, and the Cook County Juvenile Court.

which these records and the statistical reports based on them are reliable. In 1915 Miss Hinricksen compared the inconsistencies in the successive arrest records of recidivists in Illinois towns. She reported many inconsistencies in regard to age, nativity, and other social characteristics. Of twenty repeaters in Rockford, Illinois, during 1915 only two gave the same birthplaces, occupations, and ages at each arrest.[2] This method of determining the reliability of criminal statistics is not entirely satisfactory, first because identification of an indivdual generally depends on the name when the other items, such as age, address, and birthplace, differ and it is quite possible that the investigator may be mistaken in a judgment that all of the records refer to one individual; secondly, even if the data regarding recidivists are proved to be inaccurate, the data regarding the much larger number of prisoners who in a particular year are not recidivists may be accurate.

A second method of evaluating the social information contained in prison records was used in a study made recently under the direction of the Institute for Juvenile Research of Illinois. A report has been made for this Institute by Edward A. Conover regarding a study at the Illinois Penitentiary at Joliet in 1931.[3] He selected at random 200 records of prisoners who had been examined by the mental-health office in the penitentiary. In all of these cases supplementary information had been secured by correspondence with members of the families, with employers, school authorities, and others. He compared the prisoners' own statements to the mental-health office with the information secured by correspondence from the other sources. The extent of the disagreement between the statements of the prisoners and of the correspondents varied widely from one item to another. The general conclusion reached was that sub-

[2] Annie Hinricksen, "Pitfalls in criminal statistics," *Proceedings of the American Prison Association* (1916), 393-401.

[3] Edward A. Conover, "An evaluation of the materials secured by social case-work procedures in the Illinois State Penitentiary at Joliet." This paper was read before the American Orthopsychiatric Association in 1931 and is to be published in the proceedings of that Association.

stantial divergence was found between the inmates and the correspondents in twenty-four per cent of the comparisons which were made; in twelve per cent of these divergences the correspondence was less favorable to the prisoner than his own version; in seven per cent the correspondence was more favorable than his own version; and in five per cent, neutral.

The original plan of the present study was to take a consecutive series of records of arrests by the Chicago police and by independent investigations made by social agencies or by our own efforts to determine the reliability of the social information on the police records and, in cases resulting in imprisonment, on the prison records. This method was abandoned after brief experimentation. Not more than ten per cent of the persons in a sample of fifty arrests could be located in the social-service exchange in Chicago. The expense of field investigations of the other ninety per cent would be very great. The police authorities were opposed to such field inquiries. Finally, it would probably be impossible to locate many of the persons even if field studies were made and those who could be located would presumably be a selected group differing in many respects from the ones who could not be located.

The following method was therefore substituted. An effort was made to measure the consistency of all the social information on the records of all the agencies which had contacts with 507 inmates of state prisons and reformatories in Illinois. The 507 prisoners had been selected for a different purpose, and prior to the inauguration of the present study, by assistants at Joliet, Pontiac and St. Charles. The general principle used by these assistants in the selection was consecutive admissions of Chicago-born criminals to these institutions. The principle of consecutive admissions was violated to some extent because of the difficulty or ease of assigning prisoners to the investigators for life histories. Also, a group of prisoners designated "Joliet Special" was added. This group consisted of thirty-two prisoners recorded as born elsewhere than Chicago but committed to the Joliet prison from Chicago. The location and composition of this group of 507 prisoners is shown in Table I.

TABLE I. Location and Race of 507 Prisoners

INSTITUTION	WHITE	COLORED	TOTAL
Joliet Penitentiary	135	7	142
Joliet Special	20	12	32
Pontiac Reformatory	219	12	231
St. Charles School for Boys	71	31	102
Total	445	62	507

The following records were secured regarding this group of prisoners:

(1) A front-office record is taken by the prison clerk at the time of admission to the institution. This furnishes the data from which the published statistics of the institution are compiled.

(2) A mental-health-office record is taken by the psychiatrist, ordinarily later than the day of admission but within the first week. In Pontiac, however, the mental-health-office record is merely a copy of the front-office record and is not utilized in this study.

(3) A special schedule was filled out for the Institute for Juvenile Research by the investigators who selected the 507 cases.

(4) The records of the arrests which resulted in the present commitments to the institutions were secured for 335 of the 405 inmates in Joliet and Pontiac but were not located in the other 50 cases in those institutions and were not secured in the 102 St. Charles cases, since the arrest file of the police department does not contain the names of juveniles.

(5) Previous arrest records of 150 of the 405 Joliet and Pontiac inmates were located. This does not represent a complete search of the police records of arrest. The prior arrest record was investigated only for the period 1930–32 unless the prisoner's name was not found in the files for that period, in which case the files for the period 1916–30 were consulted.

(6) Juvenile court records of 57 of the 175 Joliet inmates,

139 of the 231 Pontiac inmates, and 97 of the 102 St. Charles inmates were located.

(7) Social-service exchange records of 86 of the Joliet inmates and 138 of the Pontiac inmates were secured, but because of the present pressure of work in the social agencies the records of the constituted agencies were not utilized. Similar social-service exchange records were presumably available in all of the St. Charles cases since the juvenile court cases are automatically cleared in the exchange, but they were utilized in only two cases which could not be located in the files of the juvenile court.

(8) Previous prison records were secured for 44 of the Joliet inmates and 1 of the Pontiac inmates. In addition to the sources listed above, in which an effort was made to locate each of the 507 cases, other sources were utilized for a few extraordinary cases. These included 5 cases located in the files of the Chicago Bureau of Identification, and 7 located in the court records which could not be located in the regular arrest records of the Chicago police department, and 4 cases located in the files of the Chicago and Cook County School which could not be located in the juvenile court files. This gave a total of 2,622 records of 507 prisoners or an average of a little more than 5 records per prisoner.

The following items of social information were taken from the records of these agencies and compared for the purpose of determining the consistency of the records: name, age, address, nativity, race, marital status, and occupation. These records were taken independently except that in principle the name of an offender was transmitted in writing from the police department to the court, from the court to the institution, and from the front office of the institution to the mental-health office and to the investigators who made the personal interview. In fact, however, the name is not always thus transmitted in writing.

The general method in this study was to compare these various and relatively independent records of identical prisoners for the purpose of determining the frequency of inconsistencies in the records. Inconsistencies in individual records are different from inconsistencies in statistical series. It is possible, for instance, that the five records of a particular prisoner may show five different dates of birth. In that case at least four of the five must be inaccurate. Nevertheless, because of the balancing of errors, the statistical distribution of the ages of all prisoners may be approximately the same in the five types of records. The effort has been made to determine both the inconsistencies in the several records of a particular prisoner and the inconsistencies in the statistical distribution of records of all the prisoners on each item of information on which distributions can be secured.

Inconsistencies were found, on the average, in 34.1 per cent of the cases. This is somewhat higher than the average of 24 per cent reported by Conover. In both studies, however, this general average is relatively meaningless, for it combines items on which the inconsistencies are practically zero with items on which inconsistencies are found (in the present study) in 70 per cent of the cases. Consequently the average is not a stable or necessary symbol but is affected decidedly by the inclusion or exclusion of a few items of information.

The general average in this present study is the result of four principal types of variations.

(*a*) A very large proportion of the variations are in the form of minor differences caused by clerical errors, ordinary human carelessness or misunderstandings. The criteria of consistency which were used were extremely rigorous, including variations in one letter of a name, one figure in an address, one day in the age, and any verbal difference in the description of occupation.

(*b*) Factual changes during the interval between the taking of the several records account for changes in some of the items. This is a much less important source of variation than the clerical errors, and is not found at all in certain items such as place of birth, date of birth, or race.

(*c*) The several agencies are seeking different information on some points, though the information is entered on the records under approximately the same rubrics. The police make a record of last occupation, the penal institutions of principal occupation; the police make a record of address of the offender at the time of arrest, the penal institutions make a record of the address of relatives to whom communications may be sent by the institution; the police classify prisoners by marital status as either single or married, while the penal institutions use five classes for the same data.

(*d*) Purposive deception is the motive in a certain part of the inconsistencies.

If correction is made for the minor variations caused by carelessness, for the factual changes in the interval between arrest record and subsequent record, and for differences in the conception of items, the inconsistencies are reduced to about 10 per cent. In other words, approximately 10 per cent of the inconsistencies in records are probably due to intentional deception on the part of prisoners. This is not a completely objective summary of the data but involves an element of subjective appraisal. Moreover, it does not necessarily mean that the unreliability of the data would be 10 per cent if the corrections listed above were made, for the reason that the records might be unreliable due to consistency in deceptions. It was found in a study of the aliases of prisoners that 17 per cent of the prisoners in the present study had at some time or other used fictitious names, evidently for the purpose of deception. An attempt to deceive in regard to the right name is probably made more frequently than on any other item of social information.

The percentage of cases in which the records of the several agencies were not entirely consistent is shown in Table II.

TABLE II. Per Cent of Prisoners Whose Records Were Inconsistent on Specified Items of Social Information

ITEM	PER CENT OF INCONSISTENCY
Race	0.8
Nativity	10.3
Marital Status	17.3
Name	39.3
Address	41.7
Age	60.8
Occupation	69.7
Average	34.1

This is based on 507 prisoners for all items except marital status and occupation, in which only 305 prisoners were used, because of the exclusion of the St. Charles boys, who are generally below the age of marriage and of regular occupation. This table shows a range of inconsistencies from 0.8 for race to 69.7 for occupation. One would expect the greatest consistency in regard to race and age, which are more completely susceptible to check by observation. This expectation is met in regard to race, but not in regard to age. The failure of age to rank next to race is probably due to the fact that variations of one day in the age, when correction is made for the passage of time, is counted as an inconsistency. In other respects, also, the ranking of the several items in regard to the percentage of inconsistencies does not represent a necessary or fixed relationship. The low rank of nativity is explained primarily by the method of selection of cases for the present study. The low rank of marital status is explained in part by the inclusion of a large group of Pontiac Reformatory inmates who are generally, in fact and according to the records, single. The items which rank highest in inconsistencies are those in regard to which the smallest units or classes are used in measuring inconsistencies, namely, one letter, one figure, or one occupational term. The record of occupation may be least consistent either because prisoners make false reports regarding occupation in order to secure desirable labor assignments in prison, because the conception held by the prison in recording occupation is different from the conception held by the police, because occupations are changed readily, or because occupational terminology is not standardized. The last is presumably the principal reason for inconsistencies. If broader criteria of occupational similarity could be utilized, it is probable that the rate of inconsistency would be greatly reduced. If the slight errors in spelling are eliminated, inconsistency in regard to name is reduced to 3 per cent of the cases. If the addresses which show a variation of less than two blocks are not counted as inconsistencies, the percentage of cases in which the addresses are not recorded consistently is reduced from 41.7 to about 20 per cent. Similarly, if the minor variations in age are eliminated, the percentage of inconsistency is reduced to 30. In general, it is fairly safe to conclude that substantial differences between the records of the agencies are found, on the average, in about 10 per cent of the cases.

The rate of inconsistency is 27.9 per cent for the inmates of St. Charles, 32.8 per cent in the Joliet cases and 37.8 in the Pontiac cases. The Pontiac cases have the highest rate of inconsistency in respect to name, age, address, and nativity; the Joliet cases have the highest rate in regard to marital status and occupation. The lower rate in St. Charles is presumably based in part on the fact that field studies were made in securing the records. The lower rate of inconsistency in Pontiac in regard to marital status is probably due to the fact that the Pontiac group is younger and has a much larger proportion of inmates who have not been married and who consistently and truthfully report themselves on each record to be single.

The rate of inconsistency in the records of white prisoners is 33.8, of colored prisoners 36.2. This difference is not great enough to be very significant, but the rate is higher for the colored than for white prisoners in regard to nativity, address, marital status, age, race, and occupation. The only item on which they have a lower rate—and it is at this point significantly lower—is in regard to the name, and this is due to the greater ease of spelling the names of colored prisoners than the names of many prisoners of foreign stock. The higher rate of inconsistencies of records of colored prisoners is probably not due to a greater frequency of efforts at deception.

The rate of inconsistencies in items which are necessarily or customarily stable and fixed (date and place of birth, race, and name) is lower than the rate in the items which more readily change (address, marital status, and occupation). Nativity is excluded from this comparison because of the method used in the selection of cases for this study. The comparison of these groups of items with regard to inconsistency in the records is shown in Table III.

TABLE III. Comparison of the Fixed Items and the Changeable Items in Regard to Per Cent of Inconsistencies

ITEMS	WHITE	COLORED	TOTAL
Items which are fixed (age, race, name)	33.6%	30.1%	33.2%
Items which change (address, marital status, occupation)	43.9	54.9	45.3
Total (all items)	39.5	42.5	39.6[a]

[a] This total is different from the total presented previously because of the exclusion of the data regarding nativity from the present table.

The rate of inconsistency is significantly higher for the items which are easily changed than for those which are fixed and stable. The rate of inconsistencies for the unchangeable group would be not more than than 5 per cent if the minor variations in the spelling of the name and errors of two years in age were eliminated. But, similarly, a large part of the inconsistency in the record on items which change would be eliminated if the approximate neighborhood rather than the specific address and the general range of occupational terminology were used as the criteria of consistency.

Variations in the records tend to balance when the data are presented as statistical tabulations. The general conclusion derived from the records of one agency would be, statistically, almost the same as the conclusions derived from the records of another of the agencies used in this study. The statistical distribution of ages shows the same general form of curve for each agency, with a variation in mean ages of about half a year. The police records tend to exaggerate the ages of the offenders, in comparison with the other records; this is true particularly in the younger age groups and is probably explained by the regulation that no child under 16 years of age is to be recorded. The statistical distribution of nativities, with reference only to the comparison of foreign-born and native-born, also shows that the police records, as compared with the other records, exaggerate the proportion of foreign-born prisoners. In the selected group used for this study, which included a very small number of foreign-born offenders, the disagreements were similar in origin, the police record indicating more often than any other type of record that a prisoner was foreign-born. This exaggeration (approximately ten per cent) is due primarily to the record form used by the police, which makes no differentiation of nativity and nationality. Similarly, the records taken within the institutions were consistent statistically in regard to marital status though they showed many individual variations. There was also wide variation between the records taken within the institutions and the police records because of the two-fold classification used by the institutions. A statistical distribution of occupations was not attempted because the information regarding occupations was not sufficiently specific to justify a classification on the basis of a single principle. The impression derived from inspection of the entries regarding occupation is that the variations are almost entirely within narrow ranges of skills and that if fairly broad class intervals could be constructed objectively, there would be little difference in the proportions of prisoners in the several occupational classes. The addresses in a group of cases selected for more intensive analysis were exactly identical according to the several records in about two thirds of the cases, and in the other third, in which variations did occur, the distances between the addresses was, on the average, about one mile. These variations, moreover, tend to balance each other so far as delinquency areas are concerned. These various comparisons tend, in general, to justify a generalization that the statistical distribution derived from the records of one agency are highly consistent with the statistical distributions on the same item derived from another agency.

The records of the police department gave rise to more inconsistencies when compared with other records that did any other agency. This is due in part to the higher average age recorded by the police department, in part to the higher proportion of foreign-born prisoners, but principally to the two-fold classification in regard to marital status and to the fact that the police inquiry regarding occupation referred to occupation at the time of arrest whereas the corresponding inquiry in the records of the other agencies had reference to general or principal occupation. On the other hand, the inconsistencies in the several police records of recidivists are less than the inconsistencies in the records of all agencies included in this study. The rate of inconsistency for fixed items in the police records of recidivists is 24.6 per cent, for the changeable items, 27.9 per cent. This lower rate of inconsistency in the police records is presumably due to the uniform definition of terms and the uniform criteria used in the several police stations as compared with different definitions and criteria used by the several agencies.

The following general conclusions may be derived from this analysis:

(1) The several agencies used in this study are exactly consistent in their records of any item of social information about a particular prisoner, on the average, in about two thirds of the cases and are substantially consistent in about nine tenths of the cases.

(2) The records of any one of the agencies yield about the same average and statistical distribution of data on any one item regarding all prisoners as do the records of any other agency.

(3) The consistency of the several records of a particular prisoner and the statistical consistency of the several records of a group of prisoners may not properly be translated into terms of reliability or truth. The records may be consistently untrue. However, it was found that at least 17 per cent of the prisoners had used fictitious names, as checked by fingerprint evidence, at some time or other.

(4) Approximately two thirds of the inconsistencies in the records of the several agencies could be eliminated by greater care in recording and by standardization of definitions and classifications.

The following recommendations[4] develop from this analysis:

(1) The terms which are used in recording data regarding criminals should be standardized. Address, occupation, nativity,

[4] In the reorganization of the Chicago Police Department some of the modifications recommended have been made already.

and the other items should mean the same thing to the several agencies. It is particularly important that nativity and nationality should not be confused.

(2) The classifications on each item should be identical. The classification used in recording marital status could easily be made uniform in all the agencies. It is highly important but much more difficult to develop a similar classification of occupations.

(3) Names should be filed in every agency phonetically rather than alphabetically.

(4) Other studies of the reliability of criminal statistics should be made. The method used by Conover in his Joliet study of comparing prisoner's statements with correspondent's statements is the easiest method from an administrative point of view, but has limitations in the form of inadequate replies and biased replies. The method used in the present study has values in the preliminary study of the reliability of the statistics but cannot yield positive conclusions regarding reliability in most states. It could perhaps be used to best advantage in a state like Massachusetts, where a large proportion of the prisoners have records verified by field investigations. It is probable that the only adequate method of testing these records will be by a system of registration of inhabitants of the United States, either in the form of European registration systems or in the form of general fingerprint records, which have been recommended by some of the police associations. With the extension of fingerprinting to the army, the postal-savings accounts, hospitals, banks, immigration departments and other groups of people, we shall soon have fingerprint records only slightly short of universal.

Appendix

Fields of Interest

My chief interest in sociology at present is in the mechanisms and processes of social life as they may be observed in the field of criminology. My changes in chief interest have been somewhat as follows:

1. An interest in the methods of improving social conditions. This was a missionary interest. My first sociology was a correspondence course under Dr. Annie Marion McLean, in which one of Dr. Henderson's books was the text. I had no courses in sociology in college and no other courses in sociology elsewhere, except this correspondence course, until I entered the University of Chicago as a graduate student, with the purpose

This autobiographical statement was prepared by Sutherland for L. L. Bernard, who was studying the backgrounds of American sociologists. It is now part of the Luther Bernard Papers of the Pennsylvania Historical Collections, University Library, Pennsylvania State University. In his covering letter of July 13, 1927, Sutherland explained that he "had plans of writing a detailed biography, in which I would try to describe my behavior as completely as possible with reference to the conditions that are of interest to sociologists. But I still am sufficiently in the dark in regard to the mechanisms by which personality develops and behavior is determined (in spite of a thorough perusal of your *Social Psychology*, and of many other books) to prevent me from putting the time on that." He did take the time to produce this account of his shifting interests from the start of his residency as a graduate student at Chicago (1906) to his professorship at Minnesota (1927).

of taking graduate work in history. I took sociology because it was required, according to the announcement, as a prerequisite for graduate work in history. During the first quarter at the University of Chicago I took a course under Dr. Henderson. Miss McLean had praised me, by correspondence, for my work in the correspondence course and had asked me to call on her when I came to Chicago. This I did. In addition she spoke to Dr. Henderson about me, so that when I entered Dr. Henderson's course, I received personal attention. He spoke to me, knew me, was interested in me. Consequently I was interested in pursuing sociology, and interested in the type of sociology that Dr. Henderson presented. I do not mean that this is a complete explanation of my interest, but it is a part of the explanation.

2. During my first year in graduate work at the University of Chicago I became impressed with the great complexity of social problems and the great difficulty of solving them. I developed a moderate skepticism regarding social reform. My brother had taken a course under Dr. Thomas and had been greatly impressed by it and by Dr. Thomas. I decided that if I placed more emphasis on ethnology, specializing in that, I could be dealing with a situation that was specific and concrete, and thus get rid of the troublesome and practically impossible problems of social reform.

3. I had started in my graduate work in sociology with economics as a minor, related somewhat to the interest in social reform. I suspect that the courses in economics added more to my skepticism in regard to social reform than did the courses in sociology. At any rate, as I became interested in ethnological material, I also developed an interest in psychology, and I changed from economics to psychology as a minor.

4. When I became an officer of the Juvenile Protective Association, I saw for the first time in my life the conditions of life in the immigrant sections of a large city. These impressed me very much, as had some of the earlier literature I had read (Jacob Riis, etc.), and I developed a somewhat radical attitude. I was impressed with the slightness of modification that could

be made by reform organization, and I wanted something like socialism, which I had never studied and which I did not understand in a constructive way, that would make a great and somewhat sudden change.

5. Life in a small town and teaching in a small college took me back somewhat to the reform type of sociology, but with a considerable increase in interest in the psychological processes involved. When I returned to graduate work in Chicago after an absence (aside from one summer quarter) of three years, I had as my dominant interest the material conditions–geographical and economic–by which life seemed to be controlled. I took as a subject for doctor's dissertation the practical problem of unemployment, and when I found this included too much, I narrowed it to the relation of public employment agencies to the problem of unemployment. This dissertation was worked out while I was doing research work for the Chicago Commission on Unemployment, under the general direction of Dr. Henderson. Dr. Hoxie was probably the guiding influence, however, in much of the work in the final preparation of the dissertation, for Dr. Henderson was in India during most of the last year I spent in graduate work. In general I had become disgusted and disappointed in the effort to secure information in regard to the thing that was called social theory. I could not find theory that amounted to anything, in my interpretation. I could not find a justification for sociology, except as it was a means of solving practical problems. About 1912 and 1913 I rather definitely abandoned the effort to study social processes or social theory and tried to concentrate on particular social problems, such as those mentioned.

6. I think that it was about 1918 when I began to have an interest, or a renewed interest, in sociology as a general theory of behavior. The methodological note of Thomas and Znaniecki's *Polish Peasant*, more than anything else, brought me to a realization that it was necessary to understand processes and mechanisms. Added to that was the appearance in the form of journal articles of some of Park and Burgess's material, and also contact with Reuter and Queen at the University of Illinois during the

summer of 1919. The change was not abrupt, but within the course of two or three years I had changed my interest from the study of social problems to the study of social processes and social mechanisms, in which the problem merely furnished the data and limited the field. That, with minor modifications, has remained my interest.

Bibliography

BOOKS BY E. H. SUTHERLAND

Criminology. Philadelphia: J. B. Lippincott Co., 1924. 643 pp.
Principles of Criminology, 2d ed. Philadelphia: J. B. Lippincott Co., 1934. 611 pp. A revision of *Criminology*.
Twenty Thousand Homeless Men (with Harvey J. Locke). Philadelphia: J. B. Lippincott Co., 1936. 207 pp.
The Professional Thief. Chicago: University of Chicago Press, 1937. 257 pp.
Principles of Criminology. 3d ed. Philadelphia: J. B. Lipincott Co., 1939. 651 pp.
Principles of Criminology. 4th ed. Philadelphia: J. B. Lippincott Co., 1947. 643 pp.
White Collar Crime. New York: Dryden Press, 1949. 272 pp.

ARTICLES AND REPORTS BY E. H. SUTHERLAND

"Unemployment and Public Employment Agencies." Appendix 3 in *Report of Mayor's Commission on Unemployment*, pp. 95–175. Chicago, 1914.

Additions and corrections to the Bibliography were supplied by Jon Snodgrass, graduate student in sociology at the University of Pennsylvania, who has prepared a doctoral dissertation on prominent American criminologists in the period 1920–50.

"What Rural Health Surveys Have Revealed." *Proceedings of Missouri Conference for Social Welfare*, published in *Monthly Bulletin State Board of Charities and Corrections*, IX (June 1916), 31–37.

"The Isolated Family." *Institution Quarterly*, XIII (September–December 1922), 189–92. Also in *Religious Education*, XIX (February 1924), 32–35.

"Report on the Work of the National Council for Social Studies." *Proceedings High School Conference, November 24, 1923*, published in *University of Illinois Bulletin*, XXI (February 23, 1924), 384–86.

"Public Opinion as a Cause of Crime." *Journal of Applied Sociology*, IX (September–October 1924), 50–56.

"Murder and the Death Penalty." *Journal of Criminal Law and Criminology*, XV (February 1925), 522–29.

"Administration of Justice in the Modern City and County." *Municipal Index*, 1925, pp. 192–94.

"Capital Punishment." *Nelson's Encyclopedia*. New York: T. Nelson and Sons, 1926.

"The Biological and Sociological Processes." *Papers and Proceedings of the Twentieth Annual Meeting of the American Sociological Society*, XX (1926), 58–65.

"Report of an Investigation of Probation in Minnesota." *Proceedings Minnesota Conference of Social Work*, 1927, pp. 219–29.

"Criminology, Public Opinion, and the Law." *National Conference of Social Work*, 1927, pp. 168–75.

"Is There Undue Crime among Immigrants?" *National Conference of Social Work*, 1927, pp. 572–79.

"Social Aspects of Crime." *Proceedings of the Conference of the National Crime Commission*, pp. 156–57. Washington, 1927.

"Is Experimentation in Case Work Processes Desirable?" *Social Forces*, VI (June 1928), 567–69.

"Crime and the Conflict Process." *Journal of Juvenile Research*, XIII (January 1929), 38–48.

"The Person versus the Act in Criminology." *Cornell Law Quarterly*, XIV (February 1929), 159–67.

"Neue Amerikanische Kriminalwissenschaftliche Literatur." *Monatsschrift für Kriminalpsychologie und Strafrechtsreform*, XIX (1929), 228–36.

"Edward Carey Hayes: 1868–1928." *American Journal of Sociology*, XXXV (July 1929), 93–99.

"The Content of the Introductory Courses for Prospective Social Workers." *Social Forces*, VIII (June 1930), 503–7.

"Prognose von Erfolg oder Fehlschlag bei Bewührungsfrist." *Monatsschrift für Kriminalpsychologie und Strafrechtsreform*, XXI (1930), 507–13.

"The Missouri Crime Survey." In *Scientific Methods in the Social Sciences: A Case Book*, ed. Stuart A. Rice, pp. 528–40. Chicago: University of Chicago Press, 1931.

"Mental Deficiency and Crime." In *Social Attitudes*, ed. Kimball Young, pp. 357–75. New York: Henry Holt and Co., 1931.

Prisons of Tomorrow (ed. with Thorsten Sellin). *The Annals of the American Academy of Political and Social Science*, CLVII (September 1931).

"The Prison as a Criminological Laboratory." Ibid., CLVII (September 1931), 131–36.

"Research Work in Prisons." *Proceedings of the American Prison Association*, 1931, pp. 428–33.

"Social Process in Behavior Problems." *Publications of the American Sociological Society*, XXVI (August 1932), 55–61.

"Housing and Delinquency" (with C. R. Shaw, C. E. Gehlke, Sheldon Glueck, and A. W. Stearns). In *Housing and the Community*, ed. J. M. Gries and James Ford, pp. 13–49. Washington, 1932.

"Recent Social Trends in Crime" (with C. E. Gehlke). In *Recent Social Trends*, II, 1115–35. New York: McGraw-Hill, 1933.

"Parole in Relation to the Institution." *Proceedings of the American Prison Association*, 1933, pp. 305–11.

"The Decreasing Prison Population of England." *Journal of Criminal Law and Criminology*, XXIV (January–February 1934), 880–900.

"The Reliability of Criminal Statistics" (with C. C. Van Vechten, Jr.). *Journal of Criminal Law and Criminology*, XXV (May–June 1934), 10–20.

"L'Interdiction aux personnes condamnées l'exercise de cette profession." *Congrès Pénal et Pénitentiare International, troisième section, deuxième question*, 1935, pp. 1–9.

"Wie der Berufsdieb der Bestrafung entgeht." *Monatsschrift für Kriminalpsychologie und Strafrechtsreform*, XXVII (1936), 449–56.

"Report on Ecological Survey of Crime and Delinquency in Bloomington, Indiana." *State Director of N.Y.A.*, Indianapolis, 1937.

"The Professional Thief." *Journal of Criminal Law and Criminology*, XXVIII (July–August 1937), 161–63.

"Die Bekämpfung des Berufsdiebes in den Vereinigten Staaten von Nordamerika." *Monatsschrift für Kriminalbiologie und Strafrechtsreform*, XXVIII (September 1937), 401–6.

"The Person and the Situation in the Treatment of Prisoners." *Proceedings of the American Prison Association*, 1937, pp. 145–50.

"Parole in Indiana." *News Bulletin of the Osborne Association*, IX (February 1938), 1–2.

"Parole." *Public Welfare in Indiana*, XLVIII (May 1938), 4–6.

"White Collar Criminality." *American Sociological Review*, V (February 1940), 1–12.

"Conviction and Probation." In *English Studies in Criminal Science*, pamphlet no. 1, 1941, pp. 24–26.

"Crime and Business." *The Annals of the American Academy of Political and Social Science*, CCXVII (September 1941), 112–18.

"Imprisonment." *Hill Topics*, Indiana State Prison, April 1941, pp. 6–7.

"Do Severe Penalties Reduce Crime?" *Bourne*, Indiana State Prison, May, 1941.

"Rejoinder" (to A. L. Leader's article entitled "A Differential Theory of Criminality"). *Sociology and Social Research*, XXIV (September–October 1941), 50–52.

"The Position in the United States with Regard to Probation and Conviction." *The American Bar Review*, XIX (September 1941), 522–24.

"The Development of the Concept of Differential Association." *Ohio Valley Sociologist*, XV (May 1942), 3–4.

"War and Crime." In *American Society in Wartime*, ed. W. F. Ogburn, pp. 185–206. Chicago: University of Chicago Press, 1943.

"Prevention of Delinquency." *Public Welfare in Indiana*, LV (March 1945), 5–15.

"Is 'White-Collar Crime' Crime?" *American Sociological Review*, X (April 1945), 132–39.

"What We Expect from Our Prisons." In *83rd Annual Report of Indiana State Prison: 1942–1943* (1945), pp. 26–27.

"Social Pathology." *American Journal of Sociology*, L (May 1945), 429–35.

"Free Enterprise and Over-Production." *Ohio Valley Sociologist*, XVI (May 1945), 2–3.

"Discussion of Norman Hayner's 'Criminogenic Zones in Mexico City.'" *American Sociological Review*, XI (August 1946), 438.

"Sex Ratio in Crime and Delinquency." *Eleusis of Chi Omega*, XLIX (September 1947), 424–26.

"Terms in Penology." *American College Dictionary*. New York: Random House, 1947.

"The White Collar Criminal." *Encyclopedia of Criminology*, pp. 511–15. New York: Philosophical Library, 1949.

"The Sexual Psychopath Laws." *Journal of Criminal Law and Criminology*, XL (January–February 1950), 543–54.

"The Diffusion of Sexual Psychopath Laws." *American Journal of Sociology*, LVI (September 1950), 142–48.

"Personality Traits and the Alcoholic" (with H. G. Schroeder and C. L. Tordella). *Quarterly Journal of Studies on Alcohol*, XI (December 1950), 547–61.

"Critique of Sheldon's *Varieties of Delinquent Youth.*" *American Sociological Review,* XVI (February 1951), 10–13.

BIOGRAPHICAL WRITING ON E. H. SUTHERLAND[1]

Cohen, Albert K. "Sutherland, Edwin H." *International Encyclopedia of the Social Sciences.* Vol. XV. New York: Macmillan Co., 1968.

Hall, Jerome. "Edwin H. Sutherland, 1883–1950." *Journal of Criminal Law, Criminology, and Police Science,* XLI (November–December 1950), 393–96.

Lindesmith, Alfred R. "Edwin H. Sutherland's Contribution to Criminology." *Sociology and Social Research,* XXXV (March–April 1951), 243–49.

Mueller, John H. "Edwin Hardin Sutherland, 1883–1950." *American Sociological Review,* XV (December 1950), 802–3.

The National Cyclopaedia of American Biography. Vol. XLII. New York: James T. White and Co., 1958.

Odum, Howard W. "Edwin H. Sutherland, 1883–1950." *Social Forces* XXIX (March 1951), 348–49.

Queen, Stuart. "In Memorium: Edwin H. Sutherland, 1883–1950." *American Journal of Sociology,* LVI (January 1951), 359.

Snodgrass, Jon. "The American Criminological Tradition: Portraits of Men and Ideology in a Discipline," chap. 5, "The Gentle and Devout Iconoclast." Ph.D. diss., Department of Sociology, University of Pennsylvania.

Vold, George. "Edwin Hardin Sutherland: Sociological Criminologist." *American Sociological Review,* XVI (February 1951), 3–9.

[1] Prepared by Jon Snodgrass.

Index